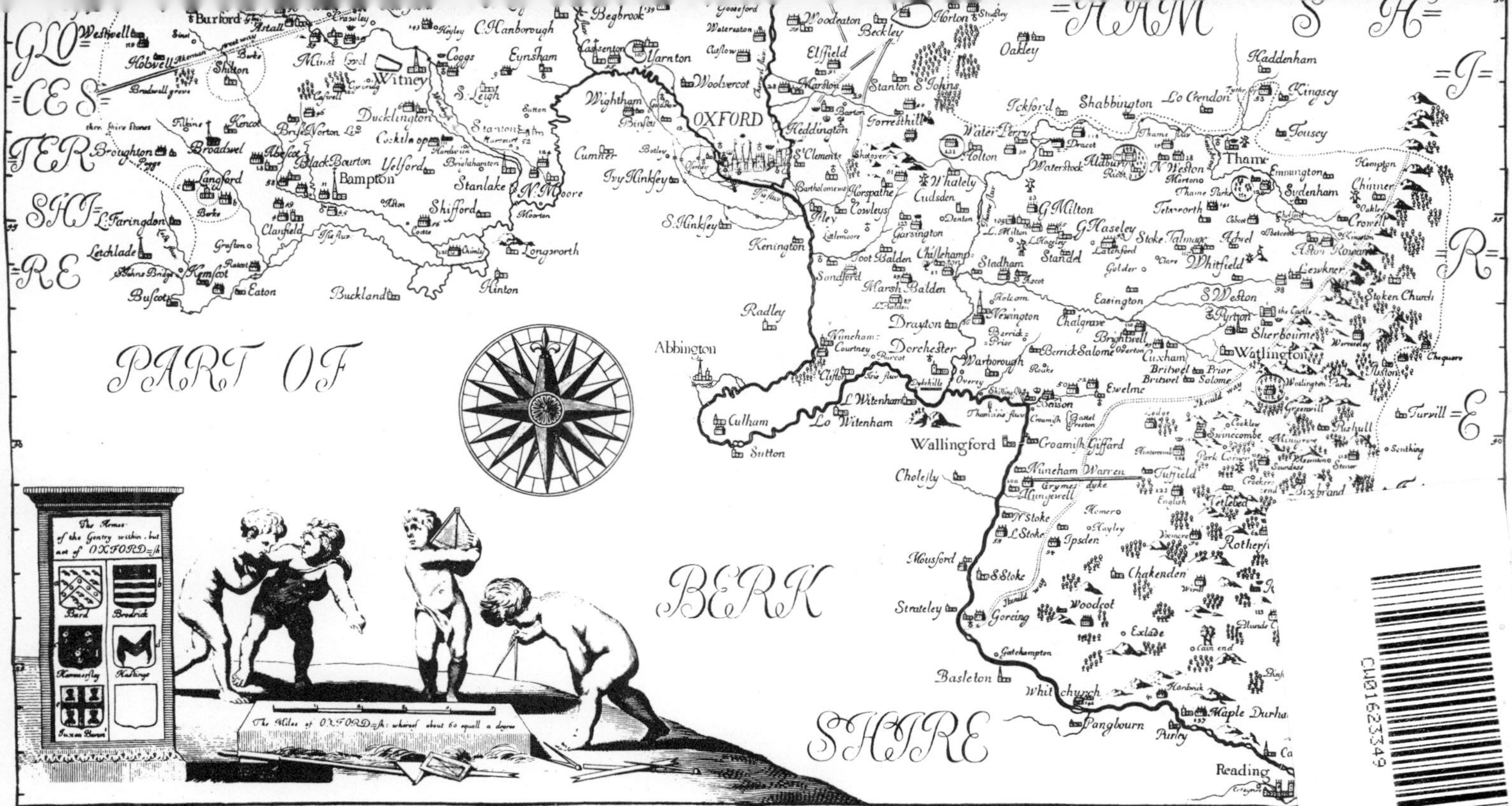

PART OF BERKSHIRE
OXFORD
Witney
Bampton
Abbington
Wallingford
Dorchester
Thame
Watlington
Reading
Woodstock
The Armes of the Gentry within, but out of OXFORD=sh
Bard
Brodrick
Hennersley
Hastings
Juxon Baron
The Miles of OXFORD=sh: whereof about 60 equall a degree

# BARRACUDA GUIDE TO COUNTY HISTORY

## VOLUME II — OXFORDSHIRE

ABOVE: Oxfordshire Volunteer Fire Brigade outside Balliol College, Oxford, 1888. BELOW: The Burford Bus, 1889. *(Henry Taunt photographs by permission of Oxfordshire County Library).*

*The Barracuda Guide to*
*County History series*

VOLUME II

# OXFORDSHIRE

by

GEOFFREY STEVENSON, MA

*Series Editor: Clive Birch*

*Barracuda Books Limited*
*Chesham, Buckinghamshire*

MCMLXXVII

PUBLISHED BY BARRACUDA BOOKS LIMITED
CHESHAM, ENGLAND

AND PRINTED BY

MALCOLM G. READ LIMITED
175 BERMONDSEY STREET
LONDON SE1

BOUND BY

LEIGHTON-STRAKER BOOKBINDING CO. LTD.
LONDON NW10

LITHOGRAPHY BY

SOUTH MIDLANDS LITHO PLATES LTD.,
LUTON, BEDFORDSHIRE



ISBN 0 86023 026 0

# CONTENTS



ENDPAPERS: Front – 1677 map of Oxfordshire *(Plot)*
Back – 1977 map of Oxfordshire

Cover Design: Shield forming part of the arms of Oxfordshire County Council after 1974.

# SERIES INTRODUCTION

This time last year this new series was born. The first volume was KENT by the late T. A. Bushell, who originated the idea in the first place. Tom Bushell was in the best tradition of amateur historianship—a man who devoted much of his leisure and all of his retirement to the study of his home county's past, with scrupulous care and much affection. It is therefore all the more pleasing that his idea should generate a whole series, several of the volumes in which are now in preparation, and the second of which has been researched and written by a professional teacher of history.

Geoffrey Stevenson has taken the idea, and the series a step further, by condensing a similar affection for his county, the resources and personal skills of a trained and professional historian, and a comprehensive knowledge of the past into a readable lexicon. To this he has added a dexterous wit which, without departing from the essential brevity of the text, gives it an astringent flavour that will entertain students, scholars and general readers alike.

The series itself is designed as a simple, easy-reference guide to the principal people, places and events of the county's history, with comprehensive cross-reference to sources for further reading and study. In this one volume, all but a thousand sources are listed.

It is possible and practical to use this guide by individual name, by place name or by date, and to readily identify relevant and accessible sources.

The book is also designed for the general reader, as a rapid, yet ample history of the county, and unusually of the City too, which can be approached as a comprehensive summary unimpeded by surplus detail or opinion.

Two further volumes are currently in preparation. *Hertfordshire* is nearing completion, and is the work of historian and teacher Gwennah Robinson, BA who authored *The Book of Hemel Hempstead & Berkhamsted* in the Town Book series, and *Berkshire* is also in preparation by Tom Middleton, professional writer and author of *The Book of Maidenhead*. It is our intention to gradually extend the series to embrace every county in the United Kingdom.

# FOREWORD

*by Robert Weir—Chairman of the Oxfordshire County Council 1974-7*

I am delighted to be asked to contribute a Foreword to this unique edition to the many books on Oxfordshire, because although my wife and I are not natives of the County, we have grown to know and love it in the 23 years we have lived within its boundaries.

Oxfordshire is a County of incomparable history and tradition, particularly when one realises that at the time the first County was created in the 10th century, the Rollright Stones had already existed for nearly 3,000 years. A thousand years later, with the addition of North Berkshire, Oxfordshire encompasses the upper Thames region once more.

An American writer, Franklyn Adams, said "I find that a great part of the information I have, was acquired by looking up something, and finding something else along the way". This book provides tremendous scope for those who, like me, enjoy this sort of exploration.

Everyone interested in local history, will be grateful to Geoffrey Stevenson for providing such a wealth of information, in a most entertaining and comprehensive form.

# INTRODUCTION

My study looks out at the reverse view of the Dorn valley to that of which W G Hoskins wrote in "The Making of the English Landscape" that 'circumscribed as it is, it contains in its detail something of every age from the Saxon to the nineteenth century'. It is this evidence of occupation over a long period, and the direct links with the continuous practical concerns of communities that for me give local history both its interest and importance. The county of Oxfordshire gave a focus to many of these events, and to an association with broader national events, for a thousand years from 912 to 1974: which is the justification of this book.

The selection of "events" and their dating remains finally my responsibility, although almost all such events are linked to one or more source to which the interested reader may go for deeper information. Reasons of space prevent the inclusion of references to manuscript primary sources, though many of these are available in their original state at the Bodleian Library or County Record Office, and many too in reproduced form in various educational agencies in the county. References to secondary material, whether books or journal articles, are numbered according to publication date, so that more recent works may be identified easily. Thus 1-200 indicates a pre-1918 date, 201-400 pre-1945, 401-600 pre-1965, 601-700 pre-1970, and 701-800 pre-1975. References to printed primary sources are numbered 900-999. Those events unnumbered thus depend either on manuscript primary sources or on local newspapers, particularly on Jackson's Oxford Journal and the Oxford Times.

The use of *circa* has been kept to a minimum, and some early dates are made specific by using the ± tolerance used by Carbon 14 dating. Inclosure awards relate to the dates given, and not the formal passing of the Act concerned.

The persons index permits the tracing of the Oxfordshire perspective of many persons of larger historical importance, and the places index leads to all Oxfordshire villages, with apologies to Newnham Murren, Warpsgrove, Nether Worton and Yelford.

Finally I must thank my Polytechnic colleagues Mary Hodges and John Brooks for their helpfulness and forebearance, and Malcolm Graham of the Oxfordshire Local History Library and his staff for their courtesy and assistance when besieged by my requests.

Middle Barton
January 1977

# CHRONOLOGICAL HISTORY

## The Upper Thames Region before the County of Oxfordshire

Before 912 AD the natural boundaries of the Upper Thames region were the North Oxfordshire Heights, the Berkshire Downs, the Chiltern Hills and a transect of the Vale of Aylesbury *(778)*, since movement and settlement were dictated by the water route up the Thames and the land trackways along the higher ridges. For a thousand years before 912 AD the natural focus of this region would have been Dorchester. The creation of a county of Oxfordshire, involving the rise of the Oxford site, the use of the Thames as a boundary, and extension to the south of the Chilterns, came in the tenth century.

**2785 BC.** (±70). A Neolithic barrow was built at Ascott-under-Wychwood *(785)*: other burial chambers of the New Stone Age were built at Steeple Barton Hoar Stone *(41, 222, 744)*, Slatepit Copse in Wychwood *(222, 744)*, Lyneham Long Cairn *(222, 744)* and Enstone Hoar Stone *(30, 222, 744)*.

**2000c BC.** Rollright Stones set up *(744, 773)*: the circle of the King's Men, the King's Stone, and the Whispering Knights are steeped in folklore *(88, 222, 231)*.

**1395** (±160). Bronze Age settlement at Hanborough, where the Beaker Folk's ring-ditch cemetery was built *(568, 773, 785)* in an area frequented by long-legged marsh birds *(778)*. Bronze age burial mound built at Hethe *(818)*.

**400c BC.** Reoccupation by agriculturists of earlier Iron Age plateau fort sites which may have been more concerned with cattle raising than defence, at Chastleton *(260, 744)*, Bozedown Camp in Whitchurch *(478, 774)*, Lyneham Camp *(521, 744)*, Wittenham Clumps, Madmarston *(533, 744)* and Blewburton Hill fort *(778)*: the region's unity was fostered by trade routes along the Thames valley and the ridges of well-drained hill-ranges: Icknield Way and the Jurassic route *(774)*. Valley settlements included Cassington *(549)*, Chinnor *(774)*, Stanton Harcourt *(569, 619)* and the Dyke Hills "oppidum" or promontory fort near Dorchester *(319, 551, 730, 744, 767, 778)*.

**150c BC.** Pottery associated with Iron Age settlements developed from the black Frilford bowls and plain Cassington and Stanton Harcourt style to more elaborate decorated ware *(771)*.

**100c BC.** Construction of the Grim's Ditches at Mongewell and between the Glyme and Evenlode *(744)*: the first was a linear earthwork from the Thames to the Chiltern crest barring progress from the lower Thames, a possible boundary between the Dobunni and Catuvellauni tribes *(631, 771)*, but intersected by the Icknield Way. The latter enclosed 22 square miles to the north-west of Woodstock *(29, 99, 259, 309, 505)*. Coin evidence suggests that Atrebatian influence from the south was gradually replaced by that of the Catuvellauni: the Belgic settlement of the northern Grim's Ditch may be modelled on their capital at Camulodunum *(771)*. These forts may have been hastily revived as defence against the Romans *(31, 309, 568, 778)*.

**43-47 AD.** The Roman invaders pacified the Civil Zone lying to the south-east of the Fosse Way, and set up forts at a uniform distance apart and from the road, such as Broxtowe, Mancetter and Sea Mills, and within the region at Alcester *(774)* where a rough square of occupation developed *(240, 331, 744)*. At Dorchester an early Roman fort was set up close to the Belgic Dyke Hills settlement *(31)*, and a civilian town later developed *(319, 551, 744, 831)*.

**70c.** Simple timber house at Ditchley preceded the stone winged-corridor villa of Trajan's period *(774)*: other villas were built at Woodeaton *(439, 469)* and five (Fawler *(158)*, Stonesfield, Shakenoak, North Leigh *(744)* and Ditchley) within the northern Grim's Ditch *(778)*. Other early Romano-British settlements included Asthall, Wilcote and Sansom's Platt where Akeman Street crossed the Windrush, Evenlode and Glyme *(731, 815)*, Beckley and Wheatley *(158)*.

**185c.** Improvement of Dorchester's defences with an earthwork rampart *(551, 786)* and probably of Alcester's defences at roughly the same time.

**250c.** Outgrowing the earlier scatter of Romano-British potteries on both banks of the Thames, production was concentrated on the Oxford potteries sited on the Dorchester-Alcester road, producing red-coated ware *(738)*.

**350c.** Rebuilding of villas at Thenford *(802)*, North Leigh *(774)* where a bath suite was installed with floors laid by the mosaic workmen of Cirencester, and Ditchley *(774)* where a granary large enough to serve a 1000 acre estate was built. Agriculture was resumed at Swalcliffe *(533)*.

**420 (±100).** Signs of the survival of active life at Dorchester soon after the collapse of Roman rule *(774)*: a large cemetery was in use outside the town *(801)*.

**571.** Success in battle by Ceawlin and Cutha over the Britons at Biedcanford gave control of the vale of Aylesbury and of four English-named settlements, Eynsham, Bensington, Aylesbury and Limbury. Yet before Ceawlin's reign, 560-93, there was evidence of west Saxon occupation in the Abingdon area *(179, 476, 701, 752, 904)*.

**584.** Cutha died fighting for Ceawlin at Fethanleag (which could well be Stoke Lyne *(752)* after which the Saxons captured many towns, yet returned "in wrath" *(701, 904)*.

**600c.** Saxon huts were built at Eynsham *(786)* and a barrow constructed at Asthall *(743)*.

**634.** Cynegils, ruler of Wessex (who in 614 had beaten the Welsh at Beandun in the south-west, killing 2065 enemies *(323, 904)* was converted to Christianity by the missionary Birinus, with Oswald of Northumbria standing godfather: the two kings gave Birinus Dorchester as the seat of a bishopric *(154)*.

**639.** Birinus baptised Cuthred, king of Wessex, at Dorchester *(904)*: at his death Agilbert the Frank was consecrated, but became bishop of Paris in Gaul about 660, about which time Birinus' bones and the bishopric were moved to Winchester for greater security *(691, 743, 752, 904)*.

**656.** Bede suggests that Diuma became first bishop of the Mercians after the death of the pagan king Penda, and there is a claim for Charlbury as his burial-place *(170, 342, 741)*: this would be close to a "frontier" Mercian federation in the Banbury area *(752)*.

**674.** A Mercian king held his court at Thame *(305, 342)*.

**679.** Mercia set up a bishop's seat at Dorchester temporarily *(323)* but this probably came to an end with Ini of Wessex's recovery of these lands *(179)*.

**700c.** Suggestion of an early religious house in the Cherwell valley, whose abbess was granted land by Bath Abbey *(305)*.

**709.** Abbot Heaha was in charge of a west Saxon monastery at Abingdon *(179)*.

**727.** Traditional date for the foundation of a monastery by St Frideswide (whether or not she fled to Binsey to escape the pantomime of Didan and Alfgar) *(58, 271, 305, 323, 467, 468)*: there is evidence of an Oxford cemetery in 816 (±100) *(820)*.

**740c.** Domestic settlement existed at Oxford along the road from Northampton to Hamwih or Southampton, which had replaced in importance the older route from Silchester to Towcester through Dorchester: wattle fences of 826 (±100) have been found *(406, 820)*.

**752.** Cuthred of Wessex continued Ini's attempt to repel the Mercians, and won a battle at Beorhforda, near Burford *(203, 323, 904)* without establishing a clear connection with the local mimic dragon procession later *(2, 3)*.

**774.** Offa of Mercia, who rose to power in 758, reputedly granted 40 hides to the church of Worcester at Swyncombe, Watlington, Shirburn, Stonor and Pishill in the Chilterns *(270)*.

**779.** Offa beat Cynewulf of Wessex in battle at Bensington and seized the town, carrying Mercian power across the Thames *(179, 323, 904)*.

**823.** Egbert of Wessex beat Ceolwulf of Mercia in battle at Cherrenhul between Oxford and Abingdon *(944)*: by 829 Wessex had supremacy over the whole of Mercia *(179, 752)*.

**849.** Birth of Alfred at Wantage *(179)*.

**871.** Raiding party of Danes was defeated outside Reading at Englefield by Ealdorman Aethelwulf *(179, 904).*

**877.** Danish pressure on east Mercia led to the removal of its bishop from Leicester and the renewal of Dorchester as his seat *(342)*: earlier (in the Pangbourne charter of 844) the bishop had insured the freedom of Thames-side monasteries by granting land to Beorhtwulf, king of a briefly-revived Mercia *(179).*

**878.** The Upper Thames region remained under English control in the Treaty of Wedmore with the Danes *(323).*

**885.** Alfred held an important council (or Witenagemot) at Shifford (whether in Bampton or, more likely, in Berkshire) *(45, 112).*

**886.** Ealhard became bishop of Dorchester *(154).* Alfred committed the defence of the navigable Thames to Ethered, from which a military importance for Oxford has been deduced *(66, 295).*

## 2. The historic County of Oxfordshire

**912.** "This year died Eathered Ealdorman of the Mercians, and King Eadward took possession of London and of Oxford (Oxna forda) and of all lands that owed obedience thereto" *(904).* The burghal hideage of this decade shows Oxford as the centre of 2400 hides, "a dependency evidently a direct forerunner of the later county" *(323, 476, 656, 757, 820).*

**914.** A Danish army "rode out from Northampton and from Leicester and broke the peace, slaying many men at Hook Norton and thereabout" *(243, 904).*

**924.** King Edward died, and within the month his son Aelfweard died at Oxford. They were both buried at Winchester *(904).*

**925.** For 12 years, Wyunelm and Ethelric, two Oxford moneyers, struck coins for Athelstan signed MO.OX.URBIS, and established a coining tradition there which lasted until 1272. Bernwald's coins marked ELFRED and OHSNAFORDA are difficult to date accurately *(295).*

**956.** King Eadwig granted land at Tadmarton to Beorhtnoth, and reallocated it to Abingdon Abbey: he also granted to Aelfhere 20 hides of land at Cuddesdon (including the area of Wheatley) *(270, 901, 981).*

**958.** Topography of Radcot Bridge and of the Dorn and Glyme rivers included in the boundaries of land conveyed by charters of King Eadwig of Wessex *(440)* and Prince Edgar of Mercia *(270, 413).*

**969.** A "fuller's isle" at Witney was described in Edgar's charter to thegn Aelfhelm *(270, 627).*

**971.** Oskytel, archbishop of York, died at Thame *(33, 285, 904).*

**977.** Another bishop, Sideman, died at Kirtlington while attending the Witenagemot there *(112, 904).*

**1002.** King Aethelred II married Emma: their son Edward (the Confessor) was in due course born at Islip *(323)*.

**13 NOV.** St. Brice's Day massacre of the Danish community in Oxford: during the disturbances the church of St Frideswide was burned down *(112, 154, 933)*.

**1004.** Secular canons established at St Frideswide's, Oxford *(154)* which was given land in Cowley, Cutteslowe and Whitehill in Tackley by Aethelred II *(270)*. Evidence of the existence of a bridge over the Cherwell in St Clements *(342, 713)*.

**1005.** Aethelmar gave land at Eynsham and Shipton-on-Cherwell to found a Benedictine monastery at Eynsham which did not survive the conquest *(154, 270, 297, 901)*. Aelfric the grammarian was its first abbot *(930)*. Thorney Abbey also received substantial lands in Beckley and Horton *(342)*.

**1009.** Aethelred spent much time in the county, at Islip and Headington *(3, 23)* and possibly with a Witan at Eynsham *(45)*, but not undisturbed, as the Danes "made an incursion away through the Chilterns, and so came to Oxford, and burned down the borough, and made their way back on both sides of the Thames towards their ships" *(904)*.

**1010.** The Danish host again entered Oxfordshire on the east but veered back to Tempsford in Bedfordshire *(904)*.

**1013.** Sweyn led the Danes in a southern raid, and Oxford immediately surrendered and gave hostages *(904)*.

**1015.** A great council at Oxford was held by Eadric, ealdorman of Mercia, for Aethelred II, absent in Normandy: during the Witan two of Cnut's thanes, Siferth and Morcar, were murdered *(323, 904)*.

**1018.** Cnut chose Oxford for the meeting where the Danes and the English swore to uphold the law of Edgar *(323, 904)*.

**1034.** Parish church of St Martin founded at Carfax, Oxford *(98, 112, 901)*: Cnut granted it to Abingdon Abbey *(901)*. St Michael's west tower built later *(786)*.

**1036.** Cnut's death led to another disputed accession, by Harold Harefoot, chosen by a Witan meeting at Oxford *(112, 323)*.

**1040.** Cnut's son, King Harold I, died at Oxford *(45, 112, 323, 904)*.

**1054.** Abbot Ordric took charge of Abingdon Abbey: during his time Oxford townsmen, anxious for a better river course through Abingdon meadows, offered 100 herrings or anchovies to the cellarer for each boat passing *(185, 901)*.

**1059.** King Edward gave Taynton to the Abbey of St Denis in France *(603)*.

**1065.** Edwin and Morcar, disaffected Northumbrian earls, marched south through Northampton forcing the Witan to meet in a rather decayed Oxford *(66)*: the damage they caused in the Cherwell valley can be traced in 1086 *(111)*. Edward negotiated a peace or amnesty *(115, 323, 904)*.

**1066.** Duke William crossed the Thames at Wallingford after his Hastings victory, and advanced along Icknield Way towards London and his coronation *(323)*. He "harried that part of the country through which he advanced until he came to Berkhamsted" *(111, 904)*.

**1067.** Death of the Saxon bishop at Dorchester, Wulfwig. He was succeeded by a Norman, Remigius, who removed the see to Lincoln *(154)*.

**1071.** Oxford's earlier defences were replaced by a motte and bailey castle for its custodian, Robert d'Oilli, to guard the river bridge to the south *(323, 555, 953)*. The destruction of Saxon houses occurred in a city where two-thirds of the property was in decay *(459)*.
Minster Lovell was alienated to the French abbey of Ivry: its vicarage was never served by more than two monks at any one time before it was taken into the king's hands for the fourth and final time in 1414 *(313)*.

**1074.** Robert d'Oilli founded the collegiate church of St George in the Castle at Oxford *(555)*: he appears to have repaired other ruined parish churches such as St Michaels *(112)*.

**1086.** Domesday Book gives a slightly larger size to the county than the 912 burghal hidage *(552)*: and names 251 settlements, though 12 more are listed in adjacent counties, and "Tew" includes Great, Little and Duns. Two estimates of population are 6645 *(323)* and 6784 *(552)*, but 50,000 would be a sensible guess. The five largest landowners, excepting the king, were Bishop Odo (in prison by 1086), Bishop Remigius of Lincoln (lands at Dorchester and in the north), Robert d'Oilli (Goring, Hook Norton, Stratton Audley and Bampton), Roger d'Ivry (Mixbury, Clanfield, Fulbrook) and Milo Crispin (Alkerton and the Wallingford area) *(518)*. These five owned almost one-third of the county outside the king's lands: in the 1873 'Domesday' the six largest landowners owned less than 14% *(518)*. The bulk of the royal estate lay in the great manors (Bensington, Bloxham, Headington, Kirtlington, Shipton and Wootton), though the king's revenue was also high from the profits of jurisdiction in the nineteen Hundred Courts *(518)*. Most tenants-in-chief had property in other counties, and only one was resident: this was Ernulf de Hesdin who retained Chipping Norton, worth £22, in demesne, until his death at Antioch on the First Crusade *(518)*. Others granted out their manors (South Weston, Tackley and Ardley were sub-infeudated by Hugh Earl of Chester). Oxford, not included in the county's size, had 1070 houses, though 559 of these were "wasted and destroyed" *(552)*. Only Oxford and Bampton had markets, though Salford had access to salt, Taynton a quarry and Bladon a pottery *(627)*. There were mills in 116 of the 251 settlements *(552)*.

**1088.** Robert Fitzhamon associated with Burford until 1107, during which period he granted a Gild Merchant to the town, establishing a Corporation which until 1861 could hold and lease land, hold a market: in six charters of 1250-1314 it received a Common Seal, Borough Court, Bailiffs *(203, 815)*.

**1093.** Robert Bloet succeeded Remigius as bishop of Lincoln, whose pet scheme to set up a monastery at Stow, transferring the properties of the former Eynsham house, was dropped: the future of a monastery in Eynsham was thus secure *(154, 297)*.

**1094.** Bishop Bloet transferred his manor of Charlbury to Eynsham Abbey *(806, 815)*.

**1096.** William II ordered Oxford's sheriff to settle with Abingdon Abbey for the misbehaviour of his agent Eadwi *(901)*.

**1100c.** d'Ivry built Beaumont castle at Mixbury *(786)*.
Hermitage founded at Musewell, a Piddington manor: the chapel and assart belonged for a time to Missenden Abbey, until re-sale *(912)*.
Causeway built over the Thames at Grandpont, south of Oxford, and the tower and porch of St Matthew, Langford *(786)*.

**1103.** Manasses Arsic built the priory of Cogges and endowed it as a cell of the Norman abbey of Fecamp *(323, 573, 786)*.

**1105.** Henry I ordered Nigel d'Oilly, sheriff of Oxford, to compensate Abingdon Abbey for the damage caused by men of Stanton Harcourt who had broken the Thames sluice there *(901)*.

**1110.** Henry I issued a deed at Hanborough exempting Eynsham men from the 'stabilitio' *(930)* or tax at the time of the emparking and walling of Woodstock Park *(51, 555, 901)*: William of Malmesbury spoke of its being filled with a menagerie of strange wild animals *(112)*.

**1117c.** Theobald of Etampes, a secular priest and 'magister Oxenefordie' *(477)* lectured in Oxford to audiences of up to a hundred clerks *(786)*.

**1122.** Gwymund, Henry I's chaplain, refounded St Frideswide's Priory for regular Austin canons *(154, 442, 777, 933)* with an endowment which included St Clement's church *(477)* and a six-day fair in Oxford *(475)*.

**1123. 8 JUNE.** Robert Bloet, bishop of Lincoln, died while riding with Henry I in Woodstock Park *(51, 904)*, soon after the consecration of St Peter's church, Cassington *(930)*. His bowels were buried at Eynsham and his heart at Lincoln *(930)*. His successor Alexander of Blois built a castle on his Oxfordshire estates at Banbury *(17, 510, 802)*.

**1126.** Henry I founded the first of five leper hospitals in the county during this century: this was the Hospital of St Bartholomew, at Cowley *(295, 670)*.

**1129.** Roger d'Oilli the younger (prompted in legend by Edith of Greystoke and the magpies) founded an Augustinian priory on the island of Oseney: the Pope raised this to Abbey status in 1154 *(154)*. About this time he also built a stone castle at Ascott d'Oilly *(786)*.

**1130.** Oxford ranked with London, York, Lincoln, Winchester and Huntingdon as a town where guilds were mentioned: it had two, weavers and shoemakers *(757)*.

**1133.** Henry I spent Easter in his new hall ("Beaumont") outside Oxford's north gate: the buildings were later given by Edward II to the

Carmelite Friars in 1318 in fulfilment of a vow made at Bannockburn *(555, 816)*.
Dame Ediva Launceline, a widow, founded Godstow Abbey for Benedictine nuns *(154, 732)*.
Robert Pullen lectured in theology at Oxford *(777, 816)*.

**1136.** Stephen of Blois, who succeeded Henry I in Dec. 1135, held a Council at Oxford *(323)*.

**1138.** Robert le Gai founded a Cistercian abbey at Oddington, on a site 'fitter for an ark than a monastery' *(3, 112, 285)* from which they gladly moved to Thame *(154, 786)*.

**1139.** Stephen's queen, Maud, Countess of Boulogne, gave all her Cowley lands to the crusading order of Knights Templar: here they established a church and preceptory *(154, 503, 973)*, soon joined by a further preceptory at Clanfield *(154)*.

**JUNE.** Stephen made powerful enemies when he arrested his kinsman, the bishop of Lincoln, together with the Chancellor and Bishop of Salisbury at Oxford *(323)*.

**1140.** Alexander of Blois, bishop of Lincoln, turned the old cathedral at Dorchester into a house for Austin canons: a new abbey church was built by 1170 *(112, 154, 786)*.

**1141.** The Pope confirmed the gift of the bishop of Lincoln's land at Thame to le Gai's Cistercian house whose abbey church was consecrated in 1145 *(285, 786)*. Empress Matilda built castles at Woodstock, Bampton (on the church tower) and Radcot (so surrounded by marsh and water as to be inaccessible *(603)* and occupied Oxford Castle.

**1142.** Stephen captured Bampton, Radcot and finally Oxford castle, Matilda escaping from St George's Tower 'on a frosty night before Christmas' and crossing the Thames to reach Wallingford *(323, 555)*.

**1144.** Matilda's supporter, William Dover, tried without success to retake Oxford. He had no better luck in 1145 *(323)*.

**1146.** Houses first recorded at Tetsworth lying south of the church *(773, 767)*: other villages recorded late are Finstock 1150, Standlake 1164, Souldern 1173, Nuffield 1181, Pishill 1195, Newton Purcell 1198, Fawler 1205, Leafield 1213 and Nettlebed 1247 *(552)*.

**1147.** Nicholas Basset founded the Cistercian abbey of Bruern, endowing it with the manor and church of Treton *(154, 277, 573)*: during Stephen's reign Robert de Sandford founded the Benedictine priory of Littlemore *(154, 675)*.

**1148c.** A further leper hospital was founded at Clattercote *(154)* and became a Gilbertine monastery after 1290. Avelina, daughter of Ernulf of Hesdin, founded the priory of Cold Norton *(154)*.

**1149.** Water Eaton township, with the exception of the Cherwell mills, and Kidlington church, previously d'Oilly property, became part of the endowment of Oseney Abbey *(709)*.

**1152.** Completion of the parish church of St Peter-in-the-East, Oxford, with help from d'Oilly, governor of Oxford castle.

**1153.** Stephen's supporters defended Britwell Castle against Henry Plantagenet, but the castle was among those pulled down when Henry became king *(743)*.

**1154.** Adulterine castles were dismantled at Swerford, where it protected the d'Oilly barony lands of Hook Norton *(320)*, Ardley, Somerton and Middleton Stoney: the king retained Banbury and Deddington castles, the FitzAlans Chipping Norton, and the d'Ivrys Mixbury *(112, 158)*.

**1155.** Henry II gave Oxford a charter *(475, 816)* confirming its right to its established gild-merchant *(786, 808)*: he also confirmed the bishop of Lincoln's Banbury market *(510, 802)*, and during his reign the borough of New Woodstock was founded *(555)*.

**1157. 8 SEPT.** Queen Eleanor bore a son, Richard, at Oxford *(112, 323)*.

**1163.** Henry II received honeyed words and homage from the rulers of Wales and Scotland at Woodstock *(555)*, but rough words from Archbishop Becket about enrolling a local tax at the Exchequer *(51, 323)*.

**1164.** Becket again at Woodstock attempting to retract his acceptance of the Constitutions of Clarendon: he finally left for France *(323)*.

**1166.** Queen Eleanor bore Henry another son, John, at Woodstock *(112, 816)*. Henry attended an ecclesiastical council of inquiry at Oxford which condemned thirty Waldensians as heretics to be branded and expelled *(112, 154)*.

**1167.** English scholars returned from France in compliance with Henry II's order, an act of retaliation for France's support of Becket *(777)*.

**1170c.** Vacarius, a Lombard jurist, lectured at Oxford on Roman law *(477)*. By this time a group of churches were complete in their aisleless, apsidal form expressing Norman taste and feeling, at Checkendon, Goring, Mongewell, Swyncombe, Woodcote and Kiddington *(280)*. During this decade "zigzag ran riot" at Iffley Church *(53, 66, 786)*.

**DEC.** Intervention on behalf of Becket by Simon, Abbot of St Albans who travelled to Woodstock, failed: Becket was killed at Canterbury on 29 Dec. *(51)*.

**1175.** Robert of Cricklade, second prior of St Frideswide's, died, but not before his book on the miracles of St Thomas of Canterbury added its measure to the Becket saga *(154, 816)*.

**1176.** Rosamund Clifford was buried at Godstow Nunnery *(154)*. As "Fair Rosamund" she lived at Woodstock as Henry II's mistress: he had imprisoned Queen Eleanor *(323)*.
Bernard of St Valery founded a Benedictine priory at Studley *(154, 323)*.

**1180.** Peter, Ralph and William, illuminators, Roger and Reginald parchment-makers, and Thomas, scribe, involved in book production at

Oxford *(94, 627)*. Death of an incluse at Hook Norton, who "held unto his death in Almys" two acres which were now sold to Oseney Abbey *(243)*. Establishment of the Hospital of St John the Baptist, Oxford, which excluded the leprous and chronic sick, but dealt with injuries, such as the severed hands of English bowmen from Bannockburn *(670)*.

**12 FEB.** Great occasion when, in the presence of the Archbishop of Canterbury and the Papal Legate, the bones of St Frideswide were translated into a new tomb, on account of a succession of miracles claimed *(154, 468)*.

**1181.** The confirmation charter for a priory of women under Augustinian rules at Goring was written *(154, 786)*.

**1182.** Gilbert Basset, whose family inherited Milo Crispin's estates *(112)*, built and endowed the priory of St Edburg, Bicester as a house of Austin canons *(3, 154, 323, 621)*.

**1183c.** Henry II granted to the bishop of Lincoln a second market in the county, at Thame, as well as two fairs *(285)*: amongst the re-affirmations by John and Henry III was permission to divert the main road down Thame High Street and through the new market *(285, 808)*.

**1184.** Henry II issued his Code of Forest Laws at Woodstock *(277, 323)*. The earliest county antiquarian rector (at Chesterton, which was served by a resident vicar) Gerald of Wales completed his Topographia and read from it at Oxford "to much applause" though he said it himself *(154, 477, 777, 816)*.

**1185.** A fulling-mill was built on the Glyme at Cleveley in Enstone on the lands of Winchcombe Abbey *(476, 773)*.

**1186.** The Dean and canons of the diocese were summoned to Eynsham for the election of a new bishop: they chose the Prior of Witham, or St Hugh *(930)*.

**1189.** At Wolvercote the King's Weir was used for trapping fish, a habit to the discomfort of those wishing to use the Thames as a means of transport *(303, 312, 497)*.

**1190.** Greater part of the city of Oxford burned in a fire *(112, 475, 777)*.

**JUNE.** Bernard of St Valery and Richard de Camville, lord of Middleton Stoney castle, left Marseilles on crusade with Richard I: they both died at the siege of Acre *(112)*.

**1191.** Bishop Hugh of Lincoln visited Banbury *(510)*, and Godstow where he declared Rosamund's shrine to be a scandal and ordered reburial outside the nunnery *(154, 944)*.

**1193.** Oseney Abbey granted an Oxford property they acquired in 1188 to Mauger the Vintner: later this became the "Golden Cross" coaching inn *(422, 486, 953)*.

**1194.** Richard I, ransomed from the Emperor, sought to make good his loss: Gerard de Camville, a supporter of John, paid 2000 marks to be confirmed in Middleton Stoney castle *(112)*. For the wider public, five stretches of open country near a great road were licensed for tournaments *(342)*. One of these was Baynard's Green, where a tournament was held in 1194 and another in 1249, with large entrance fees *(323, 621)*: the church then forbade them *(112)*.

**1196.** Edmund, a monk of Eynsham, had a trance in Holy Week when he claimed to see a vision of Hell *(154, 930)*: well-attested story as the earliest Eynsham Cartulary began to be written in the next year *(297)*.

**1197.** Walter Map, early wit, became Archdeacon of Oxford: he later had to confiscate all the county property of Gerald of Wales *(25, 154, 816, 933)*.

**1199.** John extended Oxford's privileges beyond Henry II's charter: Lawrence Kepeharme was the first recorded Mayor *(475)*.
John also granted to Robert Harcourt the manor of Bensington and the "town and manor of Henley" which acquired a gild merchant in 1269 *(815)*.

**1200.** Great Tew inhabitants fined for concealing a stag which strayed into their fields *(170)*.

**1201.** John Grim was "master of the schools" at Oxford *(477, 777)*.

**1202.** John granted a two-day weekly market at Middleton Stoney and the next year sent deer from Woodstock Park to Gerard de Camville *(765)*.
He also granted a fair at Witney to the Bishop of Winchester *(906)*.
In this period a fair at Bampton was granted to William de Valence *(22)*.

**1204.** Court spent time at John's hunting lodge at Langley in Wychwood *(112, 277)*.

**1205.** John granted William Fitzalan a four day fair at Chipping Norton *(436)*. Oseney Abbey, rectors of Great Barton, allowed Roger de St John to set up a private chapel there *(154, 953)*.

**24 FEB.** Philip Mimecan, serjeant of Shotover Forest, took the Cross, and John made arrangements for the stewardship of his Headington estates: fighting seems to have been his metier, as he died in prison in 1235 charged with murdering Andrew de Scaccario of Horspath *(912)*.

**1207.** John built another hunting lodge at Finmere with easy access to the forests of Bernwood and Whittlewood: it cost less than £40, and the site was restored to a local hermit in 1218 *(555)*. Other incluses have been noted at Hook Norton, Tetsworth and Iffley.

**1208.** Radcot bridge over the Thames reported "in need of repair": in this period others similarly referred to are at Lechlade 1226, Osney c1210, Newbridge c1250, and Wallingford c1250 *(603)*.

**1209.** Oxford townsmen having hanged two clerks to revenge the alleged murder of a woman, the community of scholars prudently left *(475, 477, 777)*.

**1213.** Disappointing turnout of barons and knights when John summoned them on their loyalty to Oxford *(816)*.

**1214. 20 JUNE.** Papal Legate issued an ordinance from Sempringham to Oxford burgesses laying down the privileges of students, and mentioning the need to appoint a University Chancellor: after Robert Grosseteste served briefly as interim "master of the schools", Geoffrey de Lucy was confirmed as Chancellor by Sept. 1215 *(301, 477, 777, 798).*

**1215.** The Great Charter contained, in Clause 23, a promise that "all weirs from henceforth shall be utterly put down by Thames and Medway..". There is some doubt that 'omnes kidelli deponantur' meant all weirs *(185).*
Oxford was besieged by the confederate barons, but escaped lightly during the national disturbances of 1215-7 *(323).*

**1216.** Faulkes de Breaute began a 7-year spell as Sheriff of Oxford *(45):* as custodian of the castle he pulled down St Budoc's church to strengthen the defences *(555).*
Hugh Gargate had church bells erected at Caversfield *(917)*: other bells to survive from this century are at Kelmscott, Shifford, Hampton Gay, Goring and St Clement's, but only 62 (4½%) of the county's bells are pre-Reformation *(917).*

**SEPT.** John stayed at Burford on his way from Cirencester to Oxford, one month before his death *(203).*

**1217c.** St Mary's Priory, Wroxton founded by Michael Belet for Austin canons *(17, 154).*

**1218.** Henry III granted to the Bishop of Winchester a weekly market at Adderbury *(17, 217)*, and disafforested accretions which had added 20,000 acres to the Domesday forests *(170).*

**1221.** Dominican order of Black Friars arrived in England in the train of Peter des Roches, reaching Oxford on Aug. 15. Thirteen of them set up a house in Little Jewry, but soon moved to a new building near Folly Bridge *(154, 816).*

**1222.** Archbishop Langton presided over a rare Provincial Council at Oseney called in pursuit of Innocent III's Lateran decrees of 1215 *(816):* it degraded a deacon who had apostasised as Haggai for love of a Jewess *(307)* and handed him to de Breaute for execution *(154, 323).*
Henry III dealt with windfalls from gale damage and ensured that trees were valued and money held in monastic safe-keeping *(170).*

**1224.** Franciscan order of Grey Friars arrived in Oxford *(154, 816).*

**1226.** St John's Hospitals at Banbury and Burford founded by this date by Robert Whiting and William of Gloucester *(203, 510).*

**1227.** Henry III's Council at Oxford threw off the yoke of his guardian Peter des Roches *(323).*
Richard Earl of Cornwall built a hunting-lodge, enclosed Beckley Park and stocked it with deer *(541, 786).*
Oxford Jews established a synagogue on land at Pennyfarthing Street given by St Frideswide's *(307).*

**1228.** Adam of Oxford, author of a life of St Hugh and narrator of Brother Edmund's vision, was deposed as Prior of Eynsham for being inefficient *(297)*: there were £152 debts to David the Jew *(930)*.
Oxford's fair was held on St Frideswide's Day, Oct. 9, in place of St Benedict's Day *(154, 933)*.

**1229.** Oxford acquired a Council chamber on the present Town Hall site, purchased by the Gild Merchant to replace the Old Yeld Hall *(475)*.

**1231.** Henry III gave St John's Hospital a new site outside Oxford's East Gate, and timber from the royal forests of Shotover and Savernake *(154, 555, 960)*: at this time the city walls were re-built *(786)* and with them the Bocardo prison over the Northgate *(808)*.
Henry III ordered that no clerk should remain at Oxford who was not 'under the discipline or tuition of one of the masters of the schools' *(556, 777)*, thus strengthening the position of university Halls *(234)*.

**1233.** Disorder in the Beckley and Ambrosden area between partisans of the Earls of Cornwall and Pembroke *(13)*.

**1234.** The Knights Hospitaller built a chapel at Gosford *(573)*.

**1237.** Henry III gave twelve oaks for the church tower at Wootton, where an incumbent was presented in 1219 by the countess of Salisbury *(413)*.

**1238.** Rioting Oxford students forced the Cardinal Legate to take refuge in the tower of Oseney Abbey, provoking an interdict on the city until Bishop Grosseteste of Lincoln restored peace *(154, 323, 477, 777)*.

**9 SEPT.** Priest entered Woodstock Palace by its unglazed windows, and attempted to kill Henry III *(45, 51, 555)*.

**1239.** Market granted to "Market End" Bicester to William de Longspee, and a fair in 1252: competition from Bignell arose only in 1377, and was resolved by a further charter for a Friday market in 1441 *(633, 815)*.

**1240.** Widowing of Lady Eva de Grey who gave to Cold Norton Priory "a new fulling mill in Standlake" for the recital of prayers *(712)*.
Evidence of brewing at Oxford *(627)*.
The Templars moved from Cowley to a new preceptory at Sandford *(477)*.
Bullingdon Hundred meeting was held at 'Cowley Sheepfold' or Bullingdon Penn *(477, 953)*.

**1241.** Association of the Stonor family with Bix documented *(456)*.

**1243.** Alan Basset founded a chantry at Bicester for two clerks to study at Oxford, which the founding of St Mary's College in 1435 made redundant *(633)*.
Ralph Chenduit, lord of Cuxham, died suddenly after mocking the Abbot of St Albans who had excommunicated him *(577)*.

**1244.** Oxford disputes between Jews and students led to curtailing of interest on loans, and to the offending clerks being handed over to the university Chancellor for punishment *(475, 477)*: other results were Henry's 1248 fixing of 2 pence per pound per week as the maximum interest rate, and the Chancellor's authority over Oxford Jews being confirmed in 1260 *(295, 477)*.

**1248.** The Chancellor gained assistance from university Proctors *(477)*, and received, until 1856, an oath promising respect from Oxford's mayor *(475)*.

**1249.** William of Durham willed the means to maintain ten or more magistri at Oxford *(777, 786, 816)*. Thus University College claimed its 700th anniversary in 1949, having prematurely feasted its millenary in 1872 somewhat misled by Alfred's activities in the Thames region *(130)*.

**1252.** Oxford students participated in a bloody affray between the Northerners (north of the Nene) and the Irish *(816)*.
Oseney Abbey was the host for the Council of the Benedictine Order *(154)*.
The Austin Friars came to Oxford, choosing the present site of Wadham College in 1268 *(786)*.

**1255.** The Cherwell was bridged at Lower Heyford *(786)*, and the new route between Bicester and Enstone led to the desertion of Steeple Barton for settlement on the other side of the Dorn *(573, 832)*.
John de Balliol's quarrels at Barnard Castle with the Bishop of Durham cost him the humiliation of being scourged in the cathedral and the expense of hiring a house in suburban Oxford near St Mary Magdalen to fulfil his promise to maintain sixteen poor scholars at Oxford *(301, 477, 556, 777, 786)*.

**1256.** Carmelite Friars arrived in Oxford *(786)*.

**7 FEB.** Henry III granted to the Abbot of Eynsham a weekly Monday market at Charlbury, and a four-day August fair *(170, 237, 741, 806, 930)*.

**1258.** A council, the "Mad Parliament", was called to Oxford because of the threat of a Welsh war: it drew up in the Provisions of Oxford a scheme of oligarchic government, but without the support of Henry's Poitevin half-brother, William de Valence, Earl of Pembroke *(323, 743)*. The meeting was in the Dominican friary *(323)*.

**1261.** The Sheriff of Oxford ordered the destruction of "Cutha's Hill" at Cuttleslowe as a dangerous lair of robbers *(476)*.

**1262.** Friars of the Sack made a brief appearance in Oxford *(786)*.
Thomas Cantilupe became university Chancellor: in exile after Montfort's defeat, he was welcomed back in 1273 by his friend Archbishop Kilwardby.
Walter de Merton, England's Chancellor, founded a college for his eight nephews and other kin, and twelve older men from the diocese of Winchester to study at Oxford *(777, 786)*. Its early centre was at Maldon, Surrey but Oxford building soon followed the promulgation of a code of Statutes for Merton College in 1274 *(113, 301, 477)*.

**1264. FEB.** Prince Edward arrived at the "king's hall outside the walls" and with Richard, King of the Romans, gathered Royalist support *(154, 302)*.

**8 MAR.** Henry III arrived at Black Friars in Oxford to wait for his army to assemble: he ordered the students to disperse, and many went to Northampton *(338)*.

**30 MAY.** Montfort, victorious over Henry III at the battle of Lewes, acted in the king's name and ordered the return of the Oxford scholars *(338)*.

**NOV.** Montfort's position in Oxford grew less secure by the failure of the Marcher Lords to join him, and by the ability of his enemies to launch a raid, unsuccessfully, from Bristol to Wallingford to rescue Prince Edward *(338)*.

**1265. 1 FEB.** Northampton "University" formally removed by the baronial council, who saw it as an unwelcome competitor to Oxford, which had become generally approved as a home of learning *(338)*.

**4 AUG.** Montfort was defeated and killed in battle at Evesham, and with him John de Dive, who thereby forfeited the castle manor of Deddington, which was granted to the canons of Windsor *(546)*.

**1268.** Riot and mayhem, first between Christians and Jews in Oxford on Ascension Day *(101, 112)*, then between John Earl of Warenne and Henry Lacy over a pasture at Bicester *(621)*.

**1270c.** Foundation of Merton College School at Oxford *(323)*.

**1272.** Henry III granted a Friday market and a three-day annual fair to Radcot *(603)*.

**1273.** Minster Lovell church endowed with a chantry priest *(313)*, and St Thomas of Canterbury church, Elsfield rededicated after alterations *(786)*.

**1274.** Code of Statutes defined the government of Merton College, Oxford *(477)*. Great Congregation appeared at the university (becoming Convocation later) *(477)*.

Meyr of Bridgnorth was an Oxford taxpayer, but was later accused of the murder of a Christian in Little Jewry and imprisoned for clipping coin *(72, 307)*.

**1277.** Oxford's Great Congregation censured thirty Thomist propositions at the insistence of the Dominican Archbishop of Canterbury, Robert Kilwardby *(777)*.

**1279.** Ownership of assorted land in Hailey belonging to the town of Witney changed by 15% each year up to the Black Death *(906)*.

Some of the Radcot inhabitants were able to pay 18s rents with only 5 acre holdings, partly from earnings related to portage on the bridge *(440, 906)*.

**1280.** Edmund Earl of Cornwall founded Rewley Abbey in Oxford as a centre for Cistercian scholars *(154, 301, 323, 816)*.

**1282.** Balliol College, Oxford received a charter, Lady Dervoguilla continuing her interest after her husband's death in 1269 *(786, 816)*.

**1283.** John Giffard of Brimpsfield founded Gloucester College, Oxford as a centre initially for thirteen monks of St Peter's Gloucester, but after

1336 for the whole Benedictine order *(154, 777, 786)*.

**1284.** Sir Osbert Giffard sought to endow his life abroad with an abducted nun from Wilton by making over his Deddington lands to his son: Edward I intervened on behalf of his wife Joan. Osbert returned in 1290 to reclaim his lands *(546)*.

**1285.** Nicholas de Kingston, wealthy Oxford vintner and many times Mayor, was charged with "black market" sale of 300 tuns of wine *(422)*.

**1286.** The Trinitarian Friars came to Oxford *(786)*.

Stone from pits at Chalgrove in Wheatley used for a bridge over the river Thame, and extensively for many Oxford buildings including Merton College *(408, 483)*.

**1288.** Merton College, Oxford acquired a horologium, which may have been a weight-driven clock *(608)*.

**1289.** Richard Holton, prior of Durham, founded Durham College, Oxford for regulars and seculars of the Benedictine Order *(777)*.

Work on the building of Merton College Chapel in Oxford began, using Wheatley "hardstone" and Taynton and Barrington "freestone": modern restoration is in Clipsham stone *(408)*.

**1290.** Oxfordshire was represented in Parliament by two knights, John the son of Gwydon, and Richard of Williamscot (actually of Kiddington) *(115, 323)*. This Parliament confirmed the university Chancellor's rights in matters of crime and contract involving "privileged persons" who by 1459 included not only college servants but also bell-ringers, laundresses and the children of poor clerks *(475)*.

**1291.** 188 churches in the county are named in Edward I's 'Taxatio' *(154)*.

**1293.** Repair of Dorchester abbey was in progress, together with the costly marble shrine for St Birinus' relics: this rebuilding was aided by Papal indulgences, whereas that of Butterfield and Scott in 1845 was not *(154, (786)*. Middleton Stoney secured market rights through the influence of Henry Lacy, later Earl of Lincoln *(13)*.

Disease in Oxford ascribed to making bread and ale with corrupt water from the Trill Mill Stream *(16, 986)*, according to Anthony a Wood.

**1295.** King's huntsman was paid 11s 8d for catching wolves in Middleton Stoney park *(765)*.

Oxford's burgesses in Parliament, Thomas de Sowy, mayor in 1294, and Andrew de Pyrie, are the first who can be named *(115)*.

**1296.** First day of Eynsham Fair was disturbed by attacks on Oxford scholars resulting in some deaths *(154, 930)*.

**1297.** Franciscan eminence began at Oxford with Duns Scotus' lectures on the Sentences until 1304, and was maintained by William of Ockham between 1317 and 1319 *(777)*.

**1298.** Carfax riots at Oxford between Oxford students and town bailiffs *(475, 777)*.

**1299.** Resolution of a dispute over the ownership of Swynford Ferry was largely in favour of Abingdon Abbey: the Abbot of Eynsham agreed to give the ferryman two breads and two pitchers of second class beer every time he crossed the Thames *(297, 642, 930)*.

**1300.** Chipping Norton had to endure sending two burgesses to Parliament, though this only lasted until 1305, and they were formally relieved of the duty in 1367 *(81, 115, 323)*.

**1301.** Death of John of Newshom, a schoolmaster, in the pursuit of duty: he drowned at Oxford whilst cutting willow rods for chastising pupils *(788)*. Cirencester Abbey acquired the barony of Broadwell *(620)*.

**5 AUG.** Queen Margaret bore Edward I's second son, Prince Edmund, at Woodstock *(45)*.

**1302.** Deddington and Woodstock both sent two burgesses to Parliament, as they did in 1305 *(97, 115, 323)*.

John, Bishop of Lincoln safeguarded Thame's market by putting down a potential rival market of the Prior of Rufford at Haddenham *(33)*.

**1304.** John de Crawel presented to the living of Upper Heyford, but within two years was deprived as Rector and degraded for thieving and robbery *(38)*.

**1305.** Witney represented in Parliament, and on four other occasions before 1330 *(115, 323)*.

**1306.** Solitary occasion when Burford sent representatives to Parliament *(115, 323)*.

**1308.** William Sautre, preceptor of Sandford, was obliged to give evidence at the trial of the Knights Templar *(154)*: on the suppression of the order, the Sandford property was transferred to the Knights Hospitaller *(786)*.

**1310.** Taynton stone transported by land to Eynsham, thence by water to the Hythe, Oxford for use at Merton College *(408)*.

**1311.** University authorities and the Friars clashed in the university church of St Mary, Oxford *(154)*.

**1312.** Edward II presented two vicars at Broadwell, but handed this, with former Templar property, to the Knights Hospitaller *(620)*.

**12 JUNE.** Edward II's caustic favourite, Piers Gaveston, having surrendered to the Earl of Pembroke was lodged in the rectory (not the castle) at Deddington while his captor visited his Bampton manor *(546)*. The Earl of Warwick, with the help of John Oddingseles, lord of Broadwell *(620)* seized Gaveston and hanged him at Warwick *(323)*: his body rested two years with the Dominicans at Oxford before being reburied at King's Langley *(154)*.

**1314.** Walter de Stapledon, bishop of Exeter, founded Stapledon Hall, Oxford which became Exeter College in 1566 *(122, 477, 786, 816)*.

**1315.** Aylmer de Valence, Earl of Pembroke, obtained royal licence to crenellate Bampton castle *(22, 112, 786)*: Broughton Castle, though of this period, received this right in 1406: eight other sites received similar licence (Garsington 1318, Chiselhampton 1319, Drayton 1329, Cuddesdon and Watlington 1338, Kingham 1346, Rotherfield Greys 1348 and Shirburn 1377) *(318)*.

**1318.** Edward II gave the royal palace at Beaumont, Oxford to the Carmelite Friars *(786)*.

**1320c.** Bishop Burghersh of Lincoln built the Holy Trinity Chapel at Banbury church by offering indulgences to contributors *(510)*: Bishop Cobham of Worcester built a Congregation House with a library above, on the north side of St Mary the Virgin, Oxford *(477)*, which acquired a new spire "more crocketed than dreaming" *(786)*.
William of Leicester, Rector of Chinnor, was commemorated in the oldest brass monument in the county *(808)*.

**1321.** Deddington saw an armed attack by men keen to destroy Despenser property and drive off his cattle *(546)*: this did not deter building at this time, such as Leadenporch House in New Street, Deddington *(786, 560)*.

**1322.** Local example of posthumous veneration of Thomas of Lancaster, the titular Earl of Lincoln and son-in-law of Hugh de Lacy, who was executed at Pontefract Mar. 22: wall-painting at South Newington church commemorates his murder *(786)*. The east end window of this period commemorates four families, of which le Scissor and Giffard have local connections *(434)*. An existing bridge at the foot of Sheep Street, Burford across the Windrush was in need of repair *(764)*.

**1323.** Burford gained a sixteen-day fair in a charter to Despenser *(77, 620)*.

**1324.** Adam de Brome founded a college at Oxford: Edward II refounded it in 1326 as King's Hall. It was soon known as Oriel College *(121, 295, 477, 777, 816)*.

**1326.** Isabella, Edward II's queen, stayed at Islip during the rebuilding of the manor-house *(254)*. She was received by Oxford university *(467)* and was preached at by the bishop of Hereford on the text "My head, my head" to the effect that she might look beyond the fall of the Despensers to the Crown itself *(323)*.

**1327.** William de Shareshull lodged at the Golden Cross, Oxford at the expense of the city when sent by Edward III to inquire into Oxford's looting of Abingdon Abbey's property *(422)*.
Gilbert given license to empark his wood at Elsfield: he was a county MP in 1324 and 1328 *(115)*. De Nowers granted a market and fair at Churchill *(283)*.

**1328.** Edward III granted the former leper hospital of St Bartholomew to Oriel College, Oxford: in 1643 it became a pest-house, and it served as a cholera hospital in 1832 *(45, 295)*.

**1330.** Robert Arden, county MP in 1314, was licensed to crenellate Wickham Park: he held Banbury Castle from 1322 to his death in

1331 *(115, 786)*.

**15 JUNE.** Edward, later the "Black Prince" was born at Woodstock: Edward III rewarded Joan of Oxford, his eldest son's nurse, and Matilda Plumpton, his rocker *(45, 323, 467)*.

**1331.** John de Broughton given permission to assign land at North Newington for chantry masses in his chapel of St John the Baptist *(83, 786)*.

**1332. 10 JUNE.** Queen Philippa bore a daughter, Isabel, at Woodstock: there were six more sons and five more daughters to come *(467)*.

**1334.** Tax returns suggest the county was the richest in England, with Norfolk second *(476)*.

Northern students fled from Oxford to Stamford, taking with them a doorknocker probably of Brasenose Hall. So serious a view did the university take that all MAs until 1827 took a special oath not to lecture at Stamford. The ring was returned to Brasenose College in 1890 *(477, 777, 786, 816)*.

**1335.** Queen Philippa bore another daughter, Joanna, at Woodstock. She died in 1348 at Bayonne on her way to marry Pedro the Cruel *(51)*.

**1336.** Violence was used, first on the prior and nine canons of St Frideswide's by Oxford townsmen, who forced them to renounce special rights during the fair *(154)*, also on Ralph Chastiloun, a county MP in 1313, by Sir Robert de Nowers, county MP 1320-30, and his two sons, not to mention Burga his wife, at Kingham. Chastiloun died, and the Nowers family were taken to the Tower *(115, 283)*. John de Lewknor, a more peaceable county MP, acquired sufficient wealth to build the hall at Lewknor, perhaps in the knowledge that his neighbour at Stonor Park had added a hall, solar and private chapel earlier *(115, 154, 562, 827)*.

**1337.** A stone and timber hunting lodge at Cornbury in Wychwood Forest was in use by the king *(773, 786)*.

**1340.** Robert Cailly killed during an affray at Crowmarsh Giffard fair *(170)*.

**1341.** Robert de Eglesfield founded the Queen's College, Oxford with Queen Philippa as its patron *(477, 777, 816)*.

**1342.** The Crutched Friars arrived for a brief spell in Oxford *(786)*.

**1344.** William de Stamford was elected Abbot of Eynsham by the monks at the insistence of the bishop of Lincoln, but Nicholas de Upton, the deposed abbot, drove out his successor with 1500 armed men *(930)*.

John Langrisshe, Oxford town clerk, was also a brewer *(766)*.

**1346.** The bishop of Lincoln, through his Archdeacon at Oxford, renounced all rights to exert control over Oxford University apart from the probate of wills *(777)*.

**1347.** Sir John de Grey received license to crenellate Rotherfield *(786)*.

**1348.** Black Death hit Oxfordshire, and affected the rural economy. Many "grounds" result from enclosing the arable area of a township into a smaller number of large pasture fields *(573)*. Two-thirds of Witney's inhabitants may have died *(188)*. Tilgarsley in Eynsham was depopulated from this time for lack of tenants *(297)*. There were six rectors at Newton Purcell in as many years *(112)*.

**1350.** Edward III permitted St Anne's chantry to be added to All Saints church, Oxford: one-third of its income came from the "Mitre" site *(220)* willed by William de Bicester. The delay was caused by the rapid deaths of his widow in Mar. 1349, his son in May 1349, and his heir Mayor Richard Cary in July 1349. Banbury was placed under an interdict by the Archbishop of Canterbury, seeking leverage in a dispute over church government with the Bishop of Lincoln *(477)*.

**1354.** Death of the Chief Justice of Common Pleas, Sir John Stonor: the effigy of a civilian jurist at Dorchester is probably Sir John *(45, 773, 786)*.

**1355.** Edward III permitted Nicholas Jordan, warden of St John the Baptist chapel at Bicester to found a new hospital there for the poor and sick *(621)*. A large sheep flock summered at Chastleton and was sheared there, while the arable sown on the Oseney estate there was only half that of 1347 *(571)*.

Merton estates at Cuxham showed reduced sowing, particularly of oats *(577)*.

**7 JAN.** Queen Philippa bore her seventh and final son, Thomas, at Woodstock *(45)*: Alas, in vain: her husband left his throne to a childless grandson.

**10 FEB.** Escalation of a student argument with the innkeeper of the Swyndlestock tavern at Carfax, Oxford (the property of John Bereford, MP in 1344 and Mayor during 1355) into the Saint Scholastica's day riots *(115, 214, 475, 777, 986)*.

**11 FEB.** Townsmen at Oxford and neighbouring villagers attacked students in Beaumont fields: the Chancellor hurried to Woodstock and the Court *(777)*.

**27 JUNE.** A new charter confirmed and extended the Chancellor's powers, and compelled Oxford townsmen to pay a substantial fine, their Mayor being imprisoned *(777)*.

**1356. 15 MAR.** An interdict was removed from Oxford as part of the settlement of the riot *(475)*.

**1358.** Tusmore, totally relieved from tax in 1354, was permitted to have its fields emparked since the labour force of villeins had died: its church was demolished in 1718 *(573)*.

Wheatley quarries began the supply of 30,000 feet of stone for the building of Windsor Castle, Taynton supplying an equal amount *(408)*. At Windsor William of Wykeham found William Wynford, master mason, as clerk of the King's Works there and used his services at New College later *(472)*.

**1360.** John Wycliff was master of Balliol College, Oxford, presumably resigning the next year when instituted rector of Fillingham *(556)*.

**1361.** Canterbury College, Oxford founded by Simon Islip, Archbishop of Canterbury: its buildings, a hall and two chambers, were begun in 1364. *(301, 477, 757, 816)*.

**1364.** Edward III granted to the Abbot of Westminster a Thursday market and annual fair at Islip *(13, 254)*.

**1365.** Archbishop Islip appointed John Wycliff warden of Canterbury College, Oxford, but he was deprived of the post when Archbishop Simon Langham converted the college to a house for regulars only, and granted it to Christ Church, Canterbury *(556)*.

**1371.** Building of Merton College library at Oxford begun *(786)*.

Chaplain led 28 men in armed attack on John de Lewknor's manor house at Dean: he lost 200 sheep *(287)*.

**1373.** Beckley hunting lodge was restored, and visited in 1378 by Richard II: the triple moats survive in the grounds of the later brick Beckley Park *(555)*.

**1376.** The moiety of Kingham manor was sold by Gilber de Chastelyn to agents of Alice Perrers, Edward III's mistress. William of Wykeham bought it later from Alice's husband, and in 1392 granted it to New College *(502, 989)*.

**1377.** Richard II granted a weekly market at Bignell, which fell away when the Market-End market at Bicester was extended to a Friday market in 1460 *(61, 621)*. The poll-tax showed Oxford's fall to sixteenth in importance in English towns *(757)*.

Gregory IX issued a bull ordering the university Chancellor to prevent Wycliff's heresies, but he was allowed to leave Oxford for Lutterworth where he died in 1384 *(477)*.

Waren de Lisle was given license to crenellate at Shirburn: he chose the moated site of the earlier manor house, and built in brick (earlier than at Stonor 1416 and Ewelme 1437) *(786)*.

**1379.** William of Wykeham, bishop of Winchester, founded the "New" College of St Mary of Winchester at Oxford, using a site described by Froissart as a particular eyesore, a "plague pit.. where thieves used to lie in wait" *(295, 477, 777, 816)*. Although anticipated by King's Hall at Cambridge, it deflected the pattern set by Merton of a graduate college into a mixed secular college which produced a morebalanced society: its statutes set aside £5 for the tutoring of younger fellows and scholars.

**1380c.** The basic wage of an ordinary mason was 6d a day, thus breaching, as a matter of course, the "social contract" of 3 - 4d laid down by the Statutes of Labourers *(472)*.

**1381. 10 MAY.** William of Wykeham presented the advowson of Adderbury church to New College, Oxford *(902)*.

**1382.** Tithe barn of cruck construction built at Church Enstone by Walter of Wynforton, Abbot of Winchcombe, for his bailiff Robert Mason *(30, 43, 773, 786)*. The new Archbishop of Canterbury (Simon of Sudbury having been executed by Wat Tyler's men) took steps to crush Lollardy and called a Council of bishops, theologians and canon lawyers to Blackfriars at Oxford to condemn Wycliff's views as heretical *(80, 777)*. Earthquake felt on May 21, as in East Kent.

**1385.** The manor of Iffley was granted to Richard Abberbury, of Donnington Castle *(53)*.

**1387.** Death of Lord Robert de Grey, whose brass effigy (58½ inches even in armour and helmet) in Rotherfield Greys church is one of the finest county examples *(786)*.

**20 DEC.** Armour and helmet was much in evidence at Radcot Bridge, where Richard II's favourite, Robert de Vere, Earl of Oxford (the family were nonetheless unconnected with county affairs) found himself trapped by the Lords Appellant, Henry Bolingbroke and Gloucester. His position was irretrievable, so he made his escape downstream to Bablockhythe ferry and ultimately abroad *(112, 323, 603)*.

**1388.** Five hundred years before County Councils, the supervision both of administration and justice by JPs in Quarter Session was emerging: Robert de Berford and Walter de Woubourne were appointed magistrates for the Banbury and Bloxham hundreds in 1331 *(510)*.

**1389.** Royal amusements at Woodstock turned sour when John Hastings, Earl of Pembroke was accidentally killed in a tournament by Sir John St John *(170)*.

**1395.** Grey's eight-year record outfaced by Sir Robert Bardolf in death, as his brass figure in Mapledurham church is 70 ins. *(786)*.
Pope Boniface IX gave a bull freeing Oxford University from interference by either the bishop of Lincoln (conceded in 1346) or the Archbishop of Canterbury, but Archbishop Arundel, 1397-1414, determined to reverse this *(777)*.

**1397.** Richard II's short-lived triumph over the Lords Appellant involved the banishment of the Archbishop, and the murder at Calais of Thomas of Woodstock, Duke of Gloucester *(555)*.

**1398. 2 SEPT.** Henry Beaufort, Bishop of Lincoln, ordered the celebration of St Frideswide's day throughout the university and county deanery, and an indulgence was granted to those who visited the shrine *(468)*.

**1399.** Eynsham Abbey appropriated the church and rectory of Combe, having re-built the church on a higher site: the village also moved *(450)*.

**1400. JAN.** Henry IV was present at the trial in Oxford of Sir Thomas Blount, one of the conspirators who sought to restore Richard II. Blount was "put to death with appropriate barbarity". *(112).*

**1403.** Sir John Drayton was indicted for failing to maintain locks and winches on the Thames at Rotherfield Pyperd *(10, 185).*

**1404.** William atte Wall commemorated by John Purfoule's will in a mass at Henley: other references to Henley's walls from 1397 *(36).*
Henry Coteler was the first seneschal or steward of Burford whose name has survived: the real local power lay with the town bailiffs *(203).*

**1406.** Sir Thomas Wykeham was licensed to fortify and crenellate his manor house at Broughton *(83, 786).*

**1407.** Thomas Chaucer of Ewelme began eight years as Speaker of the House of Commons. A wealthy merchant man *(944)*, his daughter Alice married William de la Pole who became Duke of Suffolk *(115).*

**1408.** New College, Oxford employed Richard Winchcombe as master mason in rebuilding Adderbury chancel in decorated style: the work took eleven years, and £86 was spent in 1421 - 3 probably on a tithe-barn. Stone was carted from Taynton, and "scappling" or rough-hewn stone cut from locally opened quarries. Local men such as Gylkes were employed as carpenters, carting their wood from Wychwood Forest *(472, 876, 902).*

**1411.** Archbishop Arundel attempted to carry out a visitation of the University, but found St Mary's Church, Oxford locked against him. He responded with an interdict: the local situation degenerated into another northerner versus southerner riot. The Bull of 1395 was withdrawn, and the University had to give ground *(777, 816).*

**1413.** Sir Thomas Wykeham, nephew of the bishop, became High Sheriff of the county: the Saye family's rise exposed them, in 1450 and 1471, to sudden death in riot or battle *(118).*
John Forest, prebendary of Banbury, was permitted to receive tenement property to set up a chantry, which in 1448 was taken over by a Guild: at dissolution in 1548 it was worth £62, the most valuable in the county *(510).*

**1414.** Alien priory of Ivry had its minster Lovell priory taken away by Henry V: it was later granted to the royal foundation at Eton *(786, 313).*

**6 NOV.** John de Wykham of Swalcliffe received a pardon for his part in adhering to Sir John Oldcastle's plot involving Lollard elements *(115).*

**1416.** Abingdon's Guild of the Holy Trinity built bridges across the Thames at Abingdon and Culham: previously there was no crossing between Wallingford and Oxford *(476, 786).*

**1417.** 200,000 bricks made at Crocker End, Nettlebed for building at Stonor Park *(627).*

**1420c.** Building began on the Divinity School at Oxford, the first fully detached University building *(786)*: John Lovell gave timber even though his father Lord Lovell was building a manor-house at Minster Lovell *(112, 323).*

**FEB.** William Taylor, principal of St Edmund Hall, who with his predecessor

Peter Payne had a strong influence on English Lollards and Czech Hussites, was examined by Archbishop Chichele, abjured his errors but later relapsed *(816)*.

**1424.** Standhill in Pyrton decayed over twenty years to a single farm and 500 acres of grassland, possibly because of plague *(912)*.

**6 NOV.** Rededication of Merton College chapel in Oxford after the rebuilding of the transepts *(757)*.

**1427.** Richard Fleming, bishop of Lincoln, founded Lincoln College, Oxford *(107, 777, 786, 816)*: its hall, old chapel, library, kitchen and chambers were built about ten years later *(757)*.

**1430.** Thomas Hokenorton became Abbot of Oseney until 1452, and during this time the tower of Hook Norton church was built *(243)*.

**1431.** Humphrey, Duke of Gloucester, seized two men at Oxford who were condemned as Lollards and executed *(148)*.

**1432.** Oxford University insisted that the principals of hostels or halls (of which 63 were listed during this period) be graduates *(475)*.

**1435.** Fulwell ceased to be a parish separate from Mixbury: by 1500 its chief Oseney tenant kept a sheep flock of 400 *(573)*.
Thomas and Elizabeth Holden founded St Mary's College, Oxford after the failure of an attempt to found a college for the Augustinian order in 1421 *(154, 786, 986)*.

**1436.** Burford had its own quarries for freestone and tiles at Whiteladies, Sterte and le Wort: in practice it relied on Taynton *(203, 764)*.

**1437.** William and Alice de la Pole, Earl and Countess of Suffolk, founded in Ewelme both an almshouse for thirteen poor men and a Free Grammar School *(39, 323, 974)*, having rebuilt St Mary's church earlier on the site of All Saints *(786)*. The Earl of Suffolk also received a charter for a market and two fairs at Hook Norton *(243)*.
Archbishop Chichele founded St Bernard College, Oxford for monks of the Cistercian order *(154, 777)*: the gate tower remains in St John's Front Quad *(786)*.

**1438.** Archbishop Chichele also founded All Souls College, Oxford for a warden and forty fellows *(114, 477, 777, 816)*: 15 to 20 masons were employed at Burford, working stone *(275)*. Cartage of Taynton stone was 3s a load, and of Headington stone 5d to 7d a load *(408)*. Oyster shells were used as a damp course *(472)*. John Glazier of Oxford appropriately glazed eight windows in the chapel *(786)*, where mass was first heard on Apr. 2 1443 *(777)*.

**1439.** Holy Trinity chapel, Stonor, was consecrated: it has seen no other form of communion than the mass since *(147, 456)*.
Death of John Cottesmore, Lord Chief Justice: buried in Brightwell church *(912)*. The Boarstall Cartulary was drawn up for his son-in-law, John Rede whose property included Headington quarries.

**1440.** The (old) Schools were built opposite the emergent Divinity School at Oxford *(777)*: Duke Humphrey of Gloucester contributed to the creation of new arts lectures, gave 281 volumes over nine years and gave support to a library to house them built above the Divinity School *(757, 556)*.

Eynsham market, granted by Stephen, moved to Monday and Friday *(297)*.

**1442.** Minster Lovell woods taken out of the royal forest of Wychwood to become free chase for the Lovell family *(170, 773)*: building of the mansion likely on the return of Lovell from the French wars in 1431 *(509)*.

**1444.** Lucy Colbrand was expelled from Oxford by the university Chancellor since her presence had occasioned sundry 'litigation, fornication, fights and homicides' *(777)*.

**1445.** The newly-formed Guild of the Holy Trinity at Deddington obtained leave to found a chantry in memory of Richard Andrew who had been Henry VI's Secretary. A wealthy Stapler, William Billing, was buried there in 1533, and the chantry was abolished in 1548 *(546, 922)*.

**1447.** Richard Quartermain, London merchant, MP and High Sheriff of the county *(743)* founded the Guild of St Christopher with a chantry at Thame *(285, 323)*: with his wife he also founded an almshouse at Thame for six poor men *(808)*. A hermit was allowed to collect alms from travellers at Tetsworth for the repair of the Wheatley to Stokenchurch road *(808)*.

**1448.** William of Wayneflete founded Magdalen Hall, Oxford for fifty scholars *(477, 777)*: a commendable answer to over-crowding, since Wood lays the Oxford pestilence of this year at the door of 'the sleeping of so many scholars in one dormitory' *(16, 986)*. Building work was much delayed, with frequent hindrance from the impressing of men for the King's works or even those of town corporations (such as the repair of Oxford's walls in 1370): a King's servant was paid 20d not to take away four masons working on Merton College bell-tower *(472)*.

**1449.** Richard Quartermain built St Michael's chapel as a chantry with three priests at Rycote, which the family held from 1415 to 1542 *(285, 786)*.

**1450.** Holy Trinity Guild founded at Chipping Norton by the vicar and certain parishioners *(323, 436)*.

**2 MAY.** Sailors who murdered the banished Duke of Suffolk landed his body at Dover. As with Humphrey Duke of Gloucester who died of a heart attack imprisoned at Bury in 1447, a sordid end was far removed from the longer-lasting Oxfordshire philanthropy in which they indulged.

**4 JULY.** Broughton was associated with the perils of high politics: Margaret Wykeham's father-in-law, Lord Saye and Sele, was killed by a mob in Cheapside who were supporters of Jack Cade. His son severed his Kentish Knole connections in 1456, and settled at Broughton.

**1452.** George Neville, brother of Warwick the Kingmaker, celebrated his Oxford degree with a two-day feast: he had more to celebrate in becoming university Chancellor in 1453 at 20, Archbishop of York and Chancellor of England at 31: he died at 43, his health broken by Edward IV's prison *(556)*.

**1453.** Fulwell slates were supplied from quarries at Cleveley in Enstone for roofing New College, Oxford: they were last produced after 1800 *(408)*.

**24 MAY.** Henry VI granted a charter to New Woodstock, and relieved it "for ever" of the duty of representation in parliament *(97, 115, 455)*.

**1456.** Great Almshouse at Burford founded by Richard, Earl of Warwick *(764)*. Taynton stone for building Eton College was carted overland to Henley and shipped from there, poor testimony for river navigation at the time *(757)*.

**1457. 18 JULY.** License given to William of Wayneflete to found Magdalen College, Oxford, incorporating both Magdalen Hall and the property of St John's Hospital: ten years later he began to surround the property with a battlemented Long Wall *(116, 295, 511)*.

**1461.** Cotswold meeting of Earl of Warwick and Edward, Earl of March, the future Edward IV at either Burford or Chipping Norton: smarting from defeat at St Albans and Queen Margaret's coup in seizing Henry VI, Warwick formed the plan that Edward should replace the king: on Feb. 27 London opened its gates to them *(347)*, and Mar. 4 acknowledged Edward as king.

**4 NOV.** Sir Edmund Hampden, MP for the county in 1453 and 1459, was attainted of high treason after Henry VI's fall *(115)*.

**1462.** James Wyllys, a Lollard weaver, was burned at Henley *(148, 154)*.

**1465.** Sir Robert Harecourte was seneschall of Burford, the only instance of a man of rank holding corporation office *(203)*.

**1466.** Bishop of Lincoln, from the Dominican house in Oxford, ordered the uniting of Asterleigh with Nether Kiddington parish because of depopulation: its parish church was demolished *(7, 573, 773)*.

**1469.** Brookend in Chastleton parish virtually abandoned, despite the efforts of the Abbot of Eynsham to encourage tenants *(573, 743)*.

**26 JULY.** Yorkist defeat at Danes Moor near Edgcote in Northamptonshire was due in part to rivalries between the Earls of Pembroke and Devon over their Banbury quarters *(510, 802)*.

**1470.** Sir Robert Danvers, MP for the county in 1437, active in the suppression of the Cade rising, ended his career as Chief Justice of Common Pleas *(115)*.

**1471. 14 APR.** William, Lord Saye and Sele killed at the battle of Barnet, and buried in Broughton church *(83)*.

**1472.** Richard Quartermain, of North Weston and Rycote, returned to the Commons as MP for the county at eighty years of age, by far the oldest

MP in this century *(296)*.

**1474.** William Orchard began building for Magdalen College, Oxford, the first college to crenellate most of its buildings *(757)*: he acquired for 10s a crane from the Abbot of Rewley, which the University requested in 1478 to aid the completion of the Divinity School *(472)*. William Orchard was master mason for this too, and worked at Eton in 1479. He held quarry land at Headington on a long lease from Magdalen College *(408)*.

**1475.** William Orchard built the west window of Magdalen College Chapel, Oxford with a rare plan and elevation *(472)*.
Great oak forest planted at Kirtlington.

**1478.** Thomas Rood, from Cologne, in partnership with the university stationer, Thomas Hunt, produced Oxford's first printed book *(475, 477, 777)*.

**1479.** Grammar teaching began in the school for which Wayneflete's statutes provided in perpetuity like any other element in Magdalen College, Oxford: a building was begun in 1480 *(126, 323, 511, 986)*.

**SEPT.** Edward IV, holding court at Woodstock, and his queen, Elizabeth Woodville, visited the new buildings of Magdalen College, Oxford and were received by the Chancellor, who was the queen's brother *(51, 67, 112)*.

**1481.** South Stoke was assessed at 14 pence in smoke-farthings (56 households) by Eynsham Abbey *(930)*.

**1483.** Rood and Hunt published in Oxford the "Compendium Totius Grammaticae" of John Anwykyll, grammar master of Magdalen College School, with a woodcut by Wynkyn de Worde on the cover *(511, 777)*.

**22 JULY.** Richard III stayed at Magdalen College, Oxford on progress from London to York, and heard disputations in which the Greek scholar, William Grocyn took part *(112)*.

**1484.** William of Waynflete bought the chantry of Brackley Hospital in Northamptonshire as a refuge for Magdalen College and school, Oxford during plagues: "migrations" were a biennial occurrence, Witney, Burford, Thame, Wallingford, Watlington, Aynho, Brailes and Highworth being used in addition to Brackley *(511)*.

**1485.** William Brampton of Burford, once the owner of the George Inn, was named in the Bill of Attainder against Richard III and his adherents *(203)*.

**1486.** Pestilential disease in St Mary Magdalene parish, Oxford: the previous year "Sudor Anglicus" struck England *(16, 986)*.

**1487.** Francis, Lord Lovell, a survivor of Bosworth Field and former Chief Butler of England of Richard III, was killed fighting for the Yorkist pretender at Stoke. His Minster Lovell lands were escheated to the Crown *(509)*.

**1488.** Sir William Stonor and Edmund Hampden were among the four county commissioners to examine archers and take the musters for the

Brittany expedition *(115)*.

**1492**. Walter Curson evicted twelve people from Ledall in Waterperry and converted 200 acres from arable to pasture *(573)*.

William Raynold was mason in charge of building the bell-tower of Magdalen College, Oxford: completed in 1505 *(757, 786)*.

**1494**. Henry VII visited Minster Lovell, as he did in 1497 and 1503 *(509)*.

**1497**. Henry VII granted Burford a second three-day fair *(203)*.

Lady Margaret, countess of Richmond, founded a public lecture in Divinity at Oxford: John Roper was the first lecturer in 1502 *(477)*.

**1498**. Thomas Wolsey was master of Magdalen College School *(323, 777)*: probably a pupil there too, as were Thomas More and John Longland *(511)*.

William Cope, Henry VII's cofferer, began the building of Hanwell Castle, the first use of brick in the north of the county *(786)*.

**1501**. John Arden converted 200 acres to pasture and evicted 42 people at Willaston in Hethe: he was Rewley Abbey's tenant, and his family continued as Pope tenants until 1590 *(573)*.

John Stanbridge gained a great reputation during his 9 years as schoolmaster of St John's Hospital, Banbury *(323, 510, 802)*, where Thomas Pope was his pupil *(510)*.

**APR**. The bishop of Lincoln set up a commission to try clerks who were held in Banbury Gaol after robbing Paul Bombyn, a London merchant, of £200 in Broadstone Field near Enstone *(30)*.

**1503**. Robert Busby, a woolgrower, converted 68 acres to pasture and destroyed a house at Grove in Sandford St Martin *(573)*.

**1504**. Burial in St Frideswide's of William Orchard, the master mason employed on the vaults of the Divinity School and St Frideswide's, and in building Magdalen College, Oxford *(786)*.

**1505**. Magdalen College bell-tower was given a clock, costing £10: in 1540 St Martin's church, Oxford regularly employed a clockkeeper *(608)*.

**1507**. Cold Norton priory became extinct for want of numbers *(154)*.

**1509**. Balliol College, Oxford was permitted to migrate in plague-time up to twelve miles from the city: Archbishop Neville had given them the farm of Moreton near Thame *(556)*.

Henry VII, on his death-bed, presented Magdalen College, Oxford with a she-bear *(511)*.

**1512**. Brasenose Hall became a College when its endowment was enriched by William Smyth, bishop of Lincoln and Sir Richard Sutton, Lady Margaret's lawyer *(777, 816)*.

John Wyse, a butcher, converted 200 acres to pasture at Chippinghurst, destroying four houses *(573, 940)*.

**1513**. Wynkyn de Worde revised 'Parvula' originally printed in 1481, and attributed to John Stanbridge *(511)*. Manchester Grammar School's statutes of 1515 speak of "Stanbryge gramyer" *(511)*.

**1515c.** Part of Pyrton, including the hamlet of Clare, inclosed: the rest c1639. *(773, 939)*.

**1516.** £29 paid by Merton College for an "uncommonly substantial" two-storeyed farmhouse which appears to be the original part of Holywell Manor, Oxford *(800, 963)*.

**1517.** Complaints of "ingrossing" of 11,587 acres in the county, three-quarters of them for pasture *(620, 940)*.
Richard Fox, bishop of Winchester, founded Corpus Christi College, Oxford *(108, 777, 786, 816)*: he was asked to remedy the mischiefs which spread pestilence and "frighted away the scholars" *(16, 986)*.

**1518.** Yet more pestilence at Canterbury College and St Mary Hall, Oxford *(16, 986)*: two plague deaths drove the summer court from Woodstock *(51)*.
Oxford printers included John Scolar and Johannes Dedicus, who secured the first example of copyright for seven years from the university Chancellor *(94, 477)*.

**1520.** A visitation of the small house of Austin canons at Bicester revealed the common lack of a novice-master and grammar-master *(633)*, and one at Stanton St John the presence of a woman in the rector's house *(503, 945)*.

**1521.** Bishop Longland's heresy hunt in Burford netted twenty conventicle-goers, including Edward 'schoolmaster of Burford' *(706)*, John Edmunds, a Burford tailor and his wife, and visitors from Asthall, Clanfield, Standlake, Upton and Witney. All recanted, but were confined to a religious house with branding and other penances *(77, 112, 203)*.

**1523.** A new charter for Oxford University, drawn up chiefly by Thomas Wolsey and Dr John London: Henry VIII accepted its surrender in 1543 after townsmen's opposition, but Elizabeth restored its main points *(475)*.

**1524.** The county, wealthiest in 1334, second wealthiest in 1086, was now only thirteenth in ranking according to tax returns *(743)*. John Dormer, a London mercer, built a manor-house on the site of a cell of Oseney Abbey at Steeple Barton: Ralph Sheldon altered it in 1679. Brewer Hall made it an "Abbey" after 1826 *(135, 251, 786, 832)*.

**1525.** Wolsey suppressed both a small Benedictine nunnery at Littlemore (now Minchery Farm) where the last visitation found a nun romping (ludendo et luctando) with boys in the cloister *(675)*, and St Frideswide's which was the core of his Cardinal College *(112, 777, 816)* where John Lubbyns and Henry Redmayne were master masons until 1529 *(317)*. In 1532 this became King Henry the Eighth's College and in 1546 Christ Church *(477)*. Holton and Headington stone was used *(408)*, a Lye Hill trough being described *(2)*: the road from Headington High Cross and possibly the bridge at 'Milhamforde' were improved for transporting materials *(503)*.

Ascott tenants in Great Milton parish complained of victimisation: in 1517 Dormer's tenant John Wylmott had been converting to pasture *(573)*.

**1526**. First of four borough charters to Henley *(823)*.

**1527**. Oxford's defiance of the 1523 university charter led to the imprisonment of its bailiffs, one in the Castle, the other in Bocardo *(475)*.

**1529**. Prolonged disturbances at Bruern Abbey against the abbot, John Chaffcombe *(154, 277)*.

**1530**. Bishop Longland erected 12 almshouses in his native Henley *(786)*. John Claymond, president of Corpus Christi College, Oxford, made a bequest for the upkeep of the new road to Headington *(503, 986)*. Henry VIII referred to the Universities the validity of his first marriage for an opinion: as in earlier times, the majority view at Oxford was compliant, and the centre of resistance was the Faculty of Arts *(477, 777)*.

**1531**. Sir Thomas Elyot, author, diplomat and resident of Combe, wrote 'The Boke named the Governor' for sons of the gentry who were destined to a life of public service *(450)*.

**OCT**. Bishop of Lincoln ordered the booksellers' stalls at Oxford's St Frideswide's Fair to be searched for heretical books *(94)*.

**1532**. Henry VIII visited Oxford, and transferred Wolsey's Cardinal College into a collegiate church in his own name *(45, 777)*.

**1533**. William Billing, a Merchant of the Staple at Calais, died and was buried at Deddington *(546)*.

**1534**. Henry VIII required an oath acknowledging royal supremacy from the Fellows of Oxford colleges: 167 submitted, but Balliol dons qualified their submission 'without prejudice to divine law and orthodox faith'. Faced with a statutory declaration in 1536, they made no more scruples *(556)*.

**1535**. Aggressive stand by Sir Walter Stonor, who reported to Cromwell that he had pulled up the weir of Walter Eaton belonging to Godstow Nunnery *(185)* and by John ap Powell, his servant, killed in a quarrel with Edmund Stonor: Edmund was pardoned after a winter in Marshalsea prison, as it was agreed his act was in self-defence *(124)*.

**1536**. Surrender of the smaller monastic houses: Bruern, whose abbot was rector of Wigginton in 1544 *(256)*, Bicester, Rewley, Dorchester, Goring and Wroxton *(154)*.

**17 MAY**. Henry Norris, courtier and keeper of Langley Park, was executed for undue familiarity with Queen Anne Boleyn *(170)*. His son Lord Norreys received Anne's daughter Elizabeth at Rycote in 1554.

**1537**. Thomas Pope was knighted for his work for Henry VIII in his Court of Augmentations: he could enjoy the familiar boast that 'he could ride in his own land from Cogges-by-Witney to Banbury' *(620)*, which Leland described in some detail *(944).* In 1542 Pope added to his possible rides, gaining Broadwell and the Sibfords by an exchange of lands *(620).*

**1538.** A donkey-wheel built at Grey's Court, Rotherfield Greys to operate over an earlier well.

**4 DEC.** Eynsham Abbey was surrendered to the King: Clattercote had done so in Aug. *(256).*

**1539.** Sir Adrian Fortescue of Stonor, Shirburn and Brightwell was executed at Tower Hill for sedition *(154).*

**NOV.** Surrender of the remaining monastic houses at Thame, Studley, Godstow and Oseney *(256).*

**1540.** Lord Williams of Thame began to enjoy monastic spoils, and remodelled a mediaeval building of Oseney at Weston-on-the-Green to make a two-storey front manor house: later restoration c1820 conspired to make it look even more "Tudor" *(786).*

**1541.** William Maltby became vicar of Hethe: he was the dispossessed prior of Snelshall in Buckinghamshire *(256).*

**17 JAN.** Henry VIII, making an allowance for his discarded wife Anne of Cleves, gave her the manors of Standlake, Broughton Poggs and Filkins *(620).*

**1542.** Henry VIII created the bishopric of Oxford, with Oseney as its centre, and the last abbot, Robert King, as its first bishop *(786).* Wood says that Oxford suffered two "pestilences" in this year *(16, 986).* John Leland, whose Itineraries *(944)* describe the county from about 1537, became rector of Haseley: he died in 1552 but lost his reason earlier *(112).* Edward Harman, courtier and barber, lived dangerously when named as a court person heretically inclined, but went on to Burford riches *(203).*

**3 JUNE.** Sir Thomas Pope, for a valuable consideration, gained the manor of Enstone from the lands surrendered by Winchcombe Abbey *(7, 30).*

**1544.** Edmund Harman bought monastic spoils at Burford: first the lands of the surrendered Hospital of St John (whose last master was given a pension of £3 to add to his stipend as vicar of Burford), then in 1546 the rectory and the land once belonging to Keynsham Abbey *(203).* In 1545 he bought one of four fulling mills on the Windrush *(203).*

**1545.** An elaborate roofed shelter called the Penniless Bench was built outside the city church of St Martin's Oxford *(475).*

**1546.** John Warner became the first Regius Professor of Medicine at Oxford *(466).*

**4 NOV.** Commissioners including Lord Williams *(115)* having arranged the surrender of Oseney Cathedral church and King Henry's College, Henry VIII established both Christ Church and St Frideswide's as the new cathedral *(154, 477, 786).* In 1528 Wolsey had planned to demolish it, and the roof of a new chapel had been made at Sonning *(786).*

**1548.** Protestant reformer Peter Martyn was installed at Christ Church as

Regius Professor of Divinity *(154)*. His wife's remains were muddled with those of St Frideswide later *(816)*.

**1549.** Chantry pickings were available: Richard Venables bought the lands of Woodstock, Standlake and Burford chantries, William Box, a London grocer, bought those at Witney, and Thomas Hawkyns bought that of St John's Hospital, Banbury for £89 *(922)*.
One crumb missing was Magdalen College School at Oxford, though the Dean of Christ Church had led the team of Visitors: a local protest from citizens wishing to use it to school and choir Oxford children may have been less effective than the founder's statutes, but the school was saved *(477, 511, 788)*.

**1 JULY.** Meeting of county gentry at Witney was ordered by Lord Grey de Wilton, on his way with 1300 troops to deal with prayer-book rebels in Devon, to deal with thirteen "traitorous persons" *(81, 112, 147)*, and an order stated the place of execution for six *(75, 154)*. Yet Henry Joyce, vicar of Chipping Norton (due to be hanged upon the steeple) appears to have died naturally in 1549 *(506, 922)*: Richard Thompson, vicar of Duns Tew (to be hanged at Banbury) was still in his post in 1554 *(506)*: John Wade, parish priest of Bloxham (intended to die on his steeple) still lived there in 1553 *(506)*; George Raves of Duns Tew made a will in 1558 *(506)*. The fate of John White, vicar of Combe *(244)*, John Brooklyns craftsman of Islip, William Boolar of Watlington, Bowldry of Haseley, Richard Whittington of Bicester and Sir Henry Mathew of Deddington is less clear, though Mathew, described as "parish priest" officiated in neither the parish nor the chantry in 1549 *(506, 546)*.

**7 AUG.** John of Ulm wrote from Oxford: "The Oxfordshire Papists are at last reduced to order, many of them having been apprehended and some gibbeted, and their heads fastened to the walls" *(81)*. The evidence is less conclusive, and less gory.

**14 AUG.** Geoffrey Mashe and Richard Noddes, Blackthorn husbandmen, were pardoned for all offences *(506)*.

**16 AUG.** James Webbe, vicar of Barford St Michael, was the only prisoner tried in London, convicted of treason as "captain of the rebels in Oxfordshire" and sentenced to be hanged, drawn and quartered at Aylesbury *(506)*.

**1550c.** A fulling mill was erected in an attempt to turn Oseney Abbey's buildings into a factory for 2000 woollen workers *(154, 311)*.
Turf maze dug at Troy Farm, Somerton *(786)*.

**1550.** John Danvers was a leader of a Banbury riot which destroyed fences enclosing land by the castle *(510)*.

**1552.** Bletchingdon Park fashioned to its present size by Vincent Poure *(773)*.

**1553.** John Pollard, county MP and settled at Nuneham Courtenay which he acquired in 1545, was elected Speaker of the House of Commons *(115)*.

**1554.** Banbury received a charter of incorporation *(17, 510, 711, 802)* and sent its first member, Thomas Denton, to parliament *(115)*.

**MAY.** Princess Elizabeth was removed from the Tower to fresh imprisonment in the Gate House of Woodstock Manor, under the considerate charge of Sir Henry Bedingfield. She remained until Apr. 1555, twice visiting Oxford, and staying at Rycote (which she three times did as Queen in 1568, 1570 and 1592) *(45, 51, 97, 285, 323)*.

**1555.** Sir Thomas Pope, having bought the site of the dissolved Durham College, Oxford *(816)* among his many speculative ventures, at first thought to found a replacement grammar school for the dissolved Trinity Guild in his native Deddington *(323)* and wrote a power, never exercised, to found a "Jesus schole" at Hook Norton *(112, 243)* into his charter for the new Trinity College, Oxford on Mar. 8 *(105, 477, 777)*: this he endowed with the manors of Broadwell, Broughton Poggs and Kencot, and the advowson of Broadwell church *(620)*.
Sir Thomas White, a London merchant tailor, founded St John's College, Oxford in place of the former St Bernard's College, to "strengthen the orthodox faith" *(110, 477)*.

**16 OCT.** Disputation on the Eucharist in the university church of St Mary was followed by the burning of Bishops Latimer and Ridley "in the Towne Ditche" of Oxford, "over against Balliol College" *(112, 475, 777)*.

**1556. 21 MAR.** Archbishop Thomas Cranmer was burned at Oxford, after retracting his recantation. 6s was paid for wood, and 3s 4d for the faggots *(777)*.

**21 JULY.** The Papal Legate, Cardinal Pole, was appointed Archbishop: as Visitor to the University of Oxford he was soon involved in the protest by the College of Physicians over the university's proposal to award a medical degree to David Laughton, an illiterate coppersmith *(466)*.

**1557.** Bicester and Oxford suffered from the "sweating sickness": green fruit prohibited from sale in Oxford *(16, 621, 986)*.
Death of Robert King, and burial in St Aldate's church, Oxford: a Cistercian monk, he rose to be abbot of Thame, his native town, and last abbot of Oseney. He was from 1528 vicar of Charlbury *(806)*. Henry VIII appointed him first bishop of Oxford in 1542, and he sat in judgment on the Protestant bishops *(464, 786)*.

**1558.** Falkland Hall in Burford High Street was built for a local clothier, Edmund Sylvester *(764)*.

**1559.** A rising courtier, Francis Walsingham, was MP for Banbury: in the following Parliament he was also elected for Lyme Regis, and chose the latter as a more advantageous seat *(115)*.

**18 MAR.** Lord Williams provided in his will for a free school at Thame: the school house was built in 1569, and his executors gave the running of the school in 1575 to New College, Oxford *(285, 323)*.

**1560.** John Bustard of Adderbury was expelled from New College, Oxford for refusing to attend divine service: he went abroad to Douai, and taught among the Jesuits until his death in 1576 *(217)*.

**1561.** Burford's market house, the Tolsey, gained "a carpet cloth" and its first mention in the records *(203, 764)*.

**1562.** Sir Francis Knollys, of a family rising in the Queen's service, was MP for the county, and from 1564 rented Cowley, Horspath, Littlemore and Garsington: his son became Earl of Banbury *(65, 503)*.

**1563.** A violent plague hit Oxford, "being the dregs of last year's mischief" *(16, 986)*: Balliol College retired to Church Hanborough leaving only the Bursar to maintain Chapel services and disinfect the rooms *(556)*.
John Foxe was appointed prebendary of Shipton-under-Wychwood: his chief fame is as martyrologist, and the Strasbourg version of his "Book of Martyrs" was published in 1554 *(277)*.
Elizabeth I granted a charter to the University replacing the contentious one of 1523 *(475)*: its matriculation statute gave the colleges control over the admission of students *(777)*.

**1564.** Plus ca change... "A pestilential disease in summer" *(986)*.

**1566. 31 AUG.** Queen Elizabeth was greeted with much oratory on her visit to Oxford: speeches at Wolvercote, Northgate, Carfax, Christ Church and then a Te Deum in the Cathedral. Undeterred, she spent a week there *(323, 467)*.

**1567.** After ten years' vacancy, Elizabeth I appointed another bishop of Oxford: Curwen resided at Swinbrook, but survived for only a year. It took the Queen twenty-one years to choose another, and thus to forego the revenues *(464)*.
William Camden, later headmaster of Westminster School, became a pupil at Magdalen College School, Oxford, and already conceived the idea of his "Britannia" *(511, 920)*.

**1568.** Robert Parsons became a Fellow of Balliol College, Oxford, where he was a popular teacher but made enemies by his scoffing manner. Expelled in 1574, he returned to Stonor in 1580 as a Jesuit priest *(556)*.

**1570.** Sir Henry Lee, ranger of Woodstock Park, lost 3000 sheep in a great storm. Over forty years he built up a vast estate including Ditchley and Spelsbury, but was unpopular as an encloser *(298, 451)*.

**17 NOV.** Growth in observance of Elizabeth's accession day *(298, 905)*.

**29 NOV.** Teaching began at Lord Williams' school at Thame *(285)*.

**1571.** Burford Corporation was under legal pressure over properties for maintaining Burford bridge which could be construed as chantries: prudently this was used, with the support of Simon Wisdom, to found a Free (grammar) School at Burford *(77, 323, 706, 974)*.

Hugh ap Rice, treasurer of St David's Cathedral, founded Jesus College, Oxford *(477)*.

**MAY.** Balliol College dispersed due to violent plague *(16, 986)* and did not re-assemble in Oxford until Feb. 1572. Lincoln College followed suit, and dispersed for similar reasons in 1512, 1526, 1536 and 1604 *(556, 777)*.

**1573.** Alderman William Noble was imprisoned by the university vice-Chancellor for twelve days for barring his entry into Oxford Guildhall where he intended to hold a court leet *(115)*. Noble was a city MP in 1584.

**1574.** Walter Calcott, a wealthy wool merchant and Stapler, having moved from Hook Norton and built a house at Williamscote in Cropredy, also built and endowed a grammar school and master's house next to his own *(323, 786)*. The school joined the National Society's scheme in 1814 as an elementary school *(741)*.

**AUG.** Elizabeth I was greeted by Burford burgesses at the Windrush bridge as she passed through from Langley *(32, 77)*.

**1576.** Mileways Act imposed on householders living within five miles of Oxford the obligation to contribute to improving the approaches to Oxford: a dead letter from about 1625 to its renewal in 1771 *(16, 503, 955)*.

Elizabeth I made Woodstock a staple of wool and yarn *(51)*.

Her plans to visit in 1575 had been cancelled due to plague reports in Chipping Norton *(436)* and Oxford *(16, 986)*.

**1577.** "A most pernicious infection" *(16, 986)* accounted for the 500 deaths emanating from the "Black Assize" which killed Sir William Babington of Kiddington during the trial in Oxford Castle of Rowland Jenkes, a "saucy, foul-mouthed bookseller" *(1, 16, 112)*.

Trinity College retreated to Sir Thomas Pope's new rectory at Garsington *(105, 310)*.

**1578.** There were at least 23 locks, 16 mills, 16 flood-gates and 7 weirs on the Thames between Oxford and Maidenhead *(185)*.

**1579.** Thame Market Hall built (on the site occupied since 1887 by the Town Hall): it replaced an earlier moot hall, on whose clock the church-wardens spent 5s on repairs in 1543 *(285)*.

**1580.** Thomas Fermor provided in his will for a school at Somerton *(61, 974)*.

**1581.** A printing press was set up at Stonor by John Harris, John Harvey and John Tucker for the Jesuit mission established there by Robert Parsons and Edmund Campion (who was seized by troops at Lyford and executed at Tyburn) *(147)*.

A turbulent landowner, George Whitton, clashed with both Sir Henry Lee, Ranger of Woodstock Park *(51, 455)* and with Woodstock Council over Sterting Grove, the latter case going to Star Chamber *(97)*.

**1582.** Plague again *(16, 986):* deaths at Chalford in Aston Rowant may have contributed to its depopulation *(573).*
Cobb family built a house on Adderbury Green, pulled down in 1815 *(786).*

**1583.** Four Godington farmers accused of sheltering priests *(520).*

**1584.** Rising lawyer Lawrence Tanfield became MP for Woodstock: by 1604 he was MP for the county, more fitting his station *(153, 203).*
Unwonted drama in church was condemned at the Archdeacon's Court: instances were noted at Duns Tew and at Blackthorn, where a possible "lord of misrule" entered church "with a paynted cloth on his back" *(905).*

**1585.** John Barnes, bookseller and wineseller, was made sole printer to the University, operating from St Mary's Entry, Oxford *(94, 295, 477).*
St Martin's established "City lectures" or Sunday sermons in Oxford which lasted until its demolition in 1896 *(475).*
Richard Cornwall bequeathed £300 for the founding of a free grammar school at Woodstock: it was finally launched in 1599 *(323).*

**1586.** Harpsden was inclosed by this date *(773, 939).*
Banbury was known for cakes described as 'bagge puddings, or parme puddings made with flower, frittars, pancakes' *(627).*
Thomas Tesdale, at Ludwell and then Glympton, raised woad for the dyeing industry *(292).*
New building included Mapledurham House for Sir Richard Blount, and Water Eaton manor house for Sir Edward Frere *(786).*

**1588.** Anthony Cope, MP for Banbury, spent three weeks in the Tower for proposing a Commons motion attacking Church government. He proposed that a Prayer Book of his own composition be solely authorised *(17, 154, 510).* Nonetheless he was knighted in 1591 and twice entertained James I at Hanwell *(115)* where he had a water-clock *(2).*

**4 SEPT.** Robert Dudley, Earl of Leicester, was taken ill and died suddenly at Cornbury on his way home from the court after the Armada crisis *(112).*

**1589.** Christopher Rawlins, vicar of Adderbury, died willing a grammar school to be built there *(323):* It was built on the Green in Adderbury East *(786).*
Thomas Belson of Aston Rowant was arrested with two seminarists, George Nichols and Robert Yaxley, at the Catherine Wheel in Oxford: all three were executed, together with a Welsh inn-servant, Humphrey Prichard: the landlady lost her property and was imprisoned *(112, 147, 154, 475).*
Underhill, a native of Oxford, made little mark in his three years as bishop of Oxford: for twelve years after his death the Crown benefited from the revenues during another vacancy *(464).* John Danvers of Calthorpe failed to stem Puritan zeal for putting down Whitsun Ales, May Games and Morris Dances at Calthorpe and Neithrop. Worsted by Cope, he left the

county *(510)*.

**1590.** Banbury Puritans won another victory in depriving Thomas Bracebridge of his vicarage: they were free to concentrate on the medieval crosses *(606)*.

One-sixth of the county's settlements, largely the smaller ones, were inclosed by this date *(941)*.

Sir Alexander Colepeper, Robert Catesby and twelve other Recusants were held at Broughton Castle from Mar. to Oct. *(510)*.

**1592.** Elizabeth visited Ditchley, where Sir Henry Lee entertained her in a 'low timber house with a pretty bowling green' *(786)*: she also visited Oxford *(323)*, and Burford *(203)*.

**1593.** Two women from Long Combe appeared before the Archdeacon's Court on a charge of witchcraft: the judge ordered them to produce four witnesses to testify their innocence *(154)*.

Plague, due to multitude "who came to Oxford to see the plays" *(986)*, which may have included Hamlet *(422)*. It also caused the Burford right of a day's hunting in Wychwood Forest to be commuted for a largesse of venison, which continued to be sent until 1854 *(32)*.

**1596.** The battle of Enslow Hill. A Witney person claimed to have seen "some ten persons with pikes and swords" there on Nov. 17. Lord Norreys wrote of the conspirators on Dec. 14 "their opinion will hardly be discovered unless it be on the rack, which they are likely to taste of". Trial on Dec. 17 decided to imprison the ring-leaders *(84, 573, 741, 743)*. Their aims were plain: to attack the chief houses (Water Eaton, Hampton Gay, Ditchley and Yarnton) and murder the gentry (Frere, Poure, Lee and Spencer) and take corn from the barns and cast down hedges and ditches. Their enemies were conspicuous enclosing landlords: they said Frere "destroyed a whole town called Water Eaton".

Activists included Roger Ibill of Hampton Gay, John Harcourt gent. of Cogges, Mr Pudsay of Elsfield, Heath, Powell and Durbridge of Yarnton. A mob from Witney had separately threatened Lee's Rest at Charlbury *(741)*.

**1597.** Spate of deaths (21 of 22) in the last four months of the year at Enstone *(30)*.

**1598.** John Howson became vicar of Bampton: in 1618 he began ten years as bishop of Oxford *(137)*.

**1599.** Burford had to give long leases on their recovered charity lands due to their poor state *(203)*.

Banbury had a Leather Hall *(510)*.

**1600. 26 JULY.** Destruction of Banbury Cross by Puritans, whose leader Henry Shewell prayed "God be thancked theire god dagon is fallen downe to the ground" *(606)*.

**1601.** Catesby's fortunes hit once more by his fine after the failure of the Essex rising, so that the mortgaged Chastleton estate was sold *(164)*.

**1602. 8 NOV.** The old University library, "Duke Humphrey's" was refurbished and opened by Sir Thomas Bodley *(477)*.

**1603.** James I removed his court to Oxford to avoid the plague, but Wood says it followed *(16, 986)*. The king was entertained at Christ Church *(45)* and in Sept. at Lee's Ditchley *(323)* and Tanfield's Burford Priory *(203)* as well as Langley.

**18 SEPT.** Shipton burial of "a French boy, out of William Whiting's house, .. the court lying at Great Langley" *(277)*.

**1604.** Woodstock had a brickworks *(627)*.

**FEB.** Adam Greene, a seminary priest, was released from Oxford Gaol to go abroad by virtue of James' proclamation *(147)*.

**12 MAR.** Oxford University given the right to elect two MPs, as a bulwark against the growing band of sectaries *(477, 777)*.

**12 NOV.** Oxford Guild of Freemasons, Carpenters, Joiners and Slaters incorporated by charter *(582)*.

**17 DEC.** James I granted a charter enabling Henley to appoint 13 governors of Henley Grammar School, endowed by legacy of Augustine Knapp in 1602 but this too was supplemented by the King *(36, 323, 823)*.

**1605.** Oxford paid £150 for a new charter confirming its privileges *(475)*. Wood noted the press of 150 or so "cottages, cabins or hovels.. have caused the plague to increase very much.. by taking in foreigners for inmates" *(986)*.

Oxford city and university representatives joined the new Oxford-Burcot Commission which built the first modern locks on the Thames *(185)*.

**NOV.** The Gunpowder Plot. Sir Richard Wenman of Thame Park was arrested with his wife and interrogated, for the Wenmans had given shelter to Father John Gerard earlier *(285)*.

**1607.** Chipping Norton received a charter of incorporation *(81, 112)*.

**1608.** Thomas Webb was elected Mayor of Banbury under new powers in James I's charter which extended that of 1554 *(711)*.

Publication of the Authorized Version of the Bible, on which John Aglionby, rector of Islip had worked with translation *(23)*.

Henry Sharpe the first bookseller recorded at Banbury *(510)*.

**1609.** William Frewin, a silk weaver, worked at Henley. The mill for silk-winding there closed in 1856 *(36)*.

Dame Elizabeth Periam endowed a school at Henley to bring up the poorer sort of boys 'in good manners and the fear of God': until 1792 it shared a building with the Free Grammar School *(323)*.

**1610.** Otho Nicholson, of Christ Church, bore the £2500 expense of piping water from above Hinksey to a conduit at Carfax, Oxford *(112)*. Nicholas and Dorothy Wadham founded Wadham College, Oxford which was built by William Arnold on the Austin Friars site outside Smith Gate *(82, 477)*.

Sir Thomas Bodley made an agreement with the Stationers' Company that a copy of every book should go to the library in Oxford he opened in 1602: this was being extended by the building of the New Schools and of Arts and Selden End *(786)*.
William Whateley became vicar of Banbury, another Puritan close to John Dod and Robert Harris, rectors at Cope's Hanwell *(112, 510, 743)*.

**1 MAY.** Woodstock paid 3s 2d for "music at the bringing home of the elm from Combe" *(97)*.

**22 AUG.** James I and Henry, Prince of Wales, visited Cornbury House: in 1615 Sir John Fortescue sold out to Danvers *(806)*.

**9 NOV.** George Napier, Oxford-born seminarist, was hanged at Oxford after his capture at Kirtlington *(147, 779)*.

**1611.** William Laud became President of St John's College, Oxford *(786)*.
Sloth over Thames improvements led to its timber being diverted to Sir Thomas Bodley for his library enlargement at Oxford *(185)*.

**1612.** Sir Richard Fermor bought Tusmore, which eventually replaced Somerton, and was the family home until 1810 *(147)*.
Houses of Correction opened at Witney and Banbury *(808)*.
Marston fields inclosed by Chancery deed *(226, 939)*.

**29 JAN.** Foundation stone of the New Schools laid, the day after the burial of Sir Thomas Bodley in Merton College, Oxford *(112, 786)*.

**1613.** John Lister founded almshouses at Mapledurham *(786)*.
Souldern's inclosure by Chancery decree resisted by freeholders *(520, 773, 939)*.

**1614.** Walter Jones completed building Chastleton House *(808)*.
Ellinor Collins received an apron-cloth from Woodstock's Mayor for her services as "our Whitsuntide lady" *(97)*.

**1615.** William Juxon became rector of Somerton, and left a legacy to it: his career led to the see of London, presence at Charles' execution, and retirement near Chipping Norton *(61)*.

**1616.** Prince Charles matriculated at Oxford university *(477)*.
Wolvercote mills (fulling and corn) sold to Sir John Walter of Sarsden *(497)*: visited later by Dr Plot *(2)*.
Carfax Conduit was made over to Oxford Corporation, which collected the complaints about its obstruction of traffic which began in 1634: in 1787 it was removed to Nuneham Courtenay *(475, 570)*.

**1617.** Henry Danvers, Earl of Danby, courtier and art lover, became Ranger of Cornbury Park and remodelled the house in the 1630s *(786)*.
Six villages (Wootton, Old Woodstock, Bladon, Stonesfield, Combe and Hanborough) petitioned successfully for removal from Wychwood Forest *(170)*.

**13 JULY.** Five prisoners in Oxford Gaol freed by warrant to be delivered to Sir Thomas Smith "to be transported into Virginia or other partes beyond the seas" *(276)*.

**1619.** Sir Henry Savile, Warden of Merton College, Oxford, founded Chairs of Geometry and Astronomy for the University *(295)*.

**1620.** Leonard Poure willed four almshouses at Bletchingdon *(229, 974)*.

**1621.** Henry Danvers, Earl of Danby, gave land formerly a Jewish burial ground outside Oxford's East Gate for a Botanic or Physic Garden: Nicholas Stone built the gateway *(777, 786, 816)*.
Witchcraft accusation at Stonesfield arose from quarrel between poacher and gamekeeper Will Huggins. The poacher was village constable who alleged Huggins bewitched cattle and horses *(806)*.
Sir Francis Stonor endowed an almshouse for six poor women and four poor men at Assendon *(974)*.
Burford races held: a stranger knifed at the George was buried. Similar evidence of racing in 1626 and 1654 *(203, 764)*.
Burford further discomfited when Judge Tanfield came down against the Corporation in Quo Warranto proceedings he instituted as a complainant in 1607 *(203)*.
A bad year for local MPs: Sir John Bennett, a University MP, was expelled for receiving bribes *(115)*, the Earl of Berkshire committed suicide on release from the Fleet, a punishment for brawling in the Lords *(285)*.

**2 OCT.** Barton Holyday's comedy was presented before James I during his Oxford visit: he was not amused. Holyday was Archdeacon from 1626 to 1661, much of this time spent "sheltering himself at Iffley" *(45)*. He was also rector of Emmington *(562)*.

**1622.** William Camden raised the tone of Oxford University by founding a Chair of History and endowing it with Bexley manor: George Ivye, student of Broadgates Hall, lowered the tone by calling William Stoner a 'cuckold and cucumber' and 'by poynting or boring with his fingers forked in the manner of hornes' *(844)*. No doubt he knew the meaning of "sending Verdingales to Broadgate" too *(1)*.
Lord Saye and Sele imprisoned in the Fleet for criticism of James I *(808)*.

**1623.** Bletchingdon inclosed by agreement with 15 freeholders *(48, 939, 773)*.

**1624.** Pembroke College, Oxford founded, nominally by James I, but with endowment of Richard Wightwick of Shropshire and Thomas Tesdale of Glympton. Tesdale's bequest to Abingdon scholars at Balliol College had encountered difficulties: Crabtree's stabbing of a Balliol freshman and pleading benefit of clergy and even avoiding the customary branding was but one *(556)*. Broadgates Hall (of which Thomas Clayton was master and John Pym a member) became a part of the new foundation *(120, 295, 477, 786)*.
An Act to make the Thames navigable from Burcot to Oxford strengthened the existing Commissioners: pound locks called "turnpikes" were

soon built at Iffley, Swift Ditch and Sandford, of which John Taylor, the "Water Poet" wrote in 1632 *(112, 185, 475).*
John Hiron and others of Great Tew petitioned the Lords against Judge Tanfield's denying them timber and Cowhill pasture: other tenants at Bledington and Asthall petitioned. Lady Tanfield "saith the inhabitants of Tu are more worthy to be ground to powder than to have any favour shewed them". *(153).*

**1625.** Thomas Lydyat, "chronologer and cosmographer" to Henry, Prince of Wales, and in 1620 discoverer of a menologium *(2)*, built the rectory at Alkerton *(786).*
Parliament came to Oxford to avoid the plague, but it followed: colleges dispersed and townsmen fled to Port Meadow *(45, 295, 986).*
Charles I visited Rycote *(285, 786).*
Great Tew gained a new lord with Tanfield's death and burial under a costly monument in Burford church *(45)*: Lucius Cary, Lord Falkland kept open house there for writers such as Ben Jonson, Cowley and Edmund Waller *(153)*. Lady Falkland even began a parish school.

**1626.** Great Tom, one of the cathedral peal, which came from Oseney Abbey, was recast (as on five other occasions in the century): Humphrey Keene of Caulcott in Lower Heyford was responsible, with his son James, who moved at this time to set up a bell-foundry at Woodstock *(917).*
William Knollys was created Earl of Banbury: he died in 1632 leaving two sons and a long-disputed inheritance *(65, 115).*

**1627.** Charles requested the punishment of Oxford students who killed his game in Woodstock Park *(97).*

**1628.** Royal Commission examined Burford charities *(203).*

**2 MAR.** One-third of Banbury destroyed by fire, the Puritan vicar, William Whateley, comforting inhabitants by blaming it on their sins *(510, 802).*

**1629. 25 MAY.** Fire at Eynsham destroyed 12 houses *(276, 773).*

**1630.** Oxford races held on Port Meadow: renewed in 1680 until 1880 *(428).*
Robert Lowe, owner of Bolshipton manor, St Clements, called to explain his distraint of knighthood *(503).*
William Laud was University Chancellor, 1630-41 *(777)*: an early act was to prohibit four-wheeled carriages on the roads from Oxford to London which were not university carriers: when Milton, Haseley, Tetsworth and Lewknor protested in 1638 he gave way *(312).*

**1632.** Bishop Bancroft built Cuddesdon Palace: earlier bishops had used Swinbrook and Marsh Baldon *(112, 154)*. It was destroyed in 1644.

**1633.** Chancellor Laud obtained a charter to the University allowing printing *(94)*: a springboard for the Civil War pamphlet and squib industry in Oxford *(816).*

**1634.** William Avery of Chipping Norton emigrated to Massachusetts *(436).*

Fall of spire and tower of Deddington church: costly rebuilding incomplete until 1685. Charles I requisitioned the bells for gunmetal in 1643 *(112, 546)*.

**1 MAY.** Tumult in St Peter-le-Bailey church in Oxford when Puritans attacked parishioners bent on garlanding the chancel screen, including a 21 year-old apprentice tailor consistently described as 'boy' or 'youth' *(844)*.

**1635.** Robert Vesey, a wool merchant of Chimney, left £300 to found a Free Grammar School at Bampton: the building was completed in 1653 *(323)*.

Charles I caused Danby to revive the Swainmote court in Wychwood Forest to raise revenue. Exactions were more severe at Headington from Shotover delinquents, and Charles tried in 1638 to create a new forest bailiwick round Shipton *(277)*.

Owen Johner subscribed (to the Thirtynine Articles) as schoolmaster of Kidlington *(709)*.

First barge to navigate the improved Thames reached Oxford *(112, 185)*.

**1636.** Plague prevalent, forcing the court to Woodstock, and the county Assizes to Burford *(203)*.

Ship money assessments laid on Oxford of £100, Chipping Norton £40, Banbury £40 (recently fired *(17)* ). Despite £800 of Welsh money "being lost for a time by accident at Ensam Ferry" *(642)*, no county fell further in arrears *(285)*.

**3 MAR.** Charles I confirmed the Laudian Statutes by which Oxford University was governed until 1854. The times prevented Laud's revival of the Archbishop's right of Visitation *(475, 777)*.

**23 AUG.** Queen Henrietta Maria visited the Enstone "waterworks" of Thomas Bushell, a pushing spirit who had been Bacon's seal-bearer and as farmer of Welsh minerals was to bring the mint to Oxford *(556)*, who had the speeches and songs printed in Oxford *(94)*. The series of grottoes and fountains in the Glyme valley, "so contrived as sportively to wet the unwary" was visited by Evelyn in 1664 and attracted the attention of Dr Plot *(2, 30, 112, 131)*. Charles wrote in 1635 to Danby urging moving the Worcester highway so as to preserve Bushell's works *(170)*: alas, they are all gone.

**29 AUG.** William Laud, not to be outdone, showed the King and Queen the new library of St John's College, Oxford, and admitted Prince Rupert to the degree of MA *(45, 306)*.

**1637.** Bulstrode Whitelock of Henley rejected the Earl of Berkshire's offer to share a royal patent for exploiting a new malt-kiln *(36)*. Lord Falkland sold Burford Priory to William Lenthall *(203)*. Reindeer Inn furnished its Globe Room at Banbury: dismantled panelling is reassembled in Banbury Museum *(786)*.

**SEPT.** Three Banbury constables imprisoned for failing to levy ship money: within a month of release the arrears were collected *(510)*.

**1638.** Edward Welchman began to make Banbury cakes at the Sign of the Unicorn in Parsons Street *(510, 802)*.

**1639.** Sir George Croke of Studley Priory endowed an almshouse for 4 men and 4 women at Studley *(15, 541, 974)*. He had sided with those judges who supported Hampden against the Crown *(45)*.

**1640.** Henry Cornish founded an almshouse at Chipping Norton for eight poor people *(808)*.
Dr Samuel Radcliffe, rector of Steeple Aston and Principal of Brasenose College, Oxford founded a Grammar School there *(251, 323)*. Nicholas Stone's "Romish" south porch of St Mary's church, Oxford, was one item in Archbishop Laud's impeachment *(777)*.
Speaker William Lenthall represented Woodstock, and civil lawyer, John Selden, the University in the new Parliament *(115)*: the proportion of university-trained MPs was higher in 1640 than ever again before 1918. Oxford trained one child in every hundred, and created a class of alienated intellectuals skrimping as curates or schoolmasters who were cast as radical incendiaries *(822)*.

**1641.** Horton-cum-Studley inclosed by this date *(733, 939)*.
Robert Skinner, bishop of Oxford, imprisoned in the Tower after opposing the Bill to exclude bishops from the Lords: in 1646 he retired to Launton *(464)*.
Lord Saye and Sele accepted a court position in the Court of Wards while being the driving force behind county petitions for the 'pulling down' of bishops *(115, 770)*.
Witney blanket makers, unincorporated at this time, petitioned the Lords about blanket sealing patents *(90)*.

**1642. 8 AUG.** Banbury guns taken by Earl of Northampton for use at Warwick: he pre-empted Puritan intentions *(76)*.

**16 AUG.** Bulstrode Whitelock and John Hampden seized the royal commissioners, including the Earl of Berkshire, at Sir Robert Dormer's house, and sent them as prisoners to London *(76)*.

**28 AUG.** Sir John Biron led a regiment to Oxford to defend the university, after a skirmish at Brackley *(76)*.

**10 SEPT.** Biron left for Worcester, accompanied by 100 student volunteers *(76, 770)*.

**12 SEPT.** Colonel Arthur Goodwyn occupied Oxford for Parliament *(76, 770)*.

**14 SEPT.** Lord Saye and Sele's troops reached Oxford, but left after six days *(76, 770)*.

**4 OCT.** Woodstock's Town Clerk, Edward Hiorns, had to explain to its MP, Speaker Lenthall, at the bar of the Commons his conduct in giving up the town armour to the King *(97)*.

**25 OCT.** Battle moved from Worcester to Edgehill *(802)*.

**27 OCT.** Banbury garrison instantly surrendered as King advanced from Aynho: reinlisted under Northampton as governor *(513)*. Broughton was also taken *(76)*.

**29 OCT.** "Our Oxford.. stands clear, gilded by the beams of Your Majesty's royal presence" *(986)* is how the university received the King *(76, 513)*.

**3 NOV.** Charles left Oxford, marching through Benson and Henley to Reading *(76, 770)* but failing to reach London.

**29 NOV.** Charles re-entered Oxford, and took up residence at Christ Church *(76, 770)*.

**23 DEC.** Prince Rupert dispersed Northamptonshire Roundheads who were besieging Banbury Castle *(76)*.

**1643. 1 JAN.** Sir John Biron wounded in the face with a poleaxe, and six soldiers killed (buried at Burford *(77)* ) in a skirmish there as Biron returned to Oxford *(76, 203)*.

**3 JAN.** Thomas Bushell arrived in Oxford with authentic dies and set up the Royal Mint: Charles requested college plate, and Magdalen sent 291 lbs, All Souls 253 lbs, Exeter College 246 lbs. *(295, 513, 770, 777)*.

**22 JAN.** Essex's troops entered Henley, and six soldiers were killed (buried at Henley) *(823)*.

**JAN.** Cavaliers had the best script-writers, with John Taylor's poems and John Birkenhead's broadsheet, Mercurius Aulicus, printed in Oxford *(513)*. Roundheads were not long content with "Spiritual Knapsack" pamphlets, and a London unofficial answer was Mercurius Britanicus, whose second editor was Marchmont Needham of Burford *(32, 513)*.

**4 FEB.** Roundhead prisoners from Cirencester were housed in St Michael's *(513)* or St Thomas' church *(247)* at Oxford.

**4 MAR.** Cat-and-mouse game at Henley: Roundhead Skippon fortified Phyllis Court to watch Cavalier d'Oyley at Greenlands *(823)*.

**20 MAR.** Parliamentary Commissioners arrived at Oxford and stayed, negotiating with Charles, until Apr. 15. Threw Falkland and Waller together into neutral "plotting" position *(76, 513)*.

**APR.** Oxford completed its fortifications, including St Clements where "all most a whole streete" was pulled down *(948)*. New College was the principal magazine, the Law and Logic schools stocked with oats. Swords were beaten at Wolvercote, a gunpowder mill set up at Oseney, and Charles commandeered Deddington bells for gunmetal *(76, 131, 513, 986)*. The Royalist garrison at Cornbury set up a battery *(806)*.

**MAY.** John Milton married Mary Powell at Forest Hill *(151, 503)*.

**6 MAY.** Banbury garrison defeated Northamptonshire Roundheads at Middleton Cheney *(76)*.

**13 MAY.** An important ammunition convoy reached Woodstock from the Duke of Newcastle *(76)*.

**10 JUNE.** At last Essex moved Roundhead forces up to Thame *(76, 770)*.

**13 JUNE.** Roundhead advance guard set up at Wheatley bridge, less than a mile from the Cavaliers on Shotover Plain. Balmore, scoutmaster of "rebel army" buried at Wheatley that week *(76, 285, 770, 981)*.

**17 JUNE.** Essex sent a strong body to seize Islip, but they retired *(76, 285)*. Rupert, with fewer men, rode out of Oxford, fell upon Luke's quarters at Postcombe and outlying billets at Chinnor, and rode back at dawn, avoiding Wheatley bridge, through Chalgrove, where they were briefly delayed in a skirmish *(76, 285, 513, 770)*.

**18 JUNE.** Brief moment at Chalgrove: in 1843 a stone obelisk was built there, largely commemorating its donors *(786)*.

**24 JUNE.** Death at Thame of John Hampden from wounds at Chalgrove *(285)*.

**25 JUNE.** Colonel Hurry repeated Rupert's tactics and raided West Wycombe *(513)*.

**10 JULY.** Cox the spy reported "there dies about 40 a week of plague in Oxford" *(948)*: allowing for occupational exaggeration, St Martin's was burying at 5, and Cuddesdon at 4 times the normal rate *(787, 981)*.

**12 JULY.** Wilmot, Biron and 1800 horse, all that could be spared at Oxford with Rupert gone north to welcome the Queen, left to aid Hopton at Devizes *(513)*.

**14 JULY.** Queen Henrietta Maria was greeted at Edgehill, and escorted on the last stage of her journey from Bridlington to Oxford, with 2000 Yorkshire troops. She set up court at Merton College *(76, 770)*. Late in the day Hopton inflicted defeat on the Roundheads at Roundway Down *(513)*.

**21 JULY.** Oxford's defence works hurried on by conscripting University labour on paid of 12d a day fine. Charles inspected on occasion, to "take notice of the small number of people at work" *(770)*.

**22 AUG.** Sir William Pennyman, governor of Oxford, died of camp sickness, which was widespread in Essex's army and spread to the army and citizens of Oxford *(475, 513, 754)* where scavengers' wages were doubled *(16, 986)*.

**2 SEPT.** Essex's army, joined by London regiments at Brackley, ran the gauntlet of Royalist cavalry and marched sixth miles across the Cotswolds to relieve Gloucester. Rupert attacked them between Chipping Norton and Stow but was driven off *(436, 513, 770)*.

**20 SEPT.** A disillusioned Lord Falkland rode as a volunteer in the King's cavalry at the battle of Newbury and was killed *(32, 513)*.

**1644.** Oxford unsettled: the Cornmarket was pulled down to use its lead for bullets and timber for military engines *(770)*, St Aldate's was full of "evacuee" royalists *(754)* and the plague continued *(16, 986)*. Anthony Wood was removed to Thame for schooling *(33)*. Charles made the county pay £2700 a month by following the Roundhead system of quartering troops free, and assessing the districts in his control *(513)*.

**22 JAN.** Royalist Parliament of Lords and Commons met in Christ Church Hall, until April, and returned in Jan. 1645 for a second session *(513)*.

**17 APR.** Charles went to Abingdon to see his pregnant Queen off to Bath and exile: they never met again *(513)*.

**MAY.** In Rupert's absence, Charles erred in withdrawing outlying garrisons at Reading and Abingdon: Essex closed on Cowley, Islip and Headington *(513)*.

**2 JUNE.** William Waller forced a crossing of the Thames at Newbridge, thus threatening Oxford with siege *(76)*.

**3 JUNE.** Charles, with 6000 troops, left Oxford down Horse and Jockey Lane to take the old road through Northleigh to Burford and Worcester *(76, 416, 754)*.

**6 JUNE.** Essex's army lay at Burford: propaganda complaints of "uncivil use" of the church *(32, 77, 203)*. He met Waller at Chipping Norton, then left to relieve Lyme Regis and attack Exeter *(513)*.

**21 JUNE.** Charles evaded Waller, and at Woodstock gathered 11,000 troops and the guns from Oxford *(513)*.

**29 JUNE.** Charles drew Waller into battle at Cropredy Bridge, but the Roundheads were allowed to retrieve a desperate situation *(76, 513)*. Charles perhaps slept better at Deddington rectory *(546)* than at the Grimsbury yeoman's house *(513)*. Two soldiers slain locally were buried this year at North Aston *(49)*.

**8 AUG.** King arrested John Wilmot whose dislike of Rupert had become disruptive. Wilmot, ennobled in the spring as Lord Wilmot of Adderbury, had married a rich widow with Roundhead kinsmen, by whom his son Rochester, the Restoration rake, was born *(217, 513)*.

**27 AUG.** Colonel John Fiennes began the siege of Banbury castle *(76)*. The town was much deserted, and 161 plague burials took place in the summer months *(510)*.

**6 OCT.** Fire destroyed 330 houses in the north-west quarter of Oxford *(87)*. Charles was in the West Country, and did not return until Oct 29 *(513)*.

**26 OCT.** Gage joined Northampton and the besiegers of Banbury Castle were driven away *(76)*.

**6 NOV.** Charles reviewed 15,000 troops on Bullingdon Green, and proclaimed Prince Rupert a general *(513)*.

**7 DEC.** Haughty Oxford governor, Sir Arthur Aston (who had been assaulted on his round of the garrison in 1643) now broke his leg "kervelling on horseback on Bullingdon Green before certain ladies" according to a malicious witness *(754)*. He was killed in the assault on Drogheda, battered with his own wooden leg.

**25 DEC.** Gage replaced Aston as governor of Oxford *(76)*.

**1645. 11 JAN.** Sir Henry Gage killed attempting to put a Royalist fort at Culham bridge to contain the Abingdon Roundheads *(76)*.

**24 APR.** Cromwell was active in disrupting Royalist movement north of Oxford: he defeated cavalry at Islip, and seized Bletchingdon House *(76)*.

**26 APR.** Cromwell routed Vaughan's regiment at Bampton *(76)*.

**3 MAY.** Colonel Windebank shot in Oxford Castle for failing to resist Cromwell at Bletchingdon *(770)*.

**7 MAY.** Charles left Oxford, to meet Rupert at Stow *(513)*.
Goring managed to recover Radcot Bridge, despite Cromwell's presence at Faringdon *(440)*.

**22 MAY.** Essex at Marston began to blockade Oxford with support from Cromwell at Wytham and Browne at Wolvercote *(76)*.

**23 MAY.** Walter's house at Godstow was fired by evacuating Royalists *(76)*.

**1 JUNE.** Gaunt House near Standlake was taken by Colonel Rainsborough *(76)*.

**13 JUNE.** Sir Peter Browne of Kiddington was wounded at Naseby, and died at Northampton *(147)*.

**13 AUG.** D'Oyley, governor of Henley, reported "mutiny" amongst his garrison soldiers *(36)*.

**28 AUG.** King spent one night in Oxford after Naseby, before setting off to relieve Hereford *(76)*.

**7 SEPT.** Royalists turned the tables. Colonel Legge, governor of Oxford, led a troop of horse to "beat up" Roundhead troops in Thame: schoolboy Wood was an eye-witness *(76, 285, 986)*.

**5 NOV.** Charles returned to Oxford *(76)*, his cause collapsing.

**1646. 22 APR.** Woodstock surrendered to Colonel Rainsborough, after a month's siege *(76)*. Labourers were paid 8s for two days' work in throwing down the bulwarks *(97)*.

**27 APR.** Charles I, "his hair closely cropped, disguised as a servant, accompanied by his chaplain and groom" left Oxford *(475, 265, 777)*, for Hambleden manor house *(823)* and St Albans.

**1 MAY.** Fairfax made Garsington his headquarters for laying siege to Oxford *(76)*.

**6 MAY.** Banbury surrendered to Colonel Whalley after three months' siege *(76)*.

**18 MAY.** Negotiations with Oxford's garrison began at Unton Croke's house at Marston *(76, 805)*.

**15 JUNE.** Holton register records "Henry Ireton, Commissary-General to Sir Thomas Fairfax, and Bridget, daughter to Oliver Cromwell, Lieutenant-

General of the Horse.. were married by Dr Dell in the Lady Whorwood her house in Holton" *(947)*.

**24 JUNE.** Sir Thomas Glenham surrendered Oxford to Fairfax, and the Royalist garrison marched out over Magdalen Bridge *(76, 777)*.
Radcot surrendered to Parliament *(76)*.

**29 JUNE.** Oxford Council met to elect as Mayor Alderman John Nixon, who had fled in 1642 *(475)*.

**1647.** Oxford University paid £155 for the repair of Sandford Lock *(312)*.
Parliament ordered the slighting of Oxford's fortifications *(475)*.
George Moorecroft was ejected as Rector of Kingham *(784)*.

**4 JUNE.** University received collective Visitors in the London Committee, who remained until Apr. 8 1658 *(777)*.

**1648.** Gilbert Sheldon in custody in Oxford for refusing to give up the Warden's Lodging at All Souls to the Visitors *(271)*.
Oxford Blues, now the Royal Horse Guards, raised in Oxford as a body-guard for Cromwell *(467)*.

**1649. 25 JAN.** Eleven ministers in the Banbury area petitioned Fairfax to spare Charles' life: Samuel Wells vicar of Banbury was one, though he was ejected at the Restoration *(510)*.

**5 MAY.** Commons declared 200 mutinous troopers at Banbury rebels, and sent Colonel Reynolds to suppress the outbreak. The leader, Captain Thompson, a corporal at Whalley's siege of Banbury, was pursued into Northamptonshire and shot *(203, 510)*.

**13 MAY.** Other mutineers from Salisbury, having marched to Wantage to join Harrison's supporters from Abingdon, crossed the Thames at Newbridge and reached Burford, still anxious to join the Banbury mutineers *(32, 203, 440)*.

**14 MAY.** Fairfax and Cromwell seized Burford and the mutineers in the night *(203)*.

**17 MAY.** Private Church, Corporal Perkins and Cornet Thompson were shot against Burford Church: Cornet Dene receiving a last-minute pardon *(112, 203)*. The two Thompsons were brothers.

**SEPT.** Further disturbances in the garrison at Oxford,caused the reversal of a plan to establish Oxford Castle as a citadel *(475, 770)*.

**1650.** A new crop, sainfoin cultivated by John Hastings at Daylesford *(131)*.
Cromwell consented to election as Oxford University's Chancellor *(112, 816)*.
Jacob the Jew opened a coffee house at the Angel Inn, Oxford *(447, 556, 957, 986)*.
Trade tokens issued at Banbury to overcome coin famine *(950)*.

**14 DEC.** Execution in Oxford of Ann Green, servant of Sir Thomas Read of Dun's Tew, for killing her infant by neglect, sentence pronounced by

Serjeant Unton Croke. Found to be alive during the preparations for dissection, she was spirited away by friends, and Plot says she later married in Steeple Barton *(1, 2)*.

**1651.** Lobbersdown Field at Thame inclosed by Chancery act *(939)*.
Peter Heylyn, Burford-born Royalist in retreat at Minster Lovell, published a 'Cosmographie' *(32)*. Others, like Bishop Juxon at Little Compton, angered local Puritans by allowing their harriers to run through Chipping Norton churchyard during public worship *(286)*. Yet others enjoyed retailing all the ill they could find about army preachers like Captain Butler, foisted on Lower Heyford *(112)*.

**1652.** Parliament ordered the sale of Woodstock Manor House *(97)*.
Inclosure of the west end of Dun's Tew township proposed *(939)*.
John Fettiplace of Swinbrook founded Dorchester Free Grammar School by this date *(323)*.

**10 AUG.** Oxford Council ordered trade tokens with the City Arms *(216)*. Retail shops, including alehouses, were prominent in issuing tokens down to 1672, particularly those (not Eynsham or Woodstock) at a distance from Oxford, such as Witney (22), Banbury (20), Thame (18), Henley (14), Burford (11), Chipping Norton (11), Watlington (9), Bicester (8), Deddington (5) *(950)*.

**1653.** Henley and Watlington Baptists sent "messengers" to the Berkshire Baptist Association and were received into it *(426)*.

**1654.** John Beckingham ejected from living of Enstone, in an area where there were many precedents, at Heythrop, Chipping Norton, Chastleton and Swerford *(784)*.
Two girls from Kendal "declared the word of the Lord.. in strange and excited fashion" in Oxford streets, but were whipped and sent away *(157, 154, 986)*. Richard Hubberthorpe distributed pamphlets in Oxford, and with support from Thomas Loe and surgeon Richard Bettris, a Quaker meeting was established there *(157)*.
John Camm and John Audland, north country Quakers, held two meetings at Banbury on their way to Bristol *(157)*.
Ann Downer, daughter of the vicar of Charlbury, became a Quaker, and "carried the message to her native place" *(157)*.

**1655. SEPT.** Banbury trial of the wives of Camm and Audland, for interrupting church services with "pratings": they spent eight months in Banbury Gaol, housed in a building erected as a wool market *(157, 786)*.

**1656.** Cote Baptist Chapel founded *(786)*.
A London Quaker, Mary Clark, spoke in Chipping Norton church: in 1657 she and eleven Friends emigrated to New England *(157)*.
Robert Gadney in business in Oxford as a clay tobacco pipe maker *(813)*.

**1657.** John Bowell, Alderman Nixon's former apprentice, produced his own trade tokens in Oxford as a mercer: he went on to be Mayor in 1680, and host to Charles II the following spring *(216, 986)*.

**1658**. Nixon's Free Grammar School began at Oxford with the city providing the school and Alderman Nixon the master's salary *(323)*.
Henley Quaker meeting began *(157)*.

**8 MAY**. Unton Croke junior in charge of Oxford troops patrolling against the 'zeal and insolence of Anabaptists and other sectaries' *(15, 986)*.

**26 OCT**. Oxford Corporation unanimously agreed to present an address congratulating Richard Cromwell as Lord Protector: practice for a similar address to Charles II as King in 1660 *(534)*.

**1659**. Andrew Holloway, Witney clothier, issued trade tokens: in his will, in 1688, he left six tenements in Corn Street to the poor *(950)*.

**1660**. Henry Box founded Witney Grammar School *(786)*.
Giles Tidmarsh, Chipping Norton Quaker, jailed for non-payment of church rates *(436)*.
William Lenthall defeated in Oxford elections to Parliament *(203, 986)*.

**1 MAY**. University Vice-Chancellor tried to saw down a maypole in the High Street, but the Oxford crowds beat him off *(112)*.

**10 MAY**. Oxford proclaimed the restoration of Charles II, and a hogshead of claret was put into Carfax Conduit to run in its east and south pipes *(112)*.

**1661**. Smallpox raged in Oxford *(112, 986)*.

**1662**. Aston and Cote, in Bampton parish, inclosed by agreement *(939)*.
Ascott Park, a Dormer house, was burned down before completion *(112, 786)*.
Shotover disafforested, reserving the Plain as common land of the parishes of Headington, Horspath, Cowley, Marston and Cuddesdon *(2, 817)*.
Hook Norton, a village "whose inhabitants (it seems formerly) were so rustical in their behaviour, that boorish and clownish people are said born at Hogs-Norton" *(1)*.
Ejection of 26 clergy from their livings *(808)* including Samuel Birch at Bampton, who took to schoolteaching *(22)* and Samuel Burnett at Enstone, who took to medicine *(30)*.

**10 JULY**. Commission visiting Woodstock displaced the Mayor, four councillors, and the Town Clerk, so that Edward Hiorne returned to the last post which he vacated in 1646 *(97)*.

**1663**. The "Chemical Club" at Oxford represented a social move beyond the coffee house to the private dining club in university life *(822)*.

**1664**. Thomas Stonor established a Free Grammar School at Watlington *(323)*.
Quaker meeting house built at Banbury *(17, 154, 157, 608)*. Those at Adderbury and Sibford Gower date from 1675 and 1681 *(608)*.
James Wilmott, pastor of a Baptist congregation at Hook Norton, was imprisoned at Oxford and Witney, and his goods auctioned.

**1665.** Watlington acquired a Town Hall with a covered space for the market when Thomas Stonor built rooms for his Grammar School, though he sold the right to appoint the master to John Tilson *(786, 974).*

**NOV.** "Oxford Gazette" produced for Parliament, in session at Christ Church, Oxford, by Leonard Litchfield, continued from 1666 as the London Gazette *(115, 467).*

**1666.** Death of Thomas Vaughan, poet and alchemist, at Albury where he was living at the rectory as guest of Samuel Kem *(503)*, Essex's chaplain *(987).*

**1667.** Finmere inclosed by agreement *(939).*
Moralising tract published, "God's Terrible Judgement" about the fate of an Adderbury woman fond of oaths and imprecations *(217).*
Ann Walker willed a Free Grammar School at Charlbury, but practical steps came only when Brasenose College was approached in 1675 *(323, 244).*

**1668.** George Fox visited Quakers at North Newington, where a meeting house began about 1705. He stayed with Bray d'Oyley at Adderbury Manor House on a further visit in 1673 *(243).*

**1669.** Sheldonian Theatre opened for University business in Oxford, in a more seemly setting than the medieval additions to the university church of St Mary's, Oxford. It was endowed by a former Warden of All Souls and Archbishop of Canterbury, Gilbert Sheldon, and designed by a Fellow, Sir Christopher Wren, who was also Savilian Professor of Astronomy. Wren presented the design to an early meeting of the Royal Society. *(777, 786).*
Quarry men at Bladon were paid 7s 6d for paving stones *(408).*
Samuel Blackwell of Lincoln College opened a school at Bicester *(323).*

**26 APR.** Flying coach leaving Oxford at 6 am reached London at 7 pm, improving on the stage coach journey with its overnight stop at Beaconsfield *(285, 475).*

**1671.** Wheatley windmill in a ruined condition (restored 1748) *(483).* Perhaps this was Aubrey's "Giant effigie" heretofore on Shotover which escaped the attention of Wood, Hearne and Plot?
Lady Anne Morton built almshouses at Kidlington: her husband, Judge Morton was "the scourge of highwaymen" who condemned Duval *(84).*

**1672.** Cowberry Field and meadow inclosed at Hook Norton *(939).*
Wolvercote Mill turned from grain to paper *(497, 808)*: other paper mills at Eynsham 1682, Upton 1741, Deddington 1742, Widford 1755, North Newington 1756, Shiplake 1780, Henley 1791, Hazelford Mill Broughton 1792, and in the nineteenth century at Hinksey, Rotherfield Peppard, Hampton Gay and Sandford *(627).*
Baptist meeting at Finstock, taught by Thomas Packer *(741).*

**1673.** Sir Henry Browne rebuilt Kiddington Hall *(280).*
Sir William Glynne bought Ambrosden from the Catholic Mildmays *(147).*

**1674**. Oxford University demonstrated ingratitude to Wren by defeating him in a parliamentary by-election *(115)*.

**1675**. Small pox was "verie brief" in Oxford, by which Wood meant quick and fatal *(475, 986)*: John Radcliffe had success in treatment by keeping patients cool and avoiding excessive bleeding. He cured Dame Jane Spencer of Yarnton Manor, but left for London in 1684 *(670)*.
Only evidence of the use of Woodstock ducking stool *(97)*.
George Ravenscroft of Henley given permission to export flint glass *(627)*.
Sand for glass making came from Finstock, Ledwell and Shotover *(2)*.

**1676**. Charles Beauclair, lovechild of the King and Nell Gwynn, was created Baron Headington and Earl of Burford and later, inevitably, Duke of St Albans *(32, 77)*.

**1677**. First mention of a Michaelmas Fair at Banbury *(641)*.
Andrew Yarranton's proposal to make the Cherwell navigable up to Banbury, so that corn could be carried by water to London *(599, 709)*.
Stonesfield slate production began in Stockey Bottom *(759)*.
Elias Ashmole presented his collection of natural curiosities to Oxford University. A building to house them, the Ashmolean, was built by 1683, and Dr Robert Plot, professor of Chemistry and author of "Natural History of Oxfordshire" was the first curator *(2, 777, 786)*.

**1678**. Richard Gilkes was apprenticed as a clockmaker to William Hancorne at Adderbury *(217)*.

**12 OCT**. Titus Oates' Popish Plot having broken the news in London, Ralph Sheldon, owner of Steeple Barton, had his Weston house in Warwickshire searched for arms: he was arrested on Nov. 22 *(147, 986)*.

**1 DEC**. University Vice-Chancellor searched Wood's papers, but found nothing compromising *(147)*.

**1679**. Dr Fell, bishop of Oxford, rebuilt Cuddesdon Palace *(786)*.

**SEPT**. Dr Titus Oates given the Freedom of Woodstock, to add to his honorary bailiff's place at Oxford *(97, 475)*.

**OCT**. Lord Lovelace, deprived of the Rangership of Woodstock Park, invited Titus Oates to preach during Woodstock races, which were the scene of one of Rochester's final escapades in winning the Woodstock Plate before his death-bed repentance to Bishop Burnet *(147, 706)*.

**1680**. Lord Lovelace gave his support and plate to the renewed Oxford races through pique at Woodstock for the respect it showed to Lord Norreys *(428)*: he and the Duke of Buckingham, along with Whorwood and Lenthall, were dropped from the county magistracy *(276)*.
Josiah Pullen's tree, before Dutch elm disease, stood on Headington Hill for two centuries until cut in 1894, and was used to mark the extent of Oxford's parliamentary borough *(805)*.

**JULY**. Death at High Lodge, Woodstock Park of James Wilmot, second Earl of Rochester, "for five years together continually drunk", at 32.

An old boy at Burford Grammar School, he was buried at Spelsbury *(32, 77, 170, 217)*.

**NOV.** Lady Abergavenny, of Shirburn, interrogated by the Lords in the Popish Plot, but released *(147)*.

**1681.** Meeting House built for Charlbury Quakers, replaced in 1779. Henry Shad's school there had been closed, and Friends were sent to prison, such as Benjamin Staple of Chadlington *(5, 741, 806)*.

**MAR.** Charles summoned Parliament to meet in Oxford, the Lords in the Geometry School, the Commons in Convocation House *(45, 115, 323, 777)*.

**17 MAR.** Charles was present at Burford Races, to which the King's Plate race had been transferred from Newmarket. On the return journey he hawked, and entered his coach at Campsfield *(77, 203)*.

**APR.** Charles removed Chief Justice Scroggs from the bench for his record of partiality and brutal effrontery. He was the son of a Deddington tradesman *(45)*.

**1682.** Wood saw the London road up to Headington Hill reconstructed "pitched with pebbles in the middle with hard white stone on either side" *(503, 986)*.

**1683.** William Blake of Cogges had the clock-turret built on Witney Butter Cross, which may be older *(22, 786)*.

Smallpox "hot and frequent in the county" *(475, 986)*.

Attempt to incorporate St Clement's parish into Oxford, supported by a trumped-up petition of the inhabitants, failed: incorporation had to wait until 1836 *(503)*.

**MAY.** Duke and Duchess of York, with Princess Anne, visited Oxford and opened the Ashmolean: they broke their journey to Windsor by dining at Rycote with the rising Bertie influence of Lord Norreys, now Earl of Abingdon: quite enough to make Lord Lovelace rage! *(285, 777)*.

**17 MAY.** Earth tremors in the county concentrated minds on "laws of piety to be founded on wonders of the middle region of air" *(131)*.

**27 AUG.** Oxford surrendered its charter, which was returned in Oct. 1684, nominating the Mayor and Town Clerk *(475)*.

**1684.** Wren's new Fawley Court completed at Henley *(823)*.

Edward Rogers, rector of Holton, left £200 for a free school to educate poor children *(503)*.

**1685.** Dovecotes built at Rousham *(37)* and Culham manor house *(786)*.

Peak of clockmakers in the county: 5 freemen and 12 apprentices *(608)*.

Book-papers being made at Wolvercote by T Quelch *(497)*.

White Kennett *(3)*, Blackwell's assistant at Bicester Free School, became vicar of Ambrosden and later Bishop of Peterborough *(13)*.

Sir Dudley North elected MP for Banbury: seven Norths held the seat from 1685 to 1818 *(741)*.

William Stone, Principal of New Inn Hall, Oxford left his estate for charitable ends chosen by trustees: his almshouses were only the second choice, as the purchase of a site for a hospital in Gloucester Green, Oxford fell through *(670)*.
Burford had a "Postmaster" *(203)*.
Captain Bertie commanded the company of militia which was raised against James, Duke of Monmouth's revolt *(276)*.
Judge Jeffreys secured the living of Whitchurch for his chaplain, Luc de Beaulieu, a Huguenot refugee *(228)*.

**1686**. Death of John Fell, Bishop of Oxford *(464)*.
Obadiah Walker, Master of University College, Oxford returned from a visit to court and declared his Catholicism *(147)*.

**1687. JULY**. James II discharged the Earl of Abingdon as Lord Lieutenant, and replaced him with the Earl of Litchfield *(947)*.

**SEPT**. James II visited Banbury, where three Wardington inhabitants were "touched for the King's Evil" *(510)* and Oxford, where he removed 26 Fellows of Magdalen College for electing Dr Hough as President against his wishes, and demanded that the Bishop of Madura be installed. He revoked this high-handedness shortly before his overthrow *(777)*.

**1688**. Rector Dowdeswell built a new rectory at Kingham, which his family was to occupy (as rectors) until 1957 *(784)*.
Reflecting on old age, John Cary, land agent at Ditchley, who lived to be 101, built almshouses at Spelsbury *(786, 974)*.
Mrs Grey of Barrington left £1 yearly for "sixty yards of calico to 20 houses" in Fifield *(500)*.

**MAR**. While Judge attended the Assize sermon at St Mary's, Oxford the Sheriff, Sir Henry Browne of Kiddington, showed his Catholic leanings by attending Dean Massey's chapel at Christ Church *(147)*.

**JULY**. Richard Holloway was removed from the Bench for refusing to pronounce the seven bishops' petition seditious: he retired to St Aldate's, Oxford *(276)*.

**AUG**. James II remodelled Woodstock's charter to allow Roman Catholic and Protestant dissenters access *(97)*.

**17 OCT**. James II revoked Charles II's remodelled charter to Banbury, and conceded the earlier charters of Mary and James I *(510)*.

**19 OCT**. The Lord Lieutenant, the Earl of Litchfield, was ordered by James II to call out the militia against the invasion threat *(97)*.

**6 DEC**. Lord Lovelace arrived in Oxford with 300 horse and read the Prince of Orange's declaration to a crowd at Penniless Bench *(112, 276)*.

**13 DEC**. Prince of Orange stayed at Phyllis Court, Henley on his way to London *(45, 36)*.

**1689**. Arrival of the new men: William Bentinck was created Viscount Woodstock as well as Earl of Portland *(51)*, Sir John Holt, a native of

Thame, became Chief Justice of King's Bench *(45)*; only John Churchill was still missing.
Walter began to rebuild Sarsden House after a costly fire *(784)*.
William Coles was deprived of the living of Charlbury as a non-juror, but lived on there for forty-five years *(806)*.

**1690.** Book-burning, in the Schools Quadrangle, Oxford of "The Naked Gospel" whose author, Arthur Bury, was deprived of his Exeter College rectorship by the visitor, Bishop Trelawney *(777)*.

**1691.** Sir John Danvers built Prescote Manor House *(786)*.

**1692.** John Troughton initiated Bicester nonconformity, but Henry Cornish in old age (he had been a Parliamentary Visitor to Oxford University in 1646) led services in a barn *(13)*.
Oxford stage coach pillaged on the road to London in daylight *(285)*.

**1693.** Anthony Wood condemned for writing "Athenae Oxoniensis" *(987)*: a copy was burned in Theatre Yard, Oxford, but carried on to his death in 1695, a fuller volume was published in 1721 *(777)*.
Henry Lardner of Ramsden saw that Quarter Sessions dealth with gossips who accused his wife of witchcraft *(535)*.
Holwell inclosed by agreement *(939)*.
William Blake of Cogges endowed a school there *(323, 974)*.
John Hinton became vicar of Great Milton, and instituted a grammar school there *(12)*.
Corn riots at Banbury and Charlbury *(711, 741)*, and at Oxford where "by clamouring the prices came down.." *(475, 986)*.

**1694.** Oxford Council let ground at Folly Bridge to a company providing the city streets with water, but took over the works in 1730 *(475)*.

**1695.** White Kennett published his local history *(3)* but it left time to enforce discipline at Ambrosden, where "solemn penances for fornication were exacted in Church" *(61, 503)*.
An Act laid down watercarriage rates through Thames locks and weirs *(185)*.

**NOV.** William III, fresh from the capture of Namur, dined at Heythrop *(45)*, visited Burford, staying with Lord Abercorn at the Priory *(203)*, went on to Cornbury *(170)* and finally to Oxford, where he spurned the University banquet *(323, 986)*.

**1696.** Act to permit the exchange of lands for inclosure at Salford *(939)*: the first inclosure legislation in the county.

**1697. APR.** John Pryor murdered at Burford: Lord Abercorn tried for the murder at Oxford, but acquitted. He had swiftly married the recently widowed Mrs Lenthall, and Pryor was trustee for her sons *(203, 276)*.

**1698.** Richard White, a London innkeeper born in Banbury, left an income for teaching poor children: his widow purchased Neithrop land from a bookseller, but his name was attached to Thorpe's Charity School. The

land was in Bluecoat School possession in 1825 *(510)*.
Lot Meadow in Wolvercote inclosed by Chancery agreement *(939)*.
Christopher Kempster built a house at Upton near Kitt's Quarr *(408)*.
Tsar Peter I visited Oxford, but did not receive an honorary degree like his successor Alexander I in 1814.

**1699**. William Talbot became bishop of Oxford until 1715 when he rose to Durham. His energies recovered at great expense for the see the manor of Hook Norton *(243, 974)*.
Sir John Cope's manor house built at Shelswell: Newton Purcell inclosed by agreement about this time *(61)*.

**1700**. John Bartholomew willed a Free School at Eynsham *(323, 526, 974)*.
Stone's almshouses built in St Clements by Peisley, an Oxford freemason *(503, 974)*.
Ardley inclosed by agreement *(939)*.
Rival mayors fought for the chair of office in Banbury Church, and the party quarrel spilled over into the return of rival MPs in 1701, but the Commons finally chose a North *(741)*.

**8 MAR.** Collapse of the spire of All Saints Church, Oxford.

**1701**. The Cobb family set up a webbing and horse cloth factory in Banbury *(311, 476)*: the last firth factory closed there in 1932 *(802)*.

**1702**. Much of Ambrosden fields inclosed, but not all until 1775 *(13)*.
Thomas Rowney, city MP, built a town house in St Giles (later the Judge's Lodging) *(475, 786)*.
Oxford University spent £344 on entertaining Queen Anne *(777)*.

**1703**. Joseph Collett became minister of Cote Baptist chapel: son of a gentleman, and an author, the disparagement in the vicar's return of 1738 should be taken as evidence of his success *(22, 974)*.
Magdalen College School severed its common origin with higher education in the College when Grammar School time could no longer count as residence for a degree *(511)*.
Elsfield inclosure by agreement completed by this date *(773, 939)*.

**1704**. Smallpox epidemic at Bicester *(13, 61, 621, 815)*.
First Palladian building in Oxford begun by Clarke: the Warden's Lodging of All Souls College *(786)*.

**13 AUG.** Battle of Blenheim: the victor, John Churchill, Duke of Marlborough, was rewarded with the manor of Woodstock and its park *(97)*.

**1705**. Banbury raised funds for a Bluecoat School which met in the upper floor of Banbury Gaol until 1817, when it joined the National School in new premises, merging in 1913 *(841)*.

**27 MAR.** Waterman's son baptised at Banbury, showing possible extent of Cherwell navigation *(907)*: in 1764 water-borne cargo reach Sir Edward Turner's house at Ambrosden, returning to Oxford with barley *(13, 773)*.

**18 JUN.** Foundation stone laid of Blenheim palace which Queen Anne had ordered the Board of Works to build to John Vanbrugh's design *(451).*

**22 JUN.** Vanbrugh opened four quarries in Woodstock Park, and called on Cornbury and Glympton stone. By 1706 there were 136 carters bringing stone from Strong's Burford and Taynton quarries. Vanbrugh's change of plan from Doric to Corinthian style increased the height by one-third, and Henry Wise's mature trees from Brompton Park all escalated the cost *(451).*

**1706** Duke of Shrewsbury bought Heythrop Park and began to build *(147, 786)* and All Saints' Church, Oxford restoration to Dean Aldrich's designs began *(786).*

**1707** House of Correction opened at Thame *(808).*

John Dormer of Rousham killed fighting at Almanza. *(115).*

Henley councillors agreed to forfeit one guinea for smoking tobacco at meetings *(36).*

**1708** Sarah, Duchess of Marlborough, humoured the races at Woodstock as the classic horse Godolphin Arabian belonged to her son-in-law *(451).* Grey Coat school founded in Oxford for University servants' sons *(974).*

**1709** Inclosure by agreement at Middleton Stoney *(939).*

Sir Simon Harcourt built on a modest scale at Cokethorpe Park *(786).* Observers thought they saw "an old castle being pulled down" at Woodstock Manor *(979)* but Vanbrugh had other ideas *(451, 786).*

**1710** William Bromley, University MP 1702-32, became Speaker, Harley having blocked his election in 1705 *(443, 777).*

Richard Jennings, master-mason of St Paul's Cathedral, created a mansion from a farm at Badgemore *(36).*

**OCT.** Duchess Sarah ordered Blenheim building to stop following Godolphin's fall from power: Cadogan and Sir Thomas Wheate were thus glad not to have opposition in their election as Woodstock MPs. *(451).*

**1711.** Nicholas Hawksmoor began building the Clarendon Building to house the University Press, previously lodged in the Sheldonian Theatre. The money came from the profits of the publication of Clarendon's "History of the Great Rebellion" *(777, 786).*

North family rebuilt almshouses at Banbury and maintained influence by supporting Bluecoat, Sprigge and church rebuilding funds *(741).*

**23 MAY.** Robert Harley created Earl of Oxford. The last of the de Vere Earls died in 1703.

**12 JUN.** First meeting of the court of the Company of Blanket Weavers of Witney *(90, 282, 311)* admitted 114 members *(24).*

**1712.** Dr South, rector of Islip, founded a Free School there for 21 boys

*(323, 974).*

**1713** Woodstock hit by smallpox and by debts for the Palace: Godolphin ordered only freemen to be employed in Blenheim gardens, and the Mayor created 25 new freemen *(451).*

**1714** Sir Thomas Cookes, a Worcestershire landowner, founded Worcester College, Oxford *(117, 786)* on the site of Gloucester Hall: buildings were erected between 1720 and 1746 *(777).*
James Tyrrell began building Shotover House *(786).*
John Radcliffe, successful London doctor, left £40,000 for a library, but no hint of the hospital founded by his executors *(295).*
The Marlboroughs returned to Blenheim on Anne's death, and John Vanbrugh was knighted, but retired in 1716 after a violent quarrel with the Duchess *(451).*

**1715** Susannah Newman willed the foundation of a charity school at South Stoke *(323, 974).*
John Potter used the see of Oxford, 1715-37 as the stepping-stone to Canterbury *(974).*
Charlbury inclosed by private agreement *(939).*
Woodstock Council allowed Dixon to build a cockpit provided their members gained admittance free *(51).*

**28 MAY** Oxford celebrated George I's birthday with anti-Whig riots, resulting in troops being quartered there *(323, 777)*: mobs sacked both Baptist and Presbyterian meeting-houses, but the sects co-operated in building a new chapel licensed in 1721 *(426).* Thomas Hearne refused the oath to George I and lost his Bodleian post *(777).*

**1716** Christopher Codrington left £6000 for a library at All Souls College, Oxford *(786)*: the rococo decoration of about 1750 was by Sanderson Miller, "gentleman architect" of Radway *(660, 773).*
Thomas Parker, Earl of Macclesfield set up a new county dynasty when he bought Shirburn: he was Lord Chancellor 1718-32 *(45).*

**1717** John Stevens founded the Green School at Henley for educating and clothing four boys and four girls *(36)*, and Dame Elizabeth Holford endowed a school at Stanton St. John *(503).*

**1718** First turnpike trust in the county, for the Stokenchurch-Woodstock road: the difficult descent to Oxford from the "old road" over Shotover Plain was cut out by a new road in 1775 *(503).*
Thomas Coke, agricultural improver, honeymooned at Minster Lovell, but built at Holkham, Norfolk, causing the Minster buildings to be dismantled in 1747 *(509).*

**1718** Swan's Nest brewery in existence at Oxford (sold to Halls in 1896 and Ind Coope in 1930) *(476).*
Baptist Chapel built at Hook Norton, the gift of William Harwood: restored 1854.

**16 JUL.** Banbury received a new charter, following disputes in the Mayoral election and Jacobite factions *(510, 711)*.

**31 JUL.** John Hewet and Sarah Drew killed by lightning at Stanton Harcourt: Alexander Pope, lodging in the tower of the ruinous manor house, recorded the epitaph on their memorial *(147, 786)*.

**19 AUG.** Bicester races held. Sir Edward Longueville broke his neck and died at Fritwell *(13, 61, 147)*.

**1719** Sir Robert Cocks, rector of Bladon, won £1000 prize with a public lottery ticket, spending it on 79 acres at Arncott, the rents going to clothe, school and apprentice the poor of Woodstock *(97)*.
Smallpox hit Charlbury, raising the poor rate by half *(741)*.

**1720** Earl of Deloraine died at Sandford St Martin: he was third son of the Duke of Monmouth, whose widow lived at Ledwell Park *(147)*.

**1721** Inclosure by agreement at Forest Hill *(773)*.
Common Hall of Witney Blanket Weavers opened during Robert Collier's term as master: in 1844 the building was sold to Early *(282, 786)*.

**1722** Ditchley House rebuilt in Palladian style by the Earl of Litchfield *(808)*.

**24 MAR.** Judge Page, of Middle Aston, son of the vicar of Bloxham, escaped Commons censure by 4 votes on the charge of having corrupted the Banbury electors to return Sir William Codrington. Both his accuser, Sir John Cope, and his father-in-law, Sir Thomas Wheate, were charter magistrates of Banbury. Page's reputation is for legal severity, particularly in the trial of the poet Savage, and family ostentation in his monument in Steeple Aston church *(45, 21, 251, 711)*.

**1723** Hawksmoor's Triumphal Arch at the entrance to Blenheim from Woodstock was built in memory of the Duke, who died in 1722: the Column of Victory was added in 1728-31 *(451)*.
Oxford University received from Wilton a bronze by Le Sueur of its Chancellor, the third Earl of Pembroke: it stands in the Schools Quadrangle *(777, 786)*.
Schools for free scholars were founded at Brize Norton by Mr Carter of Alvescot *(974)* and at Witney by John Holloway's will: the latter was a Bluecoat foundation *(323, 526, 974)* and associated with almshouses for the widows of blanket-makers *(786)*.

**1724** "Sudden and terrible fire" in Waterlane, Bicester *(621)*: fires also in 1718 and 1730 *(815)*.

**11 MAR.** Henry Allnutt, a wealthy London barrister, died leaving his estate to found an almshouse for twelve men with a chaplain and a schoolmaster. He first planned a hospital at Cassington, but the almshouse was built in 1726 at Goring Heath: the inmates were to be six of Goring, 2 of Cassington and Checkendon, and 1 of South Stoke and Ipsden *(245)*.

**1725** Hook Norton parish bought a "fire-engine" *(243)* about this time,

and was the site of a private lunatic asylum until 1854 *(726)*.
Caversham Park was built on the site of an old manor house by the first Earl of Cadogan: burned down by 1770, its successor is the BBC monitoring station *(786)*.

**16 OCT.** John Wesley's first sermon preached at South Leigh *(112, 154, 244)*.

**1726** John Castle, a physician, established almshouses for four widows in Guildenford, Burford *(32)*.

**1727.** Stone wall of Blenheim Park rebuilt to conserve the deer *(773)*.
Inclosure by agreement of part of Britwell Salome *(939)*, where Sir Edward Simeon had built a new house by 1729 *(147, 786)*.

**5 JAN.** Storm destroyed the spire and tower of Chalgrove church *(149, 974)*.

**1728** Woodstock freemen at View of Frankpledge fined an outsider 1*s* for trading as a tailor, the last intervention to restrict trade *(97)*.
John Morse, a London banker, began to build a small Georgian house at Waterperry *(786)*.

**1729.** First freemasons' lodge met at Crown Inn, Oxford *(582)*.

**1730.** Mixbury inclosed by Parliamentary Act, and Mapledurham in a piecemeal way without one *(221, 939)*.

**1732** Charles Knollys, claimant to the earldom of Banbury (65) became resident vicar of Black Bourton *(974)*.
Bell for Bicester Town Hall cast by Edward Hemmings, whose foundry there closed with his death by 1744 *(542, 621, 917)*.

**9 DEC.** Hostile letter about the Wesleys' Holy Club activities in the local Oxford newspaper, "Fog's Journal" *(777)*.

**1733** Jethro Tull, author of 'Horse Hoeing Husbandry'. His practical experience had begun at Howberry in the county *(285)*.

**1734** James Dawkins, born in Jamaica and purchaser of Over Norton, became MP for Woodstock, with a Jacobite reputation *(115)*.

**7 SEP.** James Figg, celebrated Thame prize-fighter, died in London *(285)*.

**1735.** John Gambold, one of Oxford's "Methodists" became vicar of Stanton Harcourt: later he joined the Moravian church *(974)*.

**1736** Edmund Boulter left money for an almshouse with a dispensary in St Clements, for "decayed neat honest men" of six parishes, only one in the county *(295, 503)*.
Charles Aldrich, rector of Henley, left a parochial library *(36)*.

**1737** James Gibbs began to build the Radcliffe Camera, Oxford to house Dr John Radcliffe's library *(777, 786, 974)*.

**1738** Rector of St Ebbe's, Oxford notes weekly meetings of thirty people called Methodists *(50, 974)*.
General Dormer employed William Kent at Rousham to lay out formal

gardens and to design two wings now masked by an 1877 mock-Elizabethan front *(37, 773, 786).*

Lenthall family provoked another Royal Commission into Burford charities: the law upheld the burgesses this time, despite the "40*s* given to maidservants if the recipients spent 20*s* in the donor's shop" *(203).*

**1739** A year of visiting: the Prince of Wales at Wroxton Abbey, commemorated by an obelisk *(45),* Alexander Pope at Adderbury *(217)* and Rousham *(251),* John Wesley at Oxford Gaol *(625)* and Burford *(808),* a London rabbi to Oxford, to circumcise the son of Hyam Levy *(447),* and the Warden of Wadham College, Oxford overseas to avoid accounting for rituals involving others' sons *(777).*

Chilworth house of the Simeon family burned down; a brief for repairs was allowed despite the family's recusancy *(12, 147).*

Completion of inclosure by agreement at Gagingwell in Enstone *(939).*

**1740** Hertford College, Oxford created out of Hart Hall *(786).*

**1741** A severe winter experienced, which raised the poor rate in every parish of a sample of 25 *(737).*

**1742** Building operations began: by Thomas Camplin in Oxford: the Holywell Music Room for Wadham College *(477, 777, 786),* and by John Sanderson and William Smith at Kirtlington Park, owing much to James Gibbs' designs. The Dashwoods moved from Northbrook House to take up residence in 1746 *(210, 786)* in a 'handsome Palladian house of local stone', and in 1750 vastly extended the old emparking *(773),* which was then landscaped between 1755-62 by Capability Brown *(786).*

**1743** Bishop Secker of Oxford wrote to Dr Doddridge, Northampton Nonconformist and hospital supporter, of his hopes that Radcliffe Trustees will turn their attention to this after the library *(670).*

Father Ignatius Brooke took the lead of the Catholic Mission in the county *(147)*: a Jesuit priest, titular Earl of Shrewsbury, died at Heythrop Park *(974).*

**1744** John Thorley, Presbyterian minister at Chipping Norton from 1701 to 1751, published a book on "the Female Monarchy . . Bees": his Chapel had become Baptist by 1773 *(308).*

**1745** Fire destroyed N wing of Rycote Park *(285, 503, 786)*: building was in progress at Thame Park for Viscount Wenman, by Smith of Warwick *(285, 786)* and at Ambrosden for Sir Edward Turner, whose father bought the estate from the Glynnes in 1727, by Sanderson Miller *(13, 660).*
Thomas Knapp was smith and wheelwright at Clanfield, where a small ironworks ceased production in the 1960s *(627).*

Association mania swept the county in the wake of the Jacobite rising: keen Whigs, such as Bishop Secker and Marlborough, joined in, but older families, Rowney, Litchfield, Dashwood, Abingdon and Shrewsbury held aloof. Lord Cornbury and the Jenkinsons of Walcot were suspect Jacobitical Tories, perhaps explaining the legend of a fugitive Pretender at

Charlbury *(670)*.

**1746** Tweed mill founded at Chipping Norton, which William Fowler sold to Thomas Bliss, a Gloucestershire Baptist cloth salesman *(311, 436, 826)*. The present building dates from 1872.

William Jackson printed "Oxford Flying Weekly Journal" in St Clement's *(503)*.

**1747** First street widening at Carfax, Oxford removed the Penniless Bench: in 1787 the Conduit was removed, and in 1896 St Martin's Church *(475)*.

Woodstock Corporation bought the first of five public lottery tickets, hoping to apply the winnings to building a Town Hall. They were less fortunate than rector Cocks in 1719 *(51)*.

Parr, a Banbury weaver, robber and murderer was the last person hanged in public there *(510)*.

**1748** Ripples of national taxation hit Bodicote township in Adderbury when Henry Grant, the Constable, paid 11*s* for "King's Carriage": they had scarcely recovered from the 7*s* Marshalsea money paid in 1741 *(913)*.

**1749 13 APR.** Handel performed at the opening of the Radcliffe Camera, Oxford *(443, 670)*.

**1751** Thomas Rowney of Dean was the second generation to sit as Oxford's MP from 1722-59: "a rough clownish country gentleman, he built Oxford Town Hall and gave the land on which the Radcliffe Infirmary was built *(532, 125)*.

Turnpike Act for the Gloucester road from Campsfield north of Oxford, also spoke of repairing an ancient horse road from Oxford to Witney over Wytham Hill, Swynford Ferry, Eynsham and Barnard Gate *(203, 297, 311, 642)*.

**1752 6 APR.** Mary Blandy hanged at Oxford for poisoning her father, former Town Clerk of Henley, with 'love philtres from Captain Cranstoun' her inamorata. *(36, 823)*.

**1753** Christ Church, Oxford, bought the only land in Pyrton not owned by the "Romanist" peer, Lord Camoys, to build a school *(430)*.

Fire destroyed the house at Middleton Stoney built about the time of inclosure in 1709 *(13, 765)*.

**5 MAY** Jackson's Oxford Journal first appeared, propsering in the atmosphere of contention between Old and New Interest in the county *(475)*.

**1754** Frederick, Lord North began 36 years as MP for Banbury, 12 of them as George III's Prime Minister *(323, 741)*: family prestige was tested in the county election, when the Old Interest of Berties, Dashwoods, Wenmans and Lees seemed to have triumphed in the open poll over the New Hanoverian-Whig families of Marlborough and Macclesfield, and Hogarth's "Chairing the Member" cartoon bears witness to the style of victory *(437, 825)*. Joseph Holloway, a sweep's boy pelted an election carriage with flints and was shot: his assailant Captain Turton was acquitted of murder in 1755 and joined the county magistracy in 1761 *(825, 947)*.

**18 JAN.** Landlord and landlady of the Hopcroft's Holt inn on the Oxford-Banbury road murdered *(112)*.

**1755** Commons unseated Sir James Dashwood and Lord Wenman, and declared Lord Parker and Sir Edward Turner the county MPs *(115, 437)*. The 52nd Regiment, which became associated with the county, was raised *(123)*.

**1756** Simon, first Lord Harcourt, began building a new house at Nuneham Courtenay with the potential of a vista over the Thames if the site was cleared *(786)*.
Middle Aston inclosed when a Private Act permitted its glebe to be exchanged with Steeple Aston lands, so that the township was wholly owned by the Page family *(251)*.

**1758** John Tilson bought land from the Stonors on which he built Watlington Park, a neat brick Georgian house *(786)*.
Smallpox outbreak at Kencot *(620)* and the Burford district *(32, 77)*.
Piddington and King's End, Bicester inclosed by Act *(939)*.
Ben Abbott was making clay tobacco pipes at Ramsden with his apprentice William Hopkins *(813)*.

**1759** North Leigh inclosed by private Act *(939)* after which rioters broke down the new fences and hedges *(773)*.

**13 APR.** The George Coffee-house in Oxford stood out against its 10 rival houses who announced a penny rise to 5*d* of a dish of chocolate or a pot of coffee *(125)*.

**1760** Smallpox deaths at Adderbury, and at Banbury whose market was being held at Weeping Cross *(217)*: Banbury inhabitants were free to be innoculated at public expenses at 5*s* a head *(711)*.
Removal of the old village at Nuneham Courtenay, where a petition to inclose arose in 1759 *(939)*, to a new site on the London-Henley turnpike road *(628)*. The new cottages were 'as regularly in line as any London street' *(951)* and the removal inspired poems both by William Whitehead, the poet laureate, and by Oliver Goldsmith *(573, 628)*. In 1764 the old parish church was replaced by a "Greek temple" *(786)*.
Neithrop and Wykham townships of Banbury parish inclosed by Act *(939)*.

**22 MAR.** Parson Woodforde, warmed by the Golden Cross's claret, madeira and port, went with a Guards Ensign recruiting for the war in Canada and India, to play unseasonal cricket in Port Meadow, Oxford *(422)*.
More money changed hands in May at Bicester when a shepherd outran a militia man, covering 10 miles in 65 minutes *(61)*.

**1761** Wendlebury church rebuilt *(13)*.
Thomas Castell ran a coach from Burford to London through Witney *(203)*.

**23 MAR.** Public execution in Oxford of highwayman Dumas *(777)*: the corpse was rescued by bargemen, according to Woodforde *(247)*.

**1762** Fire at Great Milton destroyed sixteen houses *(773)*. Fringford and Wardington inclosed by Act *(939)*.

**1763** Sheep roasted whole on the frozen Thames at Oxford *(777)*. Ending of the "Terrae Filius" of university licensed buffoon, except in a chastened form at All Souls College, Oxford *(556, 777)*.
Shillingford turnpike bridge authorised by Act *(642)*, and Merton similarly inclosed *(939)*.
Chiselhampton Church built *(66, 743)*.

**1764** Capability Brown enlarged Blenheim Lake, and in ten years earned £16,437 there *(451)*.

**17 JAN.** John Wesley 'crost Eynsham Ferry. The water was like a sea on both sides!' on his way to preach at Witney *(90, 642)*. He had chosen a winter of prolonged flood *(13)*.

**1765** Henley's old Guildhall and Shambles pulled down *(36)*.
Inclosure by Act of the remaining Banbury townships *(939)*: Thus William Poole of Charlbury began to supply "crab setts to gentlemen concerned in enclosures" and in 1773 James Wakelin of Thame began selling white-thorns and elms for the same purpose *(773)*.

**1766** Horley, Hornton and Shutford inclosed by Act *(939)*.
Oxford mob attacked flour-mills *(323)*: JPs took serious view of Oxford and Woodstock disorders committed "under pretence of distress" *(125)*.
The Duke of Marlborough obliged where the lottery tickets had failed, and had Sir William Chambers build a Town Hall at Woodstock *(97, 786)*.
William Fermor paid £11,305 for a Georgian mansion by Robert Mylne at Tusmore Park: pulled down in 1960 *(773, 786)*.

**27 MAY** "The great cock match" at Mr Kilby's at Chipping Norton *(436)*.

**1767** Bladon, Great Tew, Kencot and Steeple Aston inclosed by Act*(939)*.
Maria Edgeworth, writer whose adult life was spent in Edgeworthstown in Ireland, born at Black Bourton.
Blackstone's influence secured Acts for Abingdon Bridge and Botley Causeway, the latter supplemented by a further Act transferring the old horse road to Witney to the Botley Trustees and abolishing all gates but one on the route *(642)*. New Road, Oxford was made at this time to improve access from Oxford to the new Causeway *(956)*.

**1768** Adderbury, Chesterton, Sandford St Martin and Shipton-on-Cherwell inclosed by Act *(939)*.
Building began of houses for Charles Peers, son of a Lord Mayor of London, at Chiselhampton *(786)* and for Mrs Smith at Headington Hill Hall *(805)*, while the 1745 manor house at Ambrosden was demolished *(786)*.
Bampton parish overseers built a workhouse, sold in 1840 *(22)*.
Oxford University expelled six students of St Edmund Hall for their

association with Lady Huntingdon's conventicles: but they were mature students, three having worked as linen-draper, baker and weaver *(125, 777)*.

**26 JAN.** The Mayor and ten Oxford aldermen were sent to Newgate Gaol for offering re-election to two MPs provided they discharged the £5,670 bond debts of the city: securing release on their knees from the Speaker, they promptly clinched a like-minded deal with the Earl of Abingdon and the Duke of Marlborough *(115, 475, 532, 670)*.

**25 OCT.** James Brindley's survey for an Oxford canal was reported to a promotion meeting at the Three Tuns Inn, Banbury: £50,000 subscribed *(599)*.

**1769** Oxford University "Lodge of Alfred" warranted: Parson Woodforde was one of its 103 freemasons in its 21 years' life *(582)*.
Joseph Hawtyn, Banbury auctioneer and John Walker, Oxford attorney handled most of the 1,223 shares subscribed to take up the Oxford Canal Company's £150,000 share capital. 75% were held by investors from Oxford, Banbury, Woodstock and the countryside near the line of the projected canal *(599, 790)*.

**3 JUN.** Dr Hornsby, Oxford's Professor of Astronomy, organised local observation of the transit of Venus across the sun's disc, as he had shared in planning Cook's voyage to see it in the Pacific. The empty Radcliffe Hospital building was used, and the Observatory proposal arose from this *(670)*.

**4 AUG.** Stroud Water stage coach to Witney, and Mr Timson's Burford Stage Waggon, crossed Lord Abingdon's new Swynford toll bridge *(297, 642, 773)*.

**1770** Kirtlington church tower collapsed: despite Dashwood's legacy, it was left for 80 years 'owing to the refusal of the parish to cart materials' *(210)*.
Inclosure by Act at Black Bourton, Over Norton, Salford, Westwell, Wootton and Chipping Norton, where it provoked riots *(815, 939)*.
Turnpike Trusts set up for the Bicester-Aylesbury and Faringdon-Burford roads *(13, 603)*.
Act permitted pound-locks on the Thames: those at Day's, Benson, Cleeve, Goring and Whitchurch were built by 1790 *(185, 599)*.

**18 OCT.** Radcliffe Infirmary opened in Oxford as a university hospital with 36 bug-ridden wooden beds: in 1837 it received metal-framed beds, in 1885 a royal charter, and in 1950 had 505 beds *(295, 443, 475, 670)*.
Oxford lost a physician, transported for thieving at the Crooked Billet in St Thomas': in Maryland he continued to practise medicine *(332)*.

**1771** Two local Acts for Oxford empowered the "Incorporation" of 11 city parishes (not St Giles nor St John's) to centralise poor relief *(475)*, and the "Mileways Commissioners" to build a new market, a new Cherwell bridge, remove obstructive gates and conduits and pave the main streets *(475, 713, 777)*.

Woodstock workhouse built: farmed out in 1779 for £140 *(51)*.

**MAR.** John Cheney of Banbury undertook, not having served articles, to cease to print: he evaded this and continued the business begun in 1767, producing many chapbooks at the sign of "the Unicorn" *(614)*.

**1772** Late example at Holton of a whitesheet penance *(503)*.

Oxford's last gates, North and East, pulled down, and with the former the city gaol or Bocardo *(414, 475)*.

Radcliffe Observatory begun by Keene, completed by James Wyatt *(777, 786)*.

Humphrey Gainsborough, Congregationalist minister at Henley and brother of the painter, designed local Thames locks *(823)*.

**FEB.** Storms and floods in Oxford caused the collapse of the western arches of Magdalen Bridge: rebuilding to the design of John Gwynn was completed in 1778, and further widening in 1882 *(713, 786)*.

**1773** Oxford removed its Butchers' Shambles from Queen Street *(297)*.

Epwell, Hanborough, Hethe and Upton inclosed by Act *(939)*: the last, where John Lenthall received 90% of the allotment, caused the ending of Burford races *(77, 203)*.

Sir Christopher Willoughby began farming at Baldon House *(503)*.

**1774** Medicinal spring at Holywell, Oxford advertised *(670)*.

Chipping Norton chimney-sweep offered old soot-bag for the return of his 'eloped' apprentice *(131)*.

Inclosure by Act at Sibford Gower, Stanton Harcourt and Hook Norton, *(939)* where two allottees promptly built Gibraltar and Belleisle Farms *(243)*.

Ann Bolton distributed small tracts to the poor at Finstock, as Wesley advised, and a Methodist meeting was held at Manor Farm until the chapel was built in 1840 *(741)*.

Oxford's New Market opened: further enlarged in 1835 *(475)*.

**12 MAR.** Floods *(125, 642)* swept away the wooden bridge at Henley: a stone bridge was completed in 1786 *(786, 823)*.

**1775** Cropredy inclosed by Act *(939)*.

Wood Eaton manor house built, with work by Sir John Soane, for banker Weyland *(786)*.

Oxford Incorporation built Wellington Square Workhouse to replace its House of Correction *(475)*: there were 25 workhouses in the county at this time *(243)*.

**1776** Admiral Sayer, who served in Goree, Senegal and Belleisle, died at Ledwell House *(40)*.

Mackarness of Chipping Norton had innoculating houses at Adderbury and Great Rollright *(436)*, Lyster of Charlbury the same at Cornbury and

Bicester *(131)*, and Mr I'Ony had tried and failed with one at Beckley in 1770 *(541)*.
Tadmarton inclosed by Act: an Act for Rousham "confirmed exchanges and set out roads" *(939)*.

**1777** Alkerton and Blackthorn inclosed by Act *(939)*.
Birmingham stage-coach held up opposite the Radcliffe Infirmary at Oxford *(244, 475)*.
Outside the city, there were 192 benefices: 28 were added, and six disappeared, in the next century: about 60% were without a resident vicar or rector, and were served only by a curate usually with a low stipend *(527, 743)*. Lionel Lampett, curate of Steeple Aston, added the duties of master of Dr Radcliffe's school, and the return on a legacy of £200 which in 1779 he invested in Oxford Canal shares *(243)*.
At Broadwell, 4 of 27 births were "love-children" (recorded later as "base-born" 1782, "illegitimate" 1792 and "bastards" in the 1800s) *(620)*.

**1778** Warden Hill Hunt established *(815)*.
Great and Little Bourton, and Stanton St John, inclosed by Act *(939)*.

**26 MAR.** Royal warrant commissioned the officers of the Oxfordshire Militia as a complete regiment *(123)*.

**30 MAR.** Oxford Canal opened as far south as Banbury *(475, 510, 599, 653)*.

**16 OCT.** John Wesley visited Thame *(285)*.

**1779** Dean and Idbury inclosed by Act *(287, 939)*.
Brakespear's Henley brewery in operation *(627)*.
John Howard reported critically on conditions in Oxford County Gaol in the Castle *(808)*.

**1780** Caversfield and Shenington, then in Buckinghamshire and Gloucestershire, Bucknell and Stratton Audley were inclosed by Act *(939)* though an appeal against the last went to Quarter Sessions in 1781 *(520)*.
Statute fair began at Deddington for hiring servants and selling cattle *(546)*.
Boulter Almshouses built in St Clements according to the will of 1736: they were pulled down in 1880 *(147)*.

**1781** Eynsham Old Heath inclosed by Act *(297, 939)* and riots took place *(773)*: the settlement of Freeland there had a Wesleyan chapel long before it became a parish with an Anglican church in 1868 *(820)*.

**1782** Witney weavers bought a "Rowing Machine" to raise the nap of blankets *(282)*.
52nd Regiment acquired the county title, an affiliation which grew to mean more when regimental depots were built later *(704)*.
Another Palladian villa arose with James Lewis' rebuilding of Bletchingdon Park for the Earl of Anglesey *(786)*.

**1783** Private Act confirmed inclosure at Hanwell *(939)*.
Mrs. Frederick and her sisters endowed an "English" school for ten boys at

Bampton, which later joined the existing Free "Latin" school *(24)*.
Robbery of members returning from a meeting which established an Association to combat highwaymen on Botley Causeway *(297)*.

**14 JUL.** John Wesley preached in the new Wesleyan Chapel in New Inn Hall Street, Oxford *(625)*.

**1784** Oxford Postmaster mentioned *(955)*: Post Office moved several times before settling in St Aldate's in 1881.
John Howard saw through "modern showy buildings" of the Radcliffe Infirmary, Oxford and commented on ventilation, bug-ridden testers and so on *(670)*.
Banbury non-electors staged a mock election, since they could not force a real one on Lord North *(125, 741)*.

**12 NOV.** James Sadler, a pastrycook, ascended in a balloon from the Physic Garden, Oxford and crossed Otmoor *(125)*.

**24 NOV.** John Wesley preached in the Presbyterian meeting house at Banbury: in 1812 a Wesleyan chapel was built *(510)*.

**1785** Thomas Warton, rector of Kiddington *(7)* became Poet Laureate.

**JUN.** Samuel Weston's survey suggested that the Cherwell could be made navigable from Oxford to Banbury: a canal was resolved instead *(599)*.

**1786** Earliest record of a mock mayor-making at Old Woodstock *(756)*.
Thomas Bloss of Chipping Norton bought a spring-loom from Early of Witney *(826)* though local memories dated its arrival in Witney later *(651)*.

**AUG.** George III and Queen Charlotte visited Oxford *(45, 590)*. *(467)*.

**SEP.** Rider attacked on Wytham Hill on his way from Oxford to Burford: assailants often "disguised countrymen" *(642)*. A bolder group of highway robbers was the Culworth gang: the daughter of a Claydon publican was mistress of one of the leaders *(17, 741)*.

**DEC.** Parking fines for 90 High Street residents in Oxford for leaving their post-chaises in the streets on market days *(475)*.

**1787** Pound lock built with prison labour at Osney by the Gaol keeper, Daniel Harris *(247)* who also supervised the building of Magdalen Bridge after Gwynn's death *(713)*.
Charles Perrot left £2,300 to endow a school at Wootton for twelve boys and "to bind them out apprentices" *(413)*.
Cogges inclosed by Act *(939)*.

**1788** Churchill, Goring and Sarsden inclosed by Act (also Little Faringdon, then in Berkshire) *(939)*.

**1789** John Horseman, rector of Souldern was appointed commissioner of his first Inclosure, at Sibford Ferris *(939)*: he acted for 8 further inclosures until 1801, equalling the busy record of William Bradley, rector of Lower Heyford 1744-68, and John Davis, vicar of Bloxham who died in 1789 *(527)*.

A new City Gaol in Gloucester Green, Oxford was built to replace the old Bocardo: it was demolished in turn in 1878 *(808)*.

**OCT.** Marlborough linked the Oxford Canal and the Thames at Wolvercote with the "Duke's Cut" *(605, 630)*.
Prize fight at Banbury between Thomas Johnson and Isaac Perrins *(421, 644)*.

**1790** George Smith began a printing business at Bicester, later to produce the "Bicester Advertiser" *(621)*. William Holloway was printing at Bampton.
Locks completed at Osney and Godstow, where a new cut west of the Trout Inn allowed eighty ton barges to pass *(732)*.

**1 JAN.** First barge arrived at New Road wharf, Oxford by canal from Banbury *(475, 653)*.

**13 DEC.** Banbury parish church collapsed: the replacement by S P Cockerell, consecrated in 1797, "more like a gaol than a Christian temple" *(510, 786, 802)*.

**1791** Oxford Canal Company declared its first dividend *(790)*.
Oddington inclosed by Act *(939)*.

**1792** Banbury Constitutional Association formed to support the established order and check French revolutionary ideas *(741)*.
Edward Tatham, rector of Lincoln College, Oxford published a strong attack on Dissenters, to answer which James Hinton, minister of New Road Baptist Chapel, Oxford wrote a Vindication *(590)*.
Burial of the Earl of Guilford (Prime Minister as Lord North) at Wroxton *(786)*.

**MAR.** Canal proposal made for Hampton Gay to Isleworth, to allow Midlands traffic to avoid the river passage to London. A rival bid, leaving the Oxford Canal at Braunston, was built in 1805 as the Grand Junction Canal *(482)*.

**NOV.** Conviction and imprisonment of an Oxford papermaker's journeyman, Thomas Nash, for conspiring to demand higher wages *(131, 497)*.

**1793** Oxford Canal shares, worth £50 in 1786, appreciated to £200 as aggressive share-brokers produced a large turnover *(790)*.
Mr Annesley of Bletchingdon and Lord Jersey were the only Ploughley subscribers to the "Racing Calendar" *(446)*.
Father Leslie decided to move the Jesuit mission from Waterperry to a more accessible site in St Clements, where he built "the grim little chapel" of St Ignatius, noting the University's welcome to refugee French priests *(503, 814)*.
Bicester-Enstone Turnpike Trust established *(13)*.
Oxfordshire Militia escorted 1000 French prisoners from Southampton to Salisbury *(123)*.
John Swann bought Wolvercote Mill from the Director of Oxford Old

Bank, Jackson: his durable tarred paper was praised by Loudon who used it for roofing at Tew Lodge *(497, 717)*.

Cottages, barns and stables at Stanton St. John proved less durable to fire *(503)*.

**4 JAN.** Spate of burnings of Tom Paine's effigy at Woodstock *(97)*, Carfax *(42)*, Headington *(125)*. Followed by a spate of "Loyalty Meetings" at Thame, Chipping Norton and Bicester *(527)* where a second meeting was required for Protestant Dissenters to concur in their loyalty *(13, 446)*.

**APR.** For those too loyal to want to read Paine, there was Cock-fighting at the White Horse Inn, Burford *(347)* and whatever the "evil-minded" Militia had been saying about Mrs Jane Diver "to injure her character" *(446)*.

"NB. Mrs. Jane has a fine breast of milk, at the service of any lady near her time" *(446)*.

**1794** Barford St Michael, King's End Bicester, Duns Tew, Milcombe, Shilton, Stoke Lyne and Little Tew inclosed by Act *(939)*. Sir Henry Dashwood, involved in five inclosures simultaneously, sold half his Oxford Canal shares and borrowed £3,778 to meet his commitments *(790)*.

Labourers complained that "farmers, instead of selling their milk to the poor, give it to their pigs" *(172)*.

Oxford Corporation defended their rights against Taman, a barber encroaching on Freemen's privileges: he shut his shop *(42)*.

James Jones founded Bicester Sunday School, aiming to teach reading, writing and arithmetic, but local opinion obliged him to limit it to reading, and Christian principles *(13)*.

Heydon, a Hethe shoemaker, licensed his house for Methodist meetings: the chapel was built in 1854 *(818)*.

**APR.** County meeting urged the formation of a Yeomanry Cavalry.

**18 MAY** James Hinton encountered an angry mob when he tried to preach to fellow-Baptists at Woodstock *(426)*.

**1795** South Newington and Burford inclosed by Act *9(939)*: only one quarter of the latter went to independent farmers *(203)*.

Dr Radcliffe's School, Steeple Aston lost its "grammar" character with the appointment of a lay master, as did Watlington at this time and Bicester in 1768 *(527)*.

Coombe Lodge, Whitchurch built by a wealthy East India merchant, to face Francis Sykes' Basildon across the Thames *(228)*.

First stage coach ran from Bicester to London *(621)*.

Act empowered Thames Commissioners to buy old locks and weirs *(482)*.

**13 JAN.** JPs in Oxfordshire Quarter Sessions resolved a scale of support payments from the rates for labourers and sent it to parish overseers, before Berkshire JPs took a similar view at Speenhamland *(172, 184)*.

**24 APR.** Chipping Norton feast to celebrate the acquittal of Warren

Hastings of Daylesford after his seven year trial *(131).*

**11 JUN.** Mayor Brakespear laid the first stone of Henley's new town hall *(36),* which was moved and re-erected as 'The Crazies' when a further Town Hall was built in 1901 *(823).*

**12 JUN.** Two Militiamen shot for riotous conduct at Brighton: one more transported to Botany Bay after receiving 300 of the 1500 lashes ordered *(123).*

**14 JUN.** Two Militiamen hanged at Horsham for stealing flour *(123).*

**JUL.** Burford farmers resolved to sell corn only to mealmen and bakers and not to merchants and distant buyers *(347)*: this year a Chipping Norton mob seized wheat from farmers' wagons *(436).*

**AUG.** "Much sourness" arose from Oxford Canal Company's sending off vast quantities of corn from its wharves *(599).*

**1796** Middle and Westcote Barton, and Wigginton, inclosed by Act *(939).*
Hitchman's Brewery founded at Chipping Norton *(436, 627).*
Thame Park used to house 50 French emigre clergy unable to find hospitality in overcrowded Winchester: they stayed until 1802 *(147).*

**1797** Alvescot, Hampton Gay and Poyle, inclosed by Act *(939).*
500 University Volunteers enrolled for the defence of Oxford were reviewed on Port Meadow by the Duke of York *(590).*
Roman Catholic chapel built at Mapledurham House *(743).*
Deddington inhabitants seized a canal boat's cargo of flour *(808).*
Banbury Academy founded by Unitarians *(421).*
James Hinton, Oxford's Baptist minister, founded four Sunday and day schools merged in 1813 as "United Charity and Sunday Schools" *(181, 788).*

**1798** Oxfordshire Militia sent to Ireland to suppress Wolfe Tone's rising *(123).*
Watlington raised the first troop of Yeomanry, and Banbury soon followed *(510).* By 1803 there were 8 strong troops in the county.
Whitchurch tollbridge erected *(487).*
Mollington inclosed by Act *(939).*
Turnpiking of the road from Witney across Ramsden waste to Charlbury and Great Tew *(535, 741).*

**1799** Rise in illegitimate births at Bicester from 28 in the first half, to 79 in the second half of the century suggested "public morality had fallen to a low ebb" *(61).*
Britwell House sheltered a community of Poor Clares from Aire in Artois until 1813 *(147).*
Kelmscott inclosed by Act *(939).*

**1800** Food riots at Fawler Mill *(244, 741)* and Banbury, where troops killed a child *(802).*
Queen Anne's Bounty used to finance perpetual curacies at two unendowed

chapelries, Wheatley and Leafield *(527)*.

**1801** Wendlebury inclosed by Act *(939)*.
Oxford University set up "Honours" degree examinations *(822)*.

**10 AUG.** Otmoor inclosure, which would permit Marlborough to drain and allot 4000 acres, was prevented by mobs at Oddington and Beckley tearing down notices: Sir Alexander Croke of Studley was also opposed to it *(172, 541)*.

**1802.** Tadpole Bridge was built over the Thames, improving Bampton's communications *(440, 476)*.
Robert Mylne surveyed the Thames between Lechlade and Mapledurham for the Thames Commissioners: he mooted an idea for linking the Thames with the Evenlode and providing navigation to Charlbury *(605)*.
Witney and Oxfordshire Bank was set up by Batt and Backshell *(565)*.
Bloxham, Brightwell Baldwin, Eynsham and Lower Heyford inclosed by Act, together with 200 acres at Drayton, where 700 acres were old inclosure *(939)*.

**21 JUL.** Admiral Nelson, with Lady Hamilton and Sir William, visited Oxford and Blenheim *(51)*.

**1803** "Kirby and Tubb" Bank was established at Bicester *(621)*.
North Newington, Spelsbury and Swerford inclosed by Act *(939)*.
Dr John Kidd was the first Aldrich Professor of Chemistry at Oxford, and one of his pupils, the poet Shelley, was "sent down" from University College in 1811 for publishing a pamphlet *(295, 822, 957)*.
Volunteer troops were set up at Woodstock *(97)* North Wootton Hundred, to which 24 Steeple Aston people belonged in 1808 *(49)*, and Henley *(36)*.

**1804** Headington, Stonesfield and Worton (in Cassington) inclosed by Act *(939)*: the new Cassington Canal cut through the Worton allotments *(605)*.
James Hinton of Oxford preached at the opening of Burford's Independent Chapel *(203)*.
William Hervey had Bradwell Grove rebuilt as a Gothic pile *(620)*.

**1805** Wroxton and Balscott inclosed by Act *(939)*.
Jersey family mausoleum built at Middleton Stoney *(786)*.
County Gaol built in the Castle bailey, Oxford, incorporating an old mill which was turned to grinding flour for the Radcliffe Infirmary bakery *(475)*.

**7 NOV.** Opening night of the Henley Theatre, on a site bequeathed in 1632 by Robert Kenton *(786, 823)*.

**1806** Oxford Herald appeared *(42)*.
Charles Abbott, Oxford University MP, elected Speaker *(115, 777)*.
Shirburn and Whitchurch inclosed by Act *(939)*.

**1807** Negligible public care for the mentally ill: within 50 years provision, through the Littlemore Asylum and the workhouses grew fifteen-fold, and the proportion in private madhouses or cared for by relatives fell *(726)*.

*(726).*

Zion Chapel opened at Launton, for an Independent congregation *(13).*

52nd Regiment formed part of the Light Division serving with Sir John Moore in the Corunna campaign *(126).*

Seven Headington Quarry men imprisoned for riot and forcible entry to a recently inclosed paddock *(817).*

**1808** Deddington, Fritwell and Islip inclosed by Act *(939).*

Death at Corunna of a Thame man who substituted for a press-ganged Long Crendon needlemaker for £20 *(285).*

William Albright revived gloving at Charlbury, where the last factory closed in 1968 *(741).*

J C Loudon took in hand 2000 acres of Redland at Great Tew Lodge, intending to create a model estate on the Scottish system *(717, 773, 786).*

**1809** Peter Burton, journeyman shoemaker of Oxford, was convicted under the Unlawful Combinations Act of organising to raise wages *(131).*

Kirtlington villagers acquitted by JPs of "leasing": had it been beans or barley they were gleaning rather than corn, a harsher verdict would have been likely *(817).*

Arthur Young observed the state of agriculture in the county *(990),* and admired the threshing machines at Juggins' Wheatley farm, commended sainfoin, neat ricks, the keenness of some of the farmers in enclosing the open fields, singling out Turner of Burford, Tuckwell of Signet, Pinnel of Westwell and Warriner of Bloxham, but 'the rest is a blank' *(476).* He advocated enclosure for Wychwood, saying "the morals of the whole surrounding country demand it imperiously" *(990).*

He noted that Bicester sent ten tons of butter weekly by wagon to London *(476).*

The Edinburgh Review, a strong critic of Oxford University as a sterile Anglican monopoly, could praise the Clarendon Press for its "whiter paper, blacker ink, and neater types" but not for the spreading of new ideas *(822).*

Oxford Subscription Library opened.

**JAN.** Henley recorded floods higher than those of 1774 which swept away the bridge *(36).*

**DEC.** Lord Eldon lost the contest for Oxford University Chancellor to Lord Grenville, possibly through votes drawn away by a local magnate, the Duke of Beaufort *(590).*

**1810** Langford inclosed by Act, but about 100 of 217 parishes remained unenclosed *(476, 939).*

William Turner, the water-colour painter was probably at his best with 'Oxford from above Hinksey' and from 1809, 'View of Wychwood Forest' *(445).*

Wytham, the sole mansion of the Earls of Abingdon after the demolition of Rycote shell in 1799, was inconveniently close to the turnpike, which was therefore removed to a lower road from Botley to Swynford Bridge *(642)*.

Baptist chapel built at Charlton-on-Otmoor, a product of James Hinton's cottage preaching *(426)*.

**1811** Oxfordshire Agricultural Society founded *(808)*.

Wolvercote Mill installed a paper-making machine powered by a coal-fed steam engine *(497)*.

**1812** Goring Heath inclosed by Act *(939)*.

Oxford to Cheltenham road diverted to avoid the descent into Burford: the Bird-in-Hand was soon built on top of the ridge *(203, 476, 764)*: in 1852 it was by-passed by the railway at Shipton.

Governors of the Radcliffe Infirmary sought subscriptions for a voluntary Lunatic Asylum in the vicinity of Oxford: with help from the trustees of Warneford, who had also endowed Leamington Hospital, a building was begun in 1821 and the first patients received in 1826 *(295, 786)*.

**OCT.** A group of county freeholders passed a ritual petition at Oxford, supported by Coker of Bicester and Ashurst of Waterperry, against Roman Catholic pretensions *(147)*.

**1813c** The Henley family bought and remodelled Waterperry House *(786)*.

Thomas Tyndale, rector of Holton, put an end to bull-baiting in Wheatley stone-pits.

End of Thomas Huntley's private boarding school at Burford after a life of about fifty years *(347)*.

**1813** Culham, Stoke Talmage, Swinbrook, Wheatley and Whitchurch Common were inclosed by Act *(939)*.

**1814** Asthall and Launton were inclosed by Act *(939)*.

W J Palmer became rector of Finmere in addition to Mixbury: he taught and fed the children, encouraged allotments, emigration and industry in his 18 cottages where "tenants were not to keep children at home after they are of fit age for service, whether boys or girls" *(61, 527)*. His son Roundell was Gladstone's Lord Chancellor *(61)*.

Oxford Baptists opened an Adult School at Middle Cowley *(426)*.

An Anti-Mendicity Society was set up in Oxford *(42)*.

Bishop Moss built a school at Wheatley *(483)*.

**14 JUN.** Dinner in the Radcliffe Camera, Oxford for the Prince Regent and the visiting sovereigns of Britain's allies, Alexander of Russia and Frederick William of Prussia, who had received honorary degrees *(45, 323, 777, 42)*.

**4 JUL.** Dinner in Radcliffe Square, Oxford for 4000 'poor but respectable' inhabitants of Oxford, by subscription *(42)*.

**1815** British School established at Charlbury: handed over to a School Board in 1888 *(741)*.

Chipping Norton Court Leet anxious about "the number of lewd and

base girls that frequent the streets in the evening . . ." *(81)*.
Soho manufacturer Matthew Boulton bought Great Tew Estate from George Stratton *(786)*.
A new Holton Park was built by Elisha Biscoe to replace the old Whorwood's house with 18 hearths in 1665 *(503, 786)*.
Act secured for rebuilding Oxford's Folly Bridge *(475)*.
Kirtlington, Newington, Lewknor, Berrick Prior and Watlington inclosed by Act *(939)*, and Otmoor proposals gave one-eighth of the land to the impropriate rectors (Sir Alexander Croke of Studley and T L Cooke) to compensate for tithes *(527)*.

**1816** Arncott inclosed by Act *(939)*.
Ramsden gamekeeper attacked by two Leafield men in Wychwood *(535)*.

**1817** Henley Savings Bank began *(36)*.
Henley Theatre's premises used to establish National and Industrial Schools *(36)*.
Duke of Marlborough's death led to a cut-back in the 100 staff of household servants at Blenheim, and affected Woodstock *(915)*.
North Bar removed at Banbury: the South, or St John's Bar, was taken down in 1786 *(510)*.
Yarrton School built at the expense of Oxford alderman William Fletcher who as an infant had been put out to nurse with the wife of the parish clerk *(28, 786)*.
National School buildings erected at Banbury *(510)*.
Ambrosden villagers formed the "Amicable Society of Tradesmen" *(503)*.
Robert Peel, one of the first to gain a "First" class degree in the new Honours Schools at Oxford, was elected a University MP *(115)*.

**1818** Begbroke School was created from the poor house, whose tenant, Widow Parker, became schoolmistress for 46 weeks in the year: the other 6 weeks of corn and hay harvest "she is to go afield" *(840)*.
One in six of 312 day schools in the county was a dame school *(915)*.
Burford vestry decided to employ a person "to learn (sic) one person in every poor family to make gloves": it did not prevent the trade slipping to Woodstock and Charlbury *(203)*.
Kidlington and Thrupp inclosed by Act *(939)*.

**FEB.** Jabez Bunting opened Wesley Memorial chapel on land in New Inn Hall street, Oxford bought from the former Gaol-keeper, Daniel Harris: within a year a Day and Sunday school was added *(625)*.

**NOV.** W H Chamberlin produced a plan *(921)* endorsed by local JPs, for equalising the wages and poor rate burdens of farmers and so ending the roundsman system: begun at Cropredy, it spread to Byfield and Chipping Warden.

**1819** Churchill church rebuilt to celebrate the coming of age of the squire of Sarsden, J H Langston, later Whig-Liberal MP for Oxford over thirty years: Sarsden House was later remodelled by Repton *(115, 786)*.

Fulbrook and Littlemore inclosed by Act *(939)*.
Richard Pretyman was presented to the living of Middleton Stoney by his father, the bishop of Lincoln: he held this with five other appointments with an income of £4006 to his death in 1866 *(112, 172, 527)*.
Telford surveyed 26 miles for a proposed Abingdon-Aylesbury canal to cross the Thames in a cast-iron aqueduct, and pass to the north of Thame: this would have linked the Grand Junction with the Wilts & Berks canal, but interested parties opposed it *(33, 285, 482)*.
A velocipede appeared in the Oxford Parks *(42)*.
High street, Oxford gas-lit from the St Ebbe's works of the Oxford Gas Light and Coke Company formed in 1818 *(475)*.
Neithrop Association for the "Protection of Persons and Property" founded *(495)*.

**1820** Eye and Dunsden inclosed by Act *(939)*.
First house built in open fields at Summertown: 562 inhabitants by 1832 *(773, 820)*: St Clements also doubled to 1400 by 1823, which its curate Newman put down to slum-clearance in central Oxford *(503)*.
Joseph and Samuel Mason set up an axletree factory at Deddington *(274, 546)*.
John Welchman, Kidlington farmer, won a battle with churchwardens over the right to appoint inmates of Morton almshouses: his later battles led him to prison during the Otmoor riots. He could have learned something from his jobbing gardener, Thomas Beecham who had a major business success with pills later *(709)*.
South Stoke chapel built for the Countess of Huntingdon's Connection *(786)* and Blackthorn Independent meeting began in a baker's house *(13)*.

**10 JAN.** Fire destroyed Magdalen Hall, Oxford and Magdalen College, Oxford saw the chance to off-load it with the dissolution of Hertford College *(42, 136, 511)*.

**10 MAR.** When a North relation, Heneage Legg, pleaded poverty at the Banbury election, the non-electors rioted against the loss of their customary entertainments *(115, 711, 741)*.

**1821** William Cobbett saw only 'a very poor, dull and uninteresting country' around Witney *(475, 925)*: he began his journey out of sorts with Cheltenham, and grew angry with an Oxford innkeeper's bill (for the last Thames salmon caught at Boulter's lock?) *(112, 228)*. No master could be found for Dr Radcliffe's School, Steeple Aston, to replace John Jepson, "once a private soldier, who vegitated . . . on a most meagre endowment of £17 p.a., eking out his living by a few fees and by measuring up labourers' and artificers' work" *(251)*.
Townesend's almshouses, Witney, built for 'six aged unmarried women' *(786)*.

**26 DEC.** St Stephens' breakfasts and Rogationtide circuiting died out in Bampton following inclosure of Bampton, Weald and Lew by Act *(22, 939)*.

**1822** Banbury New Bank, owned by Heydon & Wyatt, 1784-1819 and by Tawneys, passed to Joseph Gillett and Joseph Gibbins: Banbury Old Bank belonged to the Cobbs *(565)*.
Great and Little Haseley, and Taynton, inclosed by Act *(939)*.
Stratford and Moreton Tramway surveyed a possible extension to Eynsham, but it was never built *(630)*.

**29 SEP.** Combe villagers resisted forceful attempt by Edward Tatham, Rector of Lincoln College, Oxford, and rector of Combe, where he dressed like a farmer and bred pigs, to displace a popular curate, Bartley Lee. Tatham's precautions, bringing a locksmith and four constables from Oxford, and paying 24*s* to eight men for 'guarding the church night and day' availed him nothing. The law was on Tatham's side, the curate was evicted, and local villagers, including Tom Slingo, a poacher, were imprisoned *(450, 527)*.

**1823** Anthony Jepson, seeking a more secure income than his father, ran a private venture school at Westcote Barton for 29 years: by 1836 it gained the rector's support and added a Sunday school *(46)*.
Elliston's began business in Oxford as linen and woollen drapers, joining Cavell in partnership by 1836, becoming the largest department store, taking over W Baker and Co in 1902 *(740)*.
Headington vestry refused poor relief to dog-owning claimants *(817)*.
Edward Batt set up a private madhouse at Witney *(726)*.
Garsington inclosed by Act *(939)*.

**1824** James Stockford ordered to take up the freedom of Chipping Norton or pay 13*s* 4*d* a month in default: the last attempt to enforce a trading monopoly there *(81)*.
Fever block at Radcliffe Infirmary, Oxford an inadequate answer to the lack of proper pest-house *(670)*.
Oxford Canal gave 4*s* premium on each ton of coal at Witney unloaded from Eynsham Wharf as a means of preventing competition from the Thames and Severn route through Lechlade *(605)*.
James Hinton, son of the New Road Baptist minister, became pastor of St Clements' Baptist church to fulfil concern over this growing suburb: he earned curate Newman's respect. The church failed, and was sold to the Rector for a parish school in 1839. *(503)*.
A school in Penson's Gardens, St Ebbe's, Oxford housed the "United Charity and Sunday Schools" *(788)*.

**1825** Oxford High street ironmonger, William Carter, moved to the canal-side as 'Jericho Iron and Brass Foundry' known from 1838 as Eagle Iron-works, with William Lucy as a partner from the 1850s *(574)*.
Oxford Union Society, the university debating club, began.
Underwood's Botanic Garden building at Oxford is the only Greek revival building in the university *(786)*.
Towersey, then in Bucks, Chadlington and Chilson inclosed by Act *(939)*:

old emparking at Middleton Stoney extended, obliterating all remains of the village site next to the church *(773, 786)*.

**11 DEC.** Banbury New Bank rescued by Joseph Gibbins' emergency trip to London to counter nervousness with 10,000 sovereigns *(421, 565)*.

**1826** Organisers of a Thame bull-baiting were fined *(285)* while those of a Holywell, Oxford cock-fight were patronised by George IV *(147)*.
A St Clements printer, Alphonso Tallboys, attacked corruption in Dawson's charity there: the 1521 scheme was thus revised in 1834 *(503)*.
Anthony Ashley Cooper (later the 8th Earl of Shaftesbury) defeated J H Langston, the retiring MP at Woodstock *(115)*.
Bicester Town Hall and Shambles pulled down in a disorderly public scramble *(61, 621)*.
John Bayzand, coachman of the "Oxonian", boasted of being the last to drive over the old Folly Bridge, and the first to cross Perry's new bridge *(786, 910)*.
Inclosure by Act of Thame, including Moreton, Priestend & Sydenham *(939)*.

**1827** Canal House built at Oxford for the Oxford Canal Company, by Richard Tawney in Greek Doric *(786)*.
Custom of going to Capp's Lodge in Wychwood Forest from Burford to "claim the bucks" ended *(77)*.
First cricket match between Oxford and Cambridge Universities: the Oxford centre was Magdalen Cricket Ground on Cowley Marsh *(511)*.
National Society survey counted 137 Sunday Schools in the county, with only Blackbourton, Cottisford, Launton, Widford, Easington and Little Rollright unprovided with day or Sunday schools *(527)*.

**24 MAY** Smallpox hit Banbury 'by a show at the Fair having a dead man only screened from view by a curtain' *(909)*: 73 died *(421, 641)*.

**1828** Oxfordshire Association for the Prosecution of Felons was set up *(495)*: some JPs advocated their persecution with a treadmill in the County Gaol *(527)*.
"Guide" coach offered a six-hour service from Oxford to London, returning the same day *(910)*.
Oxford Mechanics Institute opened with two rooms as a library in Queen Street.
Independent chapel opened at Witney *(24)*.

**14 JUN.** Foundations laid of Robertson's "freak Norman" St Clements' church: the old church was later demolished, its graveyard remaining until traffic improvements in 1951 *(475, 676, 786, 830)*. As curate, J H Newman had raised much of the local money.

**1829** Conference Wesleyan chapel opened at Upper Heyford, joined in 1851 by one for the Reformed Connection *(38)*.
William IV's son, by the acress Mrs Jordan, Lord Augustus Fitz-Clarence, was instituted as vicar of Mapledurham *(786)*.

**27 FEB.** Sir Robert Inglis, 'champion of the Protestant church' beat Sir Robert Peel in a University by-election following Peel's measure of Catholic Emancipation. Inglis sat until 1854 *(115, 324)*.

**7 JUN.** Oxford won the first boat race against Cambridge University, rowing 2¼ miles against the summer stream from Hambleden Lock to Henley bridge *(63, 823)*. The boat was built by Davis and King, of Oxford. The next race, in 1836, was rowed at Putney. William Gladstone was a spectator *(777)*.

**1830** Oxford had a co-operative society: later Captain Wilson started an "Adelaide Association" in the 1860s, and a co-operative of workmen was set up during the building of the University Museum, 1855-60 *(411)*.

Father Newsham of St Ignatius, St Clements began a Catholic boarding school there for eight boys: he left the Jesuit order rather than discontinue it in 1848 *(481, 503)*, taking his school to Dorchester *(147)*.

Daniel Robertson completed the University Press in Walton Street, Oxford *(786)*.

**18 MAY** Bicester vestry arranged for 85 paupers to go to Liverpool for emigration to America *(61, 621, 743)*: during the next decade only 7 cottages were built in 34 closed parishes, while 1,352 were built in 86 open parishes *(820)*.

**6 SEP.** Officers of the Militia were involved in Otmoor riots over the inclosures awarded in 1829 at Noke, Fencot and Murcot *(939)*: their prisoners escaped into St Giles Fair *(613)*. The Militia was disembodied from 1831 to 1852 *(123)*, and the ballot discontinued *(421)*.

**8 NOV.** Edward Feild, curate of Kidlington who refused to preach at rowdy old Club Days, began a National School there *(235)*.

**21 NOV.** "Swing" riots spread to Crowmarsh (where inclosure was being prepared) Ewelme and Rofford *(645)*.

**23 NOV.** Mob of 200 from Drayton St Leonard, Stadhampton and Chiselhampton broke Weller's thrashing machine at Little Milton: local JPs swore in 152 special constables in the next 3 days, but "not above 2 or 3 could be persuaded to be sworn" at Haseley *(645)*.

**24 NOV.** Incidents at Barton *(645)*.

**27 NOV.** A mob destroyed machines at Chalford, Broadstone Hill and Dunthrop before attacking the hay-making machine at Heythrop House: entering the house they demanded "Bread or Blood" under the leadership of the "King", Thomas Hollis of Sandford *(286, 645, 832)*.

**29 NOV.** A town mob from Banbury destroyed a threshing machine at Neithrop, aided by a chimney-sweep admirer of Cobbett *(421, 645)*.

Machines were destroyed at College and Ashleaze Farms in Broadwell, before the labourers moved into Southrop (Glos.): John Keble was drawn into an attempt to pacify them *(620, 645)*.

A draining plough and other machines were destroyed at Tadmarton:

James Bodfish received 15 months' prison for his part. In 1872 his namesake Isaac was thrashed by a local farmer for his union activity. The coincidence was mentioned in Parliament *(616, 645).*

**30 NOV.** Further incidents at Bodicote *(645).*

**1831** Yarnton ordered 25 Constables' staves for one guinea *(84)*, and Steeple Aston Fire Engine Company formed by local farmers *(527)* in the wake of the Swing riots.
Oxford Incorporation set up an Industrial School at Cowley *(503).*

**24 FEB.** Heythrope House burned down, probably through accident from a bedroom fire *(286).*

**20 OCT.** Terill of Bodicote tried to forward a "resurrected" corpse by the Union Coach to London from the Red Lion Inn, Banbury *(421).* The body was of a Broughton girl who died suddenly after a visit to Banbury Fair.

**15 NOV.** Oxford set up a Board of Health to take precautions against cholera which had reached Sunderland *(16).* It was too late for 50 emigrants from Deddington to America, for cholera broke out on their ship, the "Brutus": it "dampened the spirit of emigration in the district" *(546).*

**1832** St Giles, Oxford inclosed by Act *(939)*: Walton House built by St John's College on their allotment of the common fields, next to the insanitary tenements called Cock's Row *(507, 670).*
Charlbury set up a branch of the British & Foreign Temperance Society *(237)* which with local Quaker help turned the Royal Oak into a coffee house in 1880 *(741).* By 1834 branches were also set up in Chipping Norton, Hook Norton, Witney, Burford, Henley, Oxford and Woodstock, and in 1836 Banbury went further into teetotalism *(644).*
Roman Catholic church built at Hethe, after the closure of the private chapel at Tusmore after the removal of the Fermors *(818).*

**FEB.** John Gibbs, Steeple Aston labourer, hanged at Oxford for firing corn ricks *(251).*
Otmoor Committee of county JPs began to meet until the disturbances finally died away in 1835 *(613).*

**17 APR.** A cholera case reported at Hagborne, Berkshire *(16).*

**22 APR.** Cholera death of Mary Leadbeater in St Ebbe's, Oxford was followed by a two months' lull *(16).*

**25 JUN.** Cholera deaths in Oxford County Gaol, including James Leech of Bicester, where 64 died in six weeks *(621).* At Blackthorn 27 died *(61, 503).* At Burford the severe attack "started that place into repentance" *(347).* Oxford set up a cholera hospital on the Pepper Hills near the Canal, an observation house in St Aldate's National School, and a convalescent house at St Bartholomew's at Cowley. 74 of the 174 cholera cases in Oxford were in St Clements: there were 86 deaths in the city *(16).* Piped drinking-water from Headington Hill was brought after this to St Clements streets, by public subscription, but the drainage was neglected until 1854

*(503).*

**SEP.** Radical temperatures were rising in Banbury, and there was a riot in the Flying Horse Inn *(421).* Neithrop's "Wellington Inn" was renamed "The Sun Rising" for a generation until the military enthusiasm of 1859 *(421).*

**10 DEC.** Elections for the Reformed Parliament were held: the County had three members, and voters had polling stations in all the market towns, not just the Oxford hustings as in 1754 *(115).* Woodstock was reduced to a single MP, and Banbury radicals elected a Whig, H W Tancred *(741).* One Oxford MP was unseated on petition for bribery *(475).*

**1833** Henley Horticultural Society was set up "for the encouragement of the industrious cottager" *(36).*

Gasworks were built at Banbury, under powers given in an 1825 Private Act *(711) (654).*

A Great Western Railway was proposed from London to Bristol with three probable branches, one of which was from Didcot to Oxford *(238).*

**14 JUL.** John Keble preached on 'National Apostasy' at the Assize sermon in St Mary's, Oxford *(777)* where Newman was vicar 1828-43 *(344).*

**1834** Company formed for lighting Henley by gas *(36).*

Poor Law Amendment Act set up Unions based on Banbury, Bicester, Chipping Norton, Headington, Henley, Thame, Witney and Woodstock, the Oxford Incorporation continuing as before *(808).*

23 parishes had free lending libraries *(527).*

Inclosure by Act at Kidmore End and Wolvercote *(939)* where Five Mile Drive was created *(773).*

James Gardner of Banbury, renowned for an 1815 machine for hay and straw cutting, and one of 1821 for cutting fat for soap and candle manufacture, now patented a turnip-cutter *(627, 802).*

Round House lock-up built by Cooper, a local Wheatley mason *(786).*

**1835** Oxford City Police Force established, but the Vice-Chancellor continued to control the night police of the city *(808).*

Aston Rowant inclosed by Act *(939).*

Manor House Ladies' School opened at Temple Cowley: in 1841 a boys' boarding school was added *(503).*

Reformers won sweeping control of Banbury Town Council under the terms of the Municipal Reform Act: they also gained control of the magistrates' bench *(741).*

Banbury Mechanics Institute founded *(741).*

A village dispensary was set up at Deddington and Steeple Aston *(527).*

Chipping Norton and Thame Union workhouses built by George Wilinson *(786):* the first, built on the Panopticon principle, is now Cotshill Hospital, the latter is Rycotewood College *(786).*

**25 APR.** End of the Duke of Beaufort's hunting in the county: he sold his pack for £400 to a landowners' committee *(286).*

**25 JUL.** Newman's mother laid the foundation stone of Littlemore Church *(344, 676, 786)*.

**OCT.** Queen Adelaide held levees at the Angel Inn on her visit to Oxford *(42)* and gave the title "Queen's Own"to the Yeomanry.

**1836** Banbury's Police Force had an establishment of one superintendent, 2 constables, 6 night-watchmen and 4 petties *(802)*: it merged with the county Force in 1921. Chipping Norton made more modest use of two men hired from the Metropolitan Force for its "Police Association" until the County Force arrived in 1856 *(758)*.

Charles Harris, violin-maker and card-sharper of Steeple Aston, showed his success by building a new "Manor House" (later the Co-op Stores) and cottages called "Harrisville" *(251)*.

Proposals for a railway from Tring to Cheltenham through Aylesbury, Thame, North Oxford, Witney and Burford were "Euston" and the London-Birmingham railway's attempt to outflank "Paddington" and the Great Western Railway. Revived in 1838, they were a bargaining lever, and never built *(238, 605)*.

Tower Hill Workhouse was built for Witney Union by Wilkinson *(786)*.

Berkshire was added to the Oxford diocese, and Buckinghamshire was added in 1845 *(112)*. St Paul's was created as a new Oxford parish, others being Holy Trinity, St Philip and St James, St Barnabas in 1869 *(194)*, and St Margaret's in 1896 *(475)*.

Holy Trinity Roman Catholic church opened at Chipping Norton *(147)*.

**1837** Weekly "Oxford Chronicle" began *(475)*.

Gas lighting was introduced in Chpping Norton *(436)*.

Leafield and Shiplake were inclosed by Act *(939)*.

Oxford branch of the Great Western Railway proposed, with a terminus in St Clements, which Christ Church disliked. Revised plans offered a Folly Bridge terminus, and power for the Vice-Chancellor to discipline junior members fleeing to London for pleasure: local landowners now opposed it. In 1838 and 1840 proposals failed, with the Duke of Wellington opposing *(238)*.

School building activity at Thame produced a National School to vie with the British "John Hampden" School *(285)*.

Bletchingdon ceased to draw its clergy from "plebeian" sons as it had from 1750, and opted for those of gentle or "armiger" class *(527)*.

Vulcan Foundry set up by Lampitt's in Banbury. At the Great Exhibition, 1851, they showed a patented horse seed-dibber *(627)*.

Old manor house at Tusmore burned down following accidents to the tenant's pheasants and dogs *(61, 645)*.

St Clement's parish was included within the Oxford City boundary *(475)*.

**1838** Ascott-under-Wychwood inclosed by Act *(939)*.

430 weavers were employed by the Banbury firms of Gillett, Harris and Baughen: the Wrench family were the only Shutford weavers in 1841.

Total figures fell rapidly to 200 in 1851 and 100 in 1861 *(565)*.

Potts produced a Poor Law record in Banbury (in which Union relief had dropped to 11*s* per head of population *(711)*: in Jul. 1843 this became the "Banbury Guardian" *(510, 802)*.

Henry Vincent, Chartist lecturer, met Banbury's new Working Men's Association *(644, 741)*.

Brunel began the building of a Thames bridge at South Stoke for the Great Western Railway's main line *(786)*.

St John's Roman Catholic church at Banbury built: the Manse and school were designed by Pugin *(786)*. Dr Tandy brought four cart-loads of bones from Warkworth and Overthorpe *(147)*.

George Wilkinson built Bampton Town Hall *(786)*.

Woodstock Corporation met for the first time since the 1831 dispute over the Recordership *(97)*.

Oxford University's Tractarian scored a victory for their faction by removing Dr Hampden, Regius Professor of Divinity, from the list of select preachers, by an overwhelming Convocation vote *(777)*.

**1839** Royal Agricultural Show first held at Oxford: exhibits included a horse-hoe and harrow from Burcot, turnip-cutters from Banbury and a scorcher from Charlbury *(808)*.

Clanfield, Ducklington and Little Milton inclosed by General Act *(939)*.

New chapels included the Baptists in Bridge-street, Banbury (now a Finefare façade *(786)*) and the Boatmen's Floating Chapel in St Thomas, Oxford provided by Henry Ward, a coal-merchant *(247)*.

**14 JUN.** First Henley Regatta (becoming "Royal" in 1851 when patronised by the Prince Consort) *(823)*.

**12 OCT.** Rector of Upper Heyford fined £5 by clerical JP Pretyman for trespassing in search of game on the lord's common *(61, 527)*.

**1840** Two middle class school ventures: at Banbury by the Diocesan Board of Education, where a Classical and Commercial Middle School did not survive its first master *(421)* and at Thame by James Marsh, whose Oxford County Middle Class School became a preparatory school and moved to London in 1908 *(285)*.

Frank Cooper's marmalade firm began behind the High street shop in Oxford, and from 1874 in Victoria Buildings *(740)*.

Henry Broadhurst, secretary of the TUC and third workingman to sit in Parliament, was born at Littlemore: as a young stonemason helped to build the new Wheatley church *(768)*.

Toot and Marsh Baldon inclosed by Act *(939)*.

John Plowman began to build the County Hall in New Road, Oxford *(786)*.

Reynolds (later Garne's) Brewery in Burford about this time provided only factory-type industry *(764)*.

John Thorp opened Oxford Diocesan Training College at Summertown, and trained 121 boys of 15-18 before its closure in 1852 *(470, 526)*.

Girls trained for teaching at Kidlington, 1845-53, subsequently at Fishponds, Bristol *(470, 840)*.

Radford Roman Catholic chapel opened to replace Kiddington chapel by Dr Wiseman: in 1853 Ullathorne, bishop of Birmingham was imprisoned on technical grounds as a trustee *(147)*.

**1841** Martyrs' Memorial erected in St Giles, Oxford to a design of Gilbert Scott *(475, 786)*.

C R Cockerell began building, in Portland and Box stone, to house the Taylorian Institute (endowed in 1788 for teaching modern languages) and the University Galleries in Beaumont Street, Oxford *(408, 786)* which housed the Ashmolean Museum after 1894 *(476)*.

Courage's Witney brewery was established *(786)*.

"Coronation" won the Derby with a Chadlington owner and Heythrop Park trainer *(286)*.

Oxford's Jewish community set up a synagogue, from 1847-78 in Paradise Square, from 1893 on its present Nelson street site *(447)*.

Gillett's, the Banbury bankers, opened a Woodstock branch filling the gap left by the closure of Morrell's *(565)*.

Sibford School established by the Friends' Quarterly Meeting for Bucks, Berks, Oxfordshire and Northamptonshire.

Banbury Chartists had Henry Vincent as their parliamentary candidate, Barnes Austin and 3 others as municipal candidates, and disrupted Anti-Corn Law meetings there *(644, 741)*.

George Inn, Burford, a former coaching inn closed in 1837, was inhabited by 46 persons in 9 families *(764)*.

**22 MAY** University baths and gymnasium opened in St Clements, the latter replaced by a building in Alfred street, Oxford *(503)*.

**JUL.** J H Newman bought disused stabling at Littlemore and converted it into a community with an Oratory: he lived there 1842-6, and was received into the Roman Catholic church in 1845 *(344)*.

**1842** Upper Heyford inclosed by Act *(939)* after which the pre-Roman boundary dyke, the Aves Ditch, was pulled down *(773)*.

Davenport Walker, Oxford bankers, merged with London and County Bank: the manager 1872-8 was the father of Mrs Mark Pattison, the future Lady Dilke *(295)*.

Caversfield House built for the Warden of Merton College *(786)*.

Ramsden church built and replaced in 1872 *(535)*.

First gas-lighting in Thame: permanent gas company set up in 1851 *(285)*.

**1843** Neat Enstone inclosed by General Act *(939)*. This, and adjacent villages, was damaged by severe hail-storm on Aug. 9: the vicar wrote a pamphlet.

Eynsham Park built in Italianate style by Sir Charles Barry: rebuilt 1900-4, and is now a Police Training College *(786)*.

Disorders at Banbury, first at Newland Wakes *(644)* then during the August races in Mill Meadow *(421)*: the races were a casualty of railway building, and the Wakes died, with a brief revival in 1855 in Grimsbury where loyalties divided between the Prince of Wales (in the new middle-class suburb) and the Woodbine Cottage (in the agricultural hamlet) *(644)*.

**1844** County grew by the addition of Caversfield from Bucks, Shenington and Widford from Gloucestershire, and Little Faringdon, with parts of Langford and Shilton from Berkshire *(552, 786)*.
Great Milton inclosed by Act, and Church Enstone and Northmoor by General Act *(939)*.

**12 JUN** Oxford's first railway station at Abingdon-road opened, on the branch from Didcot *(475)*. The GWR had been united with the Oxford Railway Company on May 10, the latter having finally got Parliament to agree to its 1843 proposal *(238)*. The Banbury line ran out of this at Millstream Junction where a ballast pit was made *(238)*.

**1845** GWR secured an Act for the Oxford-Rugby line and, through another company, the Oxford-Worcester-Wolverhampton railway. But both were central to the gauge controversy: in 1850 the GWR tried to open the line north of Oxford with broad-gauge tracks only, while in 1851 the Oxford, Worcester and Wolverhampton mutinied and proposed to operate on the narrow-gauge. "Holding" proposals for lines from Oxford to Cambridge, and Cheltenham to London junction, were produced *(238, 971)*.
Gas was produced at Bicester *(621)*.
Britwell Salome, Britwell Prior, Chalgrove and Curbridge were inclosed by Act *(939)*.

**9 OCT.** J H Newman was received into the Roman Catholic church *(777)*.

**14 NOV.** Policemen killed a man in Chipping Norton incident: only two men materialised from the Mayor's appeal for the Yeomanry. The PC was later acquitted of manslaughter *(758)*.

**30 NOV.** Samuel Wilberforce became bishop of Oxford until 1869 *(470)*.

**1846** Bernhard Samuelson's interest in Britannia Works at Banbury began: by 1859 he employed 300 people *(743, 802)*.
Dr Henry Acland was appointed Lee's Reader in Anatomy at Christ Church: he also bought a medical practice in Broad Street, Oxford, living there to his death in 1900 *(295)*.
Grafton inclosed by Act *(939)*.
Shillingford's brewery began making ales and mineral waters at Bicester *(621)*: closed in 1926 *(542)*.

**20 JUN.** First Banbury interest in Chartist Land Society by John Hone, a Banbury weaver *(636)*.

**1847** Littlemore Hospital opened for mental patients from Berkshire and Oxfordshire *(295)*.
Rev C Jerram had St John's church built at Curbridge.

**MAY** John Buswell of Banbury won a three acre site in the Chartist land ballot: in Nov. Emma Adams (aged 9) won two acres at Snig's End. The

The family settled and farmed there *(636)*.

**24 JUN.** Feargus O'Connor bought 300 acres of upland meadow and pasture at Minster Lovell for £11,000: the Chartist Land Company planned and built a settlement there called Charterville with 78 cottages and a meeting house *(666, 773, 786)*.

**12 JUL.** British Association for the Advancement of Science met at Oxford: Henry Acland instigated a petition calling for a University Museum *(133, 786)*.

**AUG.** Gladstone elected as a University MP, remaining so until his defeat in Jul 1865 *(115)*.

Eight months' lay-off for construction workers on the Oxford to Rugby railway line: many at Lower Heyford dispersed for harvest work *(565)*.

**NOV.** The vicar of Eynsham, a clerical JP, charged a man with selling one pennyworth of walnuts on a Sunday *(527)*.

**1848** Mixed gauge was laid down for the Oxford-Birmingham line, partly through the 1847 success of the Buckinghamshire railway in getting Acts for Oxford-Bletchley and Aylesbury-Banbury lines *(238)*. Cuxham and Denton inclosed by General Act *(939)*.

**30 MAR.** Charterville allottees were prevented by JPs from taking part in Minster Lovell vestry business: the Archdeacon disallowed the Easter vestry's election of George Bubb, an allottee, as churchwarden *(666)*.

**APR.** "New World" took 15 Lower Heyford emigrants to America *(565)*.

**15 MAY** A public soiree at Charterville to raise funds for a clock: by Jul the allottees' title was being questioned by lawyers *(666)*.

**NOV.** O'Connor used Witney JPs and troops to enforce distraint orders on allottees who were rent defaulters *(666)*.

**1849** Samuel Hiron, a Deddington printer, produced "North Oxfordshire Monthly Times and Agricultural Advertiser" until 1859.

Chipping Morton, Fencot and Milton-under-Wynchwood inclosed by General Act *(939)*.

Warneford Asylum at Headington separated from the Radcliffe Infirmary with its own Royal Charter *(670)*.

John Harris began brewing at Hook Norton: one speciality was a potent "haymaker beer" at 8*d* a gallon.

Bishop Wilberforce consecrated Holy Trinity, Headington Quarry "to deliver the poor from unclean spirits that infested it" *(817)* and instituted Edward Elton to the living of "turbulent and ill-conditioned" Wheatley *(527)*. Holy Trinity, Wood Green and St Birinus Roman Catholic church, Dorchester opened *(147)*.

Buckler began new buildings for Magdalen College School, Oxford *(786)*: Miss Nicholls began a girls' school at Thame using the old Grammar School premises 1877-1908, then those of the preparatory school: for long it provided the only girls' secondary education in the south of the county

*(285).*
Book burning once more, by the sub-Rector of Exeter College, William Sewell (founder of Radley College): the book was Froude's "Nemesis of Faith" *(816).*

**MAY** Neithrop inhabitants petitioned for a Local Board of Health, and T W Rammell reported on the township's public health *(510, 607).*

**AUG-OCT.** Oxford had 52 cholera deaths of 144 cases, St Clements' suffering less than in 1832; Dr Greenhill, one of Dr Arnold's former pupils, reported fully *(27,670,966).*

**1850** Kingham inclosed by General Act *(939).*

**23 APR.** Heywood's motion overcame Gladstone's opposition and a Royal Commission was set up to enquire into the ancient universities. The Oxford Commission got little co-operation from College heads, and had to deal with the Tutors' Association and zealous reformers wanting strong professorial leads. Acts of 1854 and 1877 were an external goad to internal reforms *(777).*

**1 MAY** First passenger train left Banbury for Bletchley on the extension to the Buckinghamshire Railway *(238,421,804).*

**AUG.** Failure of Charterville allottees to stave off foreclosure on their properties. Three were gaoled until 1852 for defaulting on their legal costs: two did well enough to buy properties at £170 and £125 *(666).*

**2 SEP.** Broad-gauge train left Banbury, reaching Paddington in 2½ hours *(238, 421)*: in this month the "Regulator" Coach, set up about 1780 by the landlord of the White Lion, Banbury, ceased running to Oxford *(644).* By 1852 Oxford Canal coal tolls were reduced from 5*s* 11*d* to 2*s* 7*d* a ton to meet railway competition *(599).*

**2 DEC.** The Buckinghamshire Railway opened the Bletchley line to Banbury Road station at Water Eaton *(605).*

**1851** Banbury's two railway stations used for promenade concerts by Banbury Mechanics Institute *(644).*
Pyrton inclosed by Act *(939).*
Samuelson gained licence to build the McCormick reaper at Banbury *(644)*, but Caird noted large farms restricting threshing machines to the wheat, exempting the barley crop "both to give employment to the labourers, and because the machines in use cut the grain too short, and thus injure it for the maltster" *(26, 918).*

**20 MAY** Opening of the second Oxford station (built with prefabricated parts on the lines of the Crystal Palace) and the completed line through Islip and Bicester to Bletchley *(503, 786)* which was absorbed into the LNWR in 1879, losing its passenger facilities in 1968 *(804).*

**JUN** Delays on the Oxford, Worcester and Wolverhampton Railway were diminished when Brunel took 2,000 men to Mickleton and turned off the delinquent contractors on the tunnel, after a struggle *(238).*

**1852** T R Cobb, Mayor of Banbury, scorned wearing his robes on the Queen's visit *(644)*.
Shipton-under-Wychwood inclosed by General Act *(939)*.
Railway proposals still appeared as bargaining counters: from Cheltenham to Church Hanborough to please the Midland Railway, and from Wolvercote by Thame to Hounslow to spite the GWR *(238, 971)*.
Duke of Marlborough installed a Watt-type double acting, rotative engine at his estate sawmill at Combe: this remained in steam until 1912, and was restored in 1972 by the Combe Mill Society.
Banbury attempt to found a plush weavers' co-operative *(644)*.
G E Street, Diocesan Architect since 1850, set up office in Beaumont street, Oxford until 1856 *(816)*.

**22 MAR.** William Kalabergo murdered his uncle, a Banbury watchmaker, on Williamscote Hill, and was executed at Oxford *(421)*.

**1 OCT.** London-Birmingham broad-gauge trains began: the track from Oxford to Banbury had been altered to double working, mixed gauge in each direction. Oxford Station was opened on its present site, the Abingdon-road station being used for goods traffic until 1872 *(238, 475)*.
Electric telegraph lines laid along GWR track *(238)*.

**OCT.** Woodstock training camp for 481 volunteer Militiamen *(123)*.

**NOV.** GWR mine flooded at Kennington, during disastrous floods from Sep. to Feb. *(238, 773)*.

**1853** Schemes for gas-lighting Woodstock and Charlbury streets (not achieved by the latter until 1880) *(97, 741)*.
S L Seckham, member of a speculative Tontine, began building Park Town estate on North Oxford land once intended for a workhouse *(786)*.
Christ Church opened as parish church of South Banbury (from which Grimsbury parish grew in 1921 *(510)*.
Cowley, Crawley, Standlake, South Stoke and Warborough inclosed by Act *(939)*.

**10 FEB.** Bloxham curate, John Hewett, began All Saints' Grammar School in his vicarage, hoping to enrol clergy sons: in 1855 Wilberforce consecrated new buildings by Street, but bankruptcy followed *(523)*.

**4 JUN.** Wolvercot Junction to Evesham section of Oxford, Worcester & Wolverhampton Railway opened *(707)* losing for Cassington Wharf its Witney and Woodstock trade *(605)* and ending Banbury's last coach service to Shipton-on-Stour *(644)*. The stone for Evenlode bridges came from 'Rally Quarr' at Taynton *(408)* and construction cost the life of Richard Coombs of Finstock *(806)*. Parliament allowed a Yarnton loop line to link the Buckinghamshire and OWW lines *(238)*, and still Parsons of the 'Old Worse and Worse' tried to spike the GWR with a Yarnton-Cheltenham proposed link through Witney and Burford, though "local support was chiefly moral" *(238)*.

**6 JUN.** Lord Derby found time on his way to installation as Oxford University's Chancellor to open Wilberforce's Diocesan Training College at Culham, whose "practising school" took in, from 1853 to 1931, many Abingdon tradesmen's sons *(470)*.

**1854** Chinnor and Cottisford inclosed by Act *(939)*: the latter involved Juniper Hill *(348)* and Bicester JPs chose leases for cottages and gardens rather than ejectment writs, but by 1883 most properties were rented for 1 or 2s a week from Bicester tradesmen *(61, 817)*.
Banbury Town Hall, in Bruton's "ponderous Gothic" turned to face the new railway *(786)*.
Banbury Advertiser founded *(802)*.

**JUN.** Openings: Oxford's Public Library, with B H Blackwell as first Librarian *(475)* and Cuddesdon Theological College, Street's first diocesan assignment *(154, 253, 474, 786)*.

**AUG-OCT.** Cholera epidemic with 194 cases in Oxford, of whom 115 died. Outbreaks at Garsington, Hailey, Witney and Headington are traceable to Oxford, but other cases were at Banbury and Little Milton *(27)*. No cases occurred in the Radcliffe Infirmary or the City Gaol: the County Gaol again suffered heavily. Dr Acland was the consulting physician to the Oxford Board of Health *(27)*. Miss Skene of St Thomas visited heroically, and was later the first woman prison visitor *(247)*: Vaughan Thomas urged his Yarnton parishioners to wear "flannel-bands and dry footwear" *(781)*.

**4 DEC.** Oxfordshire Militia left for Portsmouth and a year's garrison duty on Corfu *(123)* under the command of Colonel Fane, a county MP from 1862-8 *(115)*.

**1855** Thame Agricultural Society founded *(285)*.
Aston Bampton, and Shifford inclosed by Act *(939)*.
Thomas Combe, superintendent of the Clarendon Press 1838-72, bought Wolvercote Mill, introduced a steam-driven mill, built cottages and a school *(497, 773)*.
Bodicote became an ecclesiastical parish separate from Adderbury *(217)*.
Bicester Herald founded: published until 1917 *(621)*.
Street replaced "hopeless conventicle" at Wheatley with a new church, on which Henry Broadhurst worked as a mason *(768, 786)*.
Banbury Band of Hope formed: needed resuscitation by 1861 *(644)*.

**10 AUG.** Chipping Norton linked by single branch line to Kingham and the Oxford Worcester and Wolverhampton Railway *(238, 436, 826)*.

**1856** Ipsden, North Stoke, South Weston, Wheatfield and Souldern common inclosed by Act *(939)*.
George Herbert, former shoemaker, a Banbury photographer *(421)*.
Banbury Water Company founded: previously supplied by wells *(644)*.
William Hervey of Bradwell Grove gave £1100 in 2½% Consols to endow schools at Broadwell, Filkins and Holwell *(620)*.

**11 MAR.** First issue of the Thame Gazette: in the 1880s it acquired a Liberal-nonconformist rival, the Observer *(285)*.

**1857** Banbury acquired two Corn Exchanges, one Liberal (Palace Arcade) the other Tory (Vine Tavern): neither a success *(786)*.
Charles Taphouse opened a Piano and Organ shop in Oxford, moving to Magdalen street in 1859 *(504)*.
Oxford Union Society building by Woodward: Waterhouse added the Debating Chamber in 1878 *(786)*.
Henry Hall, of Barton Abbey, Master of the Heythrop Hunt, built new kennels on the outskirts of Chipping Norton *(286)*.
Electric telegraph, spreading rapidly along railway lines after 1852, reached Banbury: GPO control came in 1870 *(510)*.
St Denys School, Oxford opened by Mother Marian's Anglican Community *(501)*.

**25 MAR.** Oxfordshire Police Force established with a Chief Constable experienced in organising Kaffirs *(495)*.

**1 JUN.** Branch line of GWR from Twyford to Henley opened *(786, 823)*.

**21 JUL.** Edward Cardwell defeated W M Thackeray in a by-election at Oxford caused by Charles Neate's unseating for bribery *(115, 664)*.

**9 NOV.** Isaac Grubb, Mayor of Oxford, refused the oath to the Vice-Chancellor, breaching the tradition begun in 1248 *(475)*.

**1858** Charlton-on-Otmoor and Horspath *(503)* inclosed by Act *(939)*.
The long-advocated 1853 Act for "disafforesting Wychwood" was carried out by awards for Ascott 1859, Asthall 1862, Chilson 1860, Cornbury 1863, Wychwood Forest 1857, Minster Lovell 1861 and Finstock 1862 *(170, 244, 277, 342, 773, 939)*.
John Salter bought King's boat-building works and in 1870 Hall's yards, and established the Folly Bridge, Oxford, business *(627)*.
Oxford was exceptional in having a Local Board of Health distinct from the Council, a consequence of University involvement *(475)*.
Wilkinson built a University Gymnasium in Alfred street, Oxford *(676)*, and Watlington Police Station (he built six other stations by 1870 at Witney, Banbury, Woodstock, Chipping Norton, Henley and Burford) *(676)*.
Kirtlington the last village celebrating Whitsun Lamb Ales *(747)*.
Fawler ironstone mines opened, stimulated by hopes of rail export to South Wales: active twice before 1886 *(707, 710)*.

**1859** Bookmakers first allocated space at Oxford races *(428)*.
Burne-Jones created stained glass for Oxford Cathedral, and later for St Edmund Hall 1865, and Manchester College 1893 *(786)*.
Philip Egerton, curate of Deddington, bought Hewett's buildings at Bloxham and re-opened a school *(168)*.
First ironstone quarries at Adderbury: Steeple Aston and Fawler in 1858

*(707).*

**FEB.** Samuelson succeeded Tancred as Liberal MP for Banbury in keenly contested by-election won from Tories only by tie-breaking vote of the police superintendent: Edward Miall had drawn off 118 radical Liberal votes bolstered by dissenting moods in the town *(741).*

**APR.** Building of Banbury Cross to commemorate the marriage of Victoria's daughter to the Prussian Crown Prince: further royal figures were added in 1914. It does not stand on the site of any of the three mediaeval crosses *(786, 802).*

**MAY** Sir Charles Douglas beat Samuelson in the general election at Banbury through a radical-Tory coalition *(741).*

**NOV.** A Volunteer Rifle Corps formed at Henley, at a time when Italy and Garibaldi were making militarism progressive *(36).*

**DEC.** Burford, as torpid as Banbury was frenetic, lost its old Corporate body and became a simple parish *(32).* Bicester became a local government district in 1858 *(815).*

**1860** Oxford Building and Investment Company founded, building in brick on a large scale, particularly at Osney *(565, 644).*
Wilkinson laid out the Norham Manor Estate in North Oxford *(676, 786).* Christ Church built six model cottages at Black Bourton and a model lodging-house for eight single young men which failed *(137)* while cottagers of Stratton Lane, Stoke Lyne faced ejectment process for squatting, but were find 1*s* damages *(61).*
Leafield parish inclosed, and Scott's church consecrated *(786, 939).* Britannia Road school opened in Banbury: two British schools there were opened at Crouch Street 1839, and Cherwell Street 1861 *(802).* John Stainer took charge of Magdalen College School, Oxford choir *(511),* and was involved in founding Oxford Philharmonic Society *(816).*
Churches like Holton and Wootton, having no organ, used gallery orchestras of string and wind instruments *(413, 503)*: Edwin Turner of Finstock began 19 summers as an itinerant harvester, going to London early to "morris the streets" *(817).*
Henry Taunt began his life of photography in Oxford district *(746).*

**JUL.** British Association met in University Museum, Oxford (built by Deane & Woodward with iron framework *(786)* and string courses of Hornton stone *(408)* ) and T H Huxley faced Wilberforce in debate on evolution *(670, 816).*

**DEC.** Victoria and Albert visited Frewen Hall, Oxford privately to see how the Prince of Wales was faring as a Christ Church undergraduate *(42, 45, 467, 942).*

**1861** Telegraph poles were put up along the Oxford-Banbury road *(251, 773).*
River Cherwell acted as a cultural break between rural communities in

terms of its contribution to the breeding population of Charlton-on-Otmoor *(617)*.
James Morrell, brewer, opted for Early Victorian treatment for Headington Hill Hall *(786)*.
Newcastle Commission reported that of 403 elementary schools in the county, 370 were Anglican and 18 British, and that only 6% of small parishes could meet the requirements for receiving State aid *(840, 915)*.

**13 NOV.** Opening of the Witney Railway to join the Oxford, Worcester & Wolverhampton line at Yarnton *(262, 807)*.

**1862** Oxford Times first published *(475)*.
Ramsden, which became a separate parish in 1861, and Finstock Common were inclosed by Act *(535, 939)*.
Salford villagers said to have consulted "Wizard Manning" in search for protection against reputed powers of local Dolly *(498, 742)*.
Oxfordshire Down recognised as a separate breed, the result of efforts since 1827 by Druce of Eynsham, Gillett of South Leigh and Blake of Stanton Harcourt *(161)*.

**1 AUG.** Thame terminus of railway from Prince's Risborough opened *(285)*.

**1863** Inclosure by Act at Benson, Berrick Salome and Stoke Row *(939)* where Oriental Wells and druidical stones are testaments to the Reade family's work for the Indian Raj *(786)*.
School on National lines, at last for Black Bourton *(137)* and for Burford *(347)* where the Grammar School had a halting life *(203)*. Thomas Chamberlain, High Anglican vicar of St Thomas, Oxford, moved his 'Osney School' into St Edward's School in New Inn Hall Street, Oxford *(247)*.
Cowley Road workhouse built for Oxford Incorporation: for affluent Gillett bankers at Banbury villadom arrived, with "Wood Green" and "The Elms" *(565, 786)*.

**23 MAR.** Last public execution at Oxford *(247)* for a murder committed at Caulcott.

**20 SEP.** Fire destroyed the Cornmarket shop of Grimbly, Hughes and Dewe the Oxford grocers *(87, 947)*.

**1864** Two abortive railway proposals, for a Watlington-Wallingford line, of which the track south of the Thames in 1866 was all that developed, and yet another Midland Railway plan near Burford *(203, 347)*.
Fifield and Idbury benefices united *(500)*: Checkendon inclosed *(939)*.
Newman's bid to build an Oxford oratory on old Workhouse site fell through: University built Wellington Square on the plot *(147)*.
Gilbert Scott rebuilt Clifton Hampden Bridge using local brick.
William Wilkinson, architect of many local buildings 1841-86, began the Randolph Hotel, Oxford *(676)*.

**AUG.** Publisher Macmillan met drill-enthusiast Archibald McLaren on holiday: Summerfields School at Oxford resulted which soon developed a strong link as preparatory school for Eton *(566)*.

**25 OCT.** GWR opened a line from Oxford through Wheatley and Tiddington to Thame *(57, 238, 503, 773)*.

**1865** Cattle plague provoked a rural crisis *(743)*.
Gladstone defeated as University's MP *(590, 777)*: country clerics more able to travel to Oxford by train to vote.
Final defeat of a railway bill from Cheltenham-Hendon through Yarnton and East Gloucestershire *(238)*. No further attempts.
Charles Dodgson, mathematical tutor at Christ Church, published "Alice's Adventures in Wonderland" and in 1871 "Through the Looking Glass, and what Alice found there" *(816)*.
Thomas Combe gave the Infirmary chapel to the Radcliffe, Oxford *(670)*.
Adwell church rebuilt by Blomfield *(562)*.

**APR.** GWR got Oxford Council's agreement to build a carriage and wagon works behind its station. Gooch's position, as GWR Chairman and MP for Cricklade, as much as "The Times" and "Punch" campaigning, saw the development go to Swindon instead *(238, 414)*.

**22 MAR** Oxford School of Art opened after a local campaign in which Holman Hunt took part: in 1871 it was sited in the basement of the Randolph Galleries *(340)*.

**1866** House-building begun included the Hamel, three-storeyed flats in St Thomas, Oxford, with open staircase similar to contemporary London building *(786)*: 23-4 Cornhill, Banbury in variegated brick by Wilkinson, now conspicuous near the 1973 Car Park *(676)*; Hailey Church by C C Rolfe at 21, who went on to build model artisan houses in 1870 in Kingston Road, Oxford *(676)*, and Street's St Philip and St James church for affluent North Oxford was completed *(786)*.
Demolition of the Angel coaching inn, Oxford *(475)*.
Co-operative movement started in Chipping Norton *(436)* and re-started in Banbury *(510, 644)*.
Radcliffe Infirmary, Oxford admitted a lady to learn nursing *(670)*.

**29 MAR.** Death of John Keble: a new (and cheaper style) Oxford college was promoted in his memory *(777)*.

**6 AUG.** Thames Conservancy created with powers from Cricklade to Yantlett Creek *(185)*.

**NOV.** Banbury reform demonstration: in 1867 the voters trebled *(741)*.

**1867** Banbury Council bought Spital Farm at Grimsbury for sewage beds *(510)*.

**1868** University control of Oxford night police ended *(475)* and students were permitted to live cheaply in lodgings (or in Butterfield's Keble College) *(786)*.
John Allen's Oxford Steam Ploughing Company started at Hockmore

Street, Cowley: by 1907 employed 200 *(462, 503, 627).*
Deane built the Clarendon Laboratory for Oxford University *(786).*
Turnpikes at east and west outlets of Oxford abolished, and the gate-houses turned into inns or demolished *(247, 503).*
Sir William Harcourt became Liberal MP for Oxford: after 1880 he looked to other seats as he rose to higher office *(115).*
Holy Trinity Convent, North Oxford *(753)*, St John's Mission House for Father Benson at Cowley *(503)* and St Barnabas church, Horton built *(541).*
Burford Cottage Hospital built: moved to new home in 1902 *(347).*

**1869** Horton Hospital, Banbury, begun by Charles Driver *(786).*
Taunton family provided a church, school and parsonage at Freeland *(786)*, while Thomas Combe bore the expense of Arthur Blomfield's St Barnabas church, Oxford with its campanile *(194, 497, 786).*

**1 APR.** Third rail taken up on Oxford-Banbury line, marking the end of broad gauge in the area *(238).*

**1870** Robert Pratley of Milton introduced New Zealand refrigerated meat to local people who rarely tasted butcher's meat *(277).*
Benjamin Jowett became Master of Balliol College, Oxford *(508)* with its new "collegiate Middle Pointed" range to Broad Street, on which Hardy's Jude left a pointed message *(786).*
Oxford School of Science and Art opened, the Science lectures taking place in the University Museum *(340).*
William Morris rented Kelmscott House to 1896: "News from Nowhere" was largely written here *(620).*
Show-time: the Royal Agricultural Show came to Diamond Farm, Oxford (the undeveloped land between St Margaret's road and Summertown) *(753)*: the Stow & Chipping Norton and the Thame societies offered prizes to youths 'who had worked the greatest number of years for the same master or on the same farm', ensuring that winners would have left school at 8 or 9 *(781).*
Volunteer Fire Brigades were formed at Oxford *(87)* and Banbury *(711).*

**1871** Cheatle reported 15 deaths from 38 scarlet-fever cases in the Burford district, where "thatched roofs have . . . disappeared" *(916).*
Religious tests ceased at Oxford University, except for Theology graduates *(777).*
Heythrop House restored by Waterhouse for Albert Brassey, son of the railway contractor *(786).*

**22 JUL.** Burford voted against the proposal for a School Board *(347).*

**1872** Local landowners' initiative opened the Watlington to Prince's Risborough railway through Chinnor, but in 1883 it was sold to GWR *(285, 476, 780).*
Fire at Bliss Tweed Mill put 300 workers idle at Chipping Norton, until rebuilding with Tuscan order chimneystack was complete *(436, 786, 826).*

Thomas Arnold's grand-daughter began married bliss on the Norham Manor Estate, Oxford: in 1888 the most famous novel, "Robert Elsmore came from the pen of Mrs Humphrey Ward *(565)*.
William Fox found rural bliss at Bradwell Grove: he was a Yorkshire steel-maker who deserted crinoline frames for umbrellas at the right time. He rebuilt the 1850 church, opened a school (closed in 1958), and by 1910 had learned to shoot 2053 pheasants, 908 partridges and 768 hares *(620)*.
Ruskin began a School of Drawing in the higher regions of the Randolph Galleries, Oxford *(340)*.
Combe sold Wolvercote Mill to the Oxford University Press *(497)*.

**16 APR.** Meeting on Milton-under-Wychwood recreation ground set up the Milton Labourers' Union with 50 members, who soon chose to join Joseph Arch's National Agricultural Labourers' Union *(795)*.

**29 MAY** Christopher Holloway, a Methodist lay preacher, became chairman of the Wootton branch of NALU which demanded 16*s* a week in place of 11*s* for labourers. 40 labourers left with their families in Jul to seek work in Sheffield ironworks, and 10 soldiers from Aldershot were used to bring in the harvest, another 40 in the Bampton area, where William Clinch had evicted labourers at Lew *(634, 903)*.

**JUL.** Four Banbury men had goods distrained to pay costs of their prosecution for failing to have their children vaccinated (1853-98 compulsory) *(781)*.
Foundation laid of A B Simeon's Woodstock Road buildings for St Edward's School, Oxford. Woodard Foundation declined to accept this or All Saints' School, Bloxham *(557)*.

**7 SEP.**Determined opposition from a fractious Carfax mob to Saturday night closing of Oxford pubs at 11: they won 30 precious minutes from local JPs *(760)*.

**7 DEC.** Benjamin Norton, a Banbury emigrant, died of yellow fever at Pernambuco during an ill-starred Brazilian emigration scheme.
Oxford Co-operative and Industrial Society began trading *(411)*.

**1873** Ambrosden School Board set up, building a school in 1876 *(786)*.
Oxford city bought Sandford land for a sewage farm *(475)*.
Village clubs still far outnumbered local branches of national Friendly Societies in this county alone in S England *(645)*.
Gladstone provoked a stir by ignoring Oxford claims in presenting to the living of Ewelme.
Tackley inclosed by Act *(939)*.

**15 JAN** Fairford to Witney section of the East Gloucestershire Railway was opened: this and Witney Railway absorbed by GWR 1890 *(238, 807)*.

**14 APR.** Hambridge's labourers at Ascott-under-Wychwood struck for a 2*s* weekly wage rise in the middle of backward barley sowing *(795)*.

**12 MAY** Thirty women went to the fields and "jostled" two young

Ramsden men *(535)*, set on by the farmer *(795)*. The vicar of Shipton and rector of Swerford, sitting as JPs at Chipping Norton, sentenced 16 women to 7 and 10 days' imprisonment at Oxford: Arch arrived and gave each prisoner £5 and a dress in the union colour of royal blue, outside Hambridge's gate on their release *(104)*. The Lord Lieutenant (Duke of Marlborough) unreservedly supported the JPs, but after a Commons question by Oxford MP Harcourt, the Lord Chancellor Selborne expressed reservations *(277, 527)*.

**6 AUG.** Joseph Malings, a Deddington chemist, had his goods cried in the Market Place for his resistance to compulsory vaccination *(52)*.

**23 DEC.** Steamship Mongol left Plymouth with 500 labourers and families recruited by Holloway to sail, at union expense, to New Zealand: they arrived on 13 Feb 1874 *(634, 743)*.

**1874** School Boards set up at Brize Norton and Burford: that at Oxford was re-elected, and T H Green, Balliol College tutor and philosopher, was elected *(146, 835)*.

Hertford College, Oxford was re-founded with help from banker Baring *(786)*.

Ruskin's students felt "the pleasure of useful muscular work" as they studied Fine Art by road-making at Ferry Hinksey *(769)*.

**4 FEB.** Lord Randolph Churchill became MP for Woodstock *(115)*: his son Winston was born in Blenheim Palace in Nov.

**14 NOV.** Idbury farmer of 60 acquitted of detaining a 15 year-old girl (his wife) against her father's will.

**DEC.** Seventeen members of two Shipton families were drowned when their ship, Cospatrick, caught fire on their way to New Zealand *(795)*.

**24 DEC.** Rail crash at Hampton Gay killed 34 and injured 100 passengers, most of whom were admitted to the Radcliffe Infirmary *(238, 670)*.

**1875** Eccentric vicars: one caused a Cowley brawl by refusing to bury "Moses Merritt" a colourful local *(503)*, another went to prison for contempt in failing to account for Eynsham charities.

More seemly novelties in St Clements were Nazareth House *(481, 786)* and T H Green's coffee tavern *(146)*.

Floods, paralleled in 1894 and 1947, cut the railway lines *(414)*.

Oxford, anxious to build a service reservoir, and John Mattock the horticulturist, acquired land in Headington *(475, 812)*.

**3 NOV.** Oxford High School for Girls opened in the Judge's Lodging, St Giles, moving to Jackson's Banbury Road building in 1879 and to Belbroughton Road in 1957 *(558)*.

**23 NOV.** St Aloysius church, Oxford dedicated into Jesuit care by Bishop Ullathorne and Cardinal Manning *(481, 814)*.

**1876** T G Jackson built the Examination Schools on the Angel site in Oxford High Street *(786)*, and the Cowley Military College founded "for

. . . the best possible education for the sons of officers and preparing candidates for commissions" in former Middle Class school buildings *(503, 786)*.
Co-operative activity began at Henley: its shop opened 1930 *(435)*.
Society for Preserving Ancient Buildings was born on the tide of William Morris' horror at restoration of Burford Church *(347)*.
George Benfield of Dean joined a northerner, N F Loxley in Oxford building partnership which "went public" in 1960 *(618)*.
St Stephen's College founded in Parks Road, Oxford *(777)*.

**22 JAN.** Vicar set up Anglican Temperance Society in Wheatley, from whose initiative the Merry Bells emerged *(981)*.

**6 MAY** Oxford tailors struck for 5½*d* an hour, with little success.

**7 JUN.** Militia band played 52nd and 85th Regiments into the newly completed Barracks in Hollow Way, Cowley *(123, 503, 786)*.

**1877** Gillett's Bank opened a Cornmarket, Oxford branch and joined with Clinch's at Witney: smaller branches at Chipping Norton 1880, and Bampton 1888 *(349, 565)*.
Garsington's village Benefit Society became a Foresters branch *(310)*, to give 17 Foresters and 16 Oddfellows branches in the county *(747)*.
Disturnpiking of Witney-Great Tew and Bicester-Enstone roads *(806)*
Dragon preparatory school founded at Oxford *(839)*.
Governor Eyre, acquitted after the Jamaica enquiry 1865, retired to Steeple Aston *(251)*.

**1878** Sidney Holland, at 21, given £100 salary to teach 102 children at Stanton Harcourt and 'to include organ and sewing' *(840)*.
Women examined in Oxford university for the first time *(777)*: Lady Margaret Hall founded for women students *(786)*. The Association for the Higher Education of Women was appropriately active in Oxford, still dispersing money on 'chaperonage' in 1919 *(777)*.
Edward Hermon, a Lancashire cotton magnate, completed Wyfold Court, now Borocourt Hospital *(786)*.

**15 FEB.** Mr Tollitt "an intelligent working man of the city" lagged only two years behind Alexander Graham Bell in providing a telephone between Oxford fire station and the engineer's house *(672)*.

**1879** Foundation of Somerville College, Oxford for women without any Anglican bias *(777, 786)*: also of the Society for Oxford Home Students, becoming St Anne's College in 1952 *(777, 786)*.
Acland Nursing Home a tribute to Sir Henry Acland's wife Sarah: its new buildings in Banbury Road, Oxford were opened in 1897 by the Prince of Wales *(295)*.
Workers' Hall opened in Magdalen Road, Cowley: soon became a Mission *(503)*.

**1 MAY** Thame Grammar School opened in Wilkinson's buildings *(786)*, and received South Kensington grants for its workshop 1891 and science block 1896: the link with New College and Rycote remained *(285)*.

**1880** John Oldrid Scott designed a Thames state barge for University College, Oxford *(786)*.

Jackson began building George Street premises for Oxford High School for Boys, supported by the Corporation rather than the old Nixon and Bluecoat foundations *(146, 786)*.

Indian Institute established in Oxford, for which Basil Champneys built a home 1883-96 *(786, 816)*.

**10 MAY** Tory victory by 54 votes when local brewer, Alexander Hall, beat Harcourt in a by-election. T H Green was active in presenting a petition for a Royal Commission, as a result of which Hall was unseated for bribery. No further election was held, and when J W Chitty became a judge in 1881, the city was unrepresented: in 1885 it was reduced to a single member *(115, 323, 475)*.

**1881** Golliwogs made an appearance as coconut shies' prizes at St Giles' Fair, Oxford *(661, 781)*.

Alderman Cavell committed suicide by jumping from the top floor of Elliston and Cavell's department store at Oxford *(664)*.

**1 JUL.** Oxfordshire Light Infantry's 1st, 2nd and 4th Battalions consisted of the 43rd (Monmouthshire), 52nd (Oxfordshire) and Oxfordshire Militia Regiments *(123, 704)*.

**1 DEC.** Oxford Tramway Company, set up in 1879, introduced horse-drawn trams on its first route from the railway station to its Cowley road terminus: it developed a horse stud of 150, and 27 routes by 1914 when it closed down; associated horse buses served Iffley turn, Wolvercote turn, Cowley village and Headington. Electric tramways were never built in Oxford *(475, 734)*.

**1882** Oxford Central School for Girls (later Cheney School) developed in New Inn Hall Street, Oxford *(788)*.

Last parliamentary inclosure at Crowell *(939)*.

Burdon-Sanderson's appointment to an Oxford chair was a key step in the university's development of modern medical education: one of the first battles was with anti-vivisectionists over the need for a Physiological Laboratory *(295)*.

**1883** Students entering Oxford University exceeded the entry of 1621 which was 784, for the first time *(670, 822)*.

Bicester Roman Catholic church and school opened *(147)*.

**JAN.** Early's blanket factory at Witney burned down *(565)*.

**1 MAY** Banbury's Mayor visited Grimsbury schools to check attendance of children whose school fees were paid by the Poor Law Guardians: this consequence of universal and compulsory education led to the abolition of school pence in the 1890s *(781)*.

**1884** Witney Wesleyan Schools, and Banbury Technical School and Mechanics Institute, were built *(90, 786)*. Lloyd's Collegiate School had a temporary existence in the Temperance Hotel in High street, Chipping Norton *(436)*.
Gratuitous advice to town and village: Thorold Rogers wished to see in Oxford "a permanent industry as active and successful as that in Banbury" (William Morris was only seven at the time) *(561, 565)*.
Henry Acland looked to see cottage hospitals, dispensaries and district nurses in rural areas *(64)*.
Culham College Volunteers formed a company in the 2nd Battalion, Oxfordshire Light Infantry *(470)*.
Turrell's Hall was short-lived as a private hall attached to Oxford University, catering for mature men *(676)*.
Pusey House, Oxford founded under Principal Gore who also set up the Community of the Resurrection at Mirfield. Its St Giles buildings are 1911-4 *(786)*.

**1885** Heythrop Hunt held its first point-to-point meeting between Gawcombe, Idbury and Fifield *(286)*.
Banbury auctioneer attempted to set up a regular stock meeting in Deddington market place *(565)*.
Oxford set up a new smallpox Isolation Hospital at Cold Arbour *(670)*.
Burford Grammar School entered its pupils for the College of Preceptors examinations, changing in 1902 to Oxford Locals, by which time they were aided by state funds for laboratories *(706)*.
Cutler-Boulter dispensaries were set up at Gloucester street and Marston street, Oxford, the almshouse being pulled down *(670)*.
Charlbury cricket club played in the White Lion Inn field *(741)*.
Deane added the Pitt-Rivers Museum to the Oxford site *(786, 816)*.

**DEC.** Third Reform Act reduced Oxford to a single MP, disfranchised Banbury and Woodstock boroughs, and divided the county seats into North, Mid and South Divisions *(115, 403)*.
Floods destroyed Osney bridge, rebuilt in 1767 under the Botley Turnpike Act.

**1886** Mansfield College, which began life as Spring Hill College in Birmingham and a mainly Congregational body moved to Oxford to become a university hall: it strengthened Nonconformity since its entry to the university in 1871 *(68, 403, 777)*.
St Hugh's College, Oxford opened as a hall for women students: full collegiate status came in 1959 *(786)*.
Salter's Oxford boatyard began a river steamer service to Kingston *(476)*.
South of England Telephone Company set up in Cornmarket, Oxford: had 57 subscribers paying £10 each when National Telephone Co. took over in the 1890s *(672)*.
Oxford Eye Hospital founded *(295)*.

Kingham Hill School founded by Charles Baring-Young as a charitable school for orphans or boys from poor homes *(300, 444)*.

**1887** Hampton Gay manor house derelict after a fire *(786)*.
Oxford and District Trades and Labour Council formed.
City Drapery Stores at Oxford (later Webber's) adopted the "Lamson Cash Railway" *(565)*.

**6 APR.** First passenger train ran on the Banbury-Cheltenham Direct Railway's line from Chipping Norton to King's Sutton through Hook Norton, where two men had been killed working on the viaduct *(243)*, Bloxham and Adderbury *(238, 484, 804)*: the last "Chippy Dick" or "Hooky Flier" ran in 1951 *(773)*.

**1888** Burford omnibus service began, giving a four-hour parcel service to London connecting with the GWR.
Thame's new Town Hall completed *(285)*.
Oxford Wesleyan Boys' School became an Organised Science School, concentrating science classes held all over the city since 1871 *(340)*.
First Oxford "Summer Meeting" connecting with the university's Extension Movement *(403)*.
County Council elected to replace JPs in Quarter Sessions dealing with administrative business.

**25 SEP.** Castle street Citadel opened in Oxford by William Booth, the Salvation Army General: previously Salvationists ran the gauntlet of the "Skeleton Army" of local roughs.

**1889** Move to Oxford of Manchester College, a Unitarian institution founded in 1786 *(263, 777)*.
Oxford Order constituted the city as a County Borough, with special direct university representation: it swept away the Local Board, Police Committee and Market Committee *(475)*.
Hook Norton's Ironstone Partnership opened quarries: by 1900 it failed, and its creditor, the GWR, took its locomotive, "Hook Norton" and used it hauling boat trains in Weymouth Harbour until 1926 *(707)*.

**1890** Hook Norton Partnership began to work ironstone south of Adderbury station. Production ended in the 1930s, and wartime Northern Aluminium Company buildings are now Twyford Seed Factory *(707)*.
Henry Tubb, the Bicester banker, built an Italianate mansion at Chesterton *(786)*.
Cotuit Hall (now a Polytechnic hostel) built at Headington *(786)*.

**19 MAY** Woodstock Railway Company's line from Kidlington to Blenheim and Woodstock (palace before people) opened *(238, 476)*: GWR took over completely in 1897 *(748)*.

**1891** Oxford School of Science and Art became the responsibility of the City's Technical Instruction Committee: from 1894-1934 it shared the use of the former Bluecoat School site *(340)*.

Coffee tavern set up on Combe village green by Miss Brooke *(450)*.
Seven ton coach-and-four driven on the Thames ice *(475)*.

**23 FEB.** Meeting at Great Milton to revive the Agricultural Labourers' Union: supported by Herbert Samuel (then a Balliol undergraduate) and Ben Tillett (the dockers' leader). Further meetings were held at Burford, Milton-under-Wychwood and Garsington, but its success was limited to raising Chalgrove, Haseley and Milton wages by 1*s* a week, and giving 10*s* union payment weekly to Worminghall strikers, but the strike collapsed *(795, 915)*.

**1892** Ill-feeling at Great Haseley assuaged by vicar's action in finding allotments for labourers and building an institute *(915)*.
Oxford's first electricity supply: its extension to domestic usage was slow until the private company was taken over in 1932 *(475)*.
Micklethwaite built a side-chapel at Keble College, Oxford to house Holman Hunt's "The Light of the World" *(786)*.

**21-22 MAY** Weekend conversion of Paddington-Exeter main line to narrow gauge: more slowly, the widening of Sonning Cutting and rebuilding of the Thames bridges at Moulsford and Basildon was involved *(238)*.

**1893** Roman Catholic boys' school opened in Radcliffe Row, Oxford *(481)*.
Islip's new school built: the old one became an Institute, and after 1919 housed the Women's Institute *(254)*.
Dr Radcliffe's School, Steeple Aston, was reorganised by the Charity Commissioners to create a fund for technical and practical agricultural education. It began humbly with cookery classes for the girls of Rousham and Heyford.
A pupil-teacher centre was established in Oxford *(788)*.
St Hilda's College, Oxford founded, with support from Cheltenham Ladies' College *(786)*. It became a full college in 1960.
Great Haseley ironworks so affected by agricultural depression that J V Gibbon, its owner and a mechanical inventor, committed suicide *(475)*.
Henry Hare won the competition for building Oxford's new Town Hall: *(786)*: it involved demolishing Nixon's School, whose endowments had been diverted to provide places for Freemen's sons at Oxford High School for Boys. After 1944 University Scholarships were provided. *(475)*.
Hilaire Belloc proposed an Oxford Union motion that undergraduates should have some share in University government: F E Smith and the majority disagreed *(777)*.
George Hawkins, organiser of Oxford Trades Council (another "Oxford Union") became President of the Co-operative Union Congress *(411)*.
Another William Morris set up a bicycle repairing business with £4 capital in James Street, Cowley *(480)*: he twice attended evening classes in Engineering Design at Oxford's School of Technology *(837)*. Morris was not the only one of Oxford's 23 cyclemakers who moved into garage

proprietorship *(837)*.

**APR.** Clarendon Press published T G Jackson's "Wadham College", the first of a series of college histories in Oxford *(445)*.

Brickmaking at Headington Quarry affected by strike *(817)*.

**1894** Co-operative Society backed Banbury's first working-class council candidates since Chartist days: they failed, but preluded the setting-up of the Independent Labour Party there in 1906.

Civil parish of Cowley St John created *(503)*.

Company of the Church Lads' Brigade formed, with the Vicar as Captain, at Kidmore End *(272)*.

**AUG.** Oxford Central Municipal Technical School opened in Church Street, St Ebbe's, moving to Southfields in 1934 *(340)*: premises shared with City of Oxford Schools of Technology, Art and Commerce, whose Art School moved from Ashmolean Museum where it began in 1865 *(340)*.

**OCT.** Oxfordshire Constabulary paid £15 for its first official bicycle, but forbade its constables to ride at night, 1917-40: in 1914 they were given their first motor-car, and in 1950 their first two-way radio *(495)*. Already they were dealing with the new-found 'juvenile delinquent' *(775, 828)*.

**DEC.** First election, with secret ballot, of parish councils: at Wigginton five labourers reversed an early "show-of-hands" decision and won all the seats *(842)*. Agricultural unionists were also successful at Horspath, Wootton, Burford, Tetsworth and Weston-on-the-Green *(903)*.

**1895** Albert Brassey, of Heythrop, won North Oxfordshire as a Unionist MP on the retirement of Sir Bernhard Samuelson *(115, 286)*.

First chaplain to Catholic students at Oxford University appointed.

Bliss family interest in Chipping Norton receded as the firm went "public" and came under Birmingham Banking Company control *(826)*.

William Carter bought 730 acres at Black Bourton from the Duke of Marlborough and, as he had elsewhere, developed a residential and small-holding colony called Carterton. Many of its 141 small free-holders were police and army pensioners *(191)*.

Burford Grammar School became an Organised Science School, with an agricultural side *(706)*.

**1896** Stokenchurch transferred to Buckinghamshire *(552)*.

Leander Club opened premises at Henley *(823)* where a rich solicitor, Sir Frank Crisp, built a bizarre folly, Friar Park *(786)*.

Charlbury Water Works Company formed through the Albright family's efforts: mains water was available in 1897, and Chipping Norton Rural District Council took over the works in 1939 *(741)*.

Demolition of all but the tower of St Martin's, Carfax, Oxford *(786)*.

Campion Hall set up as a Jesuit private hall in Oxford University *(481, 777, 786, 816)*.

William Morris died and was buried at Kelmscott: his tomb was designed by Philip Webb *(786)*.

Hook Norton Ironstone Company began quarrying and calcining, but when Brymbo took over in 1901 the bulk of the output was sent by rail to Wales. Redlands quarry was opened in 1904 following the failure of Hook Norton Partnership, but all production ended in 1946. The wagons were shipped to Tanganyika for developing ground-nuts schemes. *(707).*

**31 MAR.** Licit union commemorated with the homecoming at Blenheim of the Duke of Marlborough and his American bride, Consuela Vanderbilt: illicit union (per 1176) by naming a "517" Class 0-4-2T engine "Fair Rosamund" during Queen Victoria's visit *(748).* Mr Broad, gentleman's outfitter at Bristol House, Woodstock, may have benefitted from the 'occasion' *(845).*

**8 AUG.** All Saints School, Bloxham transferred to the Provost and Fellows of St Nicholas College, Lancing (the Woodard Foundation) *(168).*

**1897** John Kibble, a Charlbury builder (author of *(237) (244)* ) designed a fountain to commemorate both piped water and the Diamond Jubilee *(741).*

St Benet's Hall founded as the Oxford house of the Benedictine monks, becoming a private University hall in 1918 *(777, 786).*

Prince of Wales visited Oxford to open the new Acland Home: "not yet regarded as a heroic figure, but his figure was the worst thing about him" *(330).*

Monastery of the Servile Fathers established at Begbroke Manor House *(147).*

Roman Catholic church, Our Lady and St John, opened at Goring *(147).*

A teachers' training college for women began in Cowley Place, Oxford but was taken over by St Hilda's College in 1921 *(786).*

**FEB.** Last throes of compulsory vaccination laws: stir at Charlbury where 19 men were charged, but only bound over *(806).*

**1898** William Morris, then the proprietor of a cycle and motorcycle repair shop in High Street, Oxford set up Morris Garages in Longwall Street to repair motor cars *(295, 475, 480, 561, 837).*

**8 MAR.** World's wonder at Asthall School: children were let out 'to see a motor car that was passing through the village' *(781).*

**JUN.** Oxford School Board took over the Central Girls' School in order to obtain a Higher Grade elementary school for Girls *(788)*: a new building in New Inn Hall Street opened in 1901.

**SEP.** Customers at St Giles Fair paid *3d* for the thrill of seeing Mr Gladstone's funeral procession on an early bioscope *(661, 781).*

**1899** Cecil Sharp rediscovered English morris at Headington Quarry *(817, 539)*, led by William Kimber.

Banbury Council voted 14-8 against a School Board: voluntary efforts produced the 550 extra places demanded by the Board of Education *(510).*

**AUG.** Seven Caversham boys fined 5*s*, seven days' hard labour in default for bathing in the Thames 'without proper bathing dress or drawers' *(781)*.

**13 DEC.** 1st Battalion, Oxfordshire Ligh Infantry marched through beflagged streets from Cowley barracks to Oxford railway station on their way to fight in South Africa *(126)*. Only two Wootton men served in the war in South Africa *(413)*.

**1900** Oxfordshire Yeomanry's first casualty was at Dreifontein where the captain of the Banbury troop was killed.
Barclays Bank absorbed the High Street, Oxford bank with strong University connections belonging to the Parsons of Elsfield and the Thomsons of Woodperry *(295)*.
Benfield & Loxley set up brickmaking plant at Sandford, closing it in 1915 when the clay became riddled with lime *(618)*.

**19 MAY** Bicester celebrated the relief of Mafeking: a watchmaker was later compensated for his damaged property *(495)*.

**AUG.** Regatta established at Radcot, continuing into the 1930s *(603)*.

**1901** Banbury was supplied by an Electric Light Supply Company which turned a malthouse into a generating station: only after a takeover in 1928 was alternating current available, and pylons were erected in the 1930s between Stourport and Banbury *(510, 673)*.
Oxford School Board built the Boys' Central School in Gloucester Green, now the bus waiting-room *(786)*.
Earl of Dudley opened Hook Norton quarries, but production was erratic, and Friswell's dismantled the works in 1920 *(707)*.

**17 MAY** Crowds once more at Oxford station to greet 3 officers, 89 NCOs and men of the 1st Battalion, Oxfordshire Light Infantry on their return to barracks from South Africa *(126)*.

**1902** Witney's secondary education was reorganised: the Bluecoat School was closed, and a Federation of the Free Grammar School with the Technical School (pioneered by Science and Art classes emerging from the Wesleyan School) was headed by the ex-head of Witney Wesleyan School: the term "grammar" was only resumed in 1909 *(526)*.
Oxford Sanitary Aid Society, later more euphoniously called Oxford Health and Housing Association, developed baby-weighing centres, arranged for cheap humanised milk from Oxford Dairy Company, and pioneered the 1921 Maternity Home *(670)*.
Great Central Railway opened a link to Banbury *(476)*.
St Mary Hall was finally incorporated into the adjacent Oriel College, Oxford *(786)*.

**1 JUN.** Oxford rags and revels, including Compton Mackenzie's youthful indiscretions, to celebrate the end of the Boer War.

**4 JUN.** Oxford Municipal Labour Representation Association more soberly launched.

**1903** Heythrop Hunt found it necessary to set up a Wire Committee, one

member defining progress as "larger fields, poorer farmers, more wire and tarred roads" *(286)*.
Nonetheless an "Automobile and Cycle Agency" in Oxford failed, and William Morris salvaged his toolkit and determination *(480)*.
Headington Quarry Pig Club established *(817)*.

**1904** Electric light first used in Bliss Tweed Mill, Chipping Norton and in the Radcliffe Infirmary *(475, 826)*.
New school for St Thomas, Oxford to replace condemned boys', girls' and infants' schools *(247)*.

**1905** Bicester received piped water *(621)*.
Shiplake Court built by Ernest George for Robert Harrison *(786)*: now Shiplake College.
City of Oxford Electric Traction Company formed to operate a modernised tramway system: local opposition to all methods, whether stud, conduit or trolley, prevented action and the motor-bus was the next transport stage in Oxfordshire *(734)*.

**1906** Milham Ford School was opened by Augustine Birrell: the Church Education Corporation bought the Cowley Place site from the Moodys who ran a private venture school from 1894. In 1923 Oxford Corporation bought this girls' school and in 1938 built new premises in Marston lane, Oxford *(488)*.
Oxford Co-operative Society set up scholarships tenable at the City Technical School *(411)*.

**JAN.** Liberal election victories in North and South Oxfordshire.

**1907** University Extension movement, going back to 1873, housed a conference at Oxford which looked at its role in working-class education. R H Tawney and A E Zimmern wrote a report, and from this concern the Workers' Educational Association was born.
Lord Curzon, elected Oxford University's Chancellor, sought by internal reforms to ward off "the less sympathetic hand of the State" *(403)* but by 1919 the University joined the University Grants Committee.

**1908** Early's of Witney protected their blankets against "foreign manufactures" by using the Merchandise Marking Act of 1887 against Yorkshire competitors *(651)*.
Basil Champneys began the Rhodes Building of Oriel College, Oxford *(786)*.
C F Jenkin became Oxford University's first Professor of Engineering Science, and Jackson began the building of an Electrical Laboratory *(295, 786)*.

**11 AUG.** Winston Churchill proposed marriage to Clementine Hozier in the Temple of Diana at Blenheim Palace: in 1975 Lady Spencer-Churchill unveiled a plaque.

**1909** Closure of Spratt's barn, the last working shaft at Stonesfield slate mines, and of the last plush factory in Banbury *(408, 773, 808)*.

**1 JAN.** Old Age Pensions available: by 1912 70% of people in the county over seventy were receiving them, one of the highest county figures. This suggests their welcome rather than reluctant acceptance *(348, 536, 762)*.

**15 SEP.** Army manoeuvres over Kingham Hill *(180, 300)*.

**18 SEP.** Conservative manoeuvres: their van touring the county with propaganda against the People's Budget ran into little local difficulties at Witney, Littlemore, Jericho and East Oxford before being overturned in Headington Quarry *(817)*.

**DEC.** Thame received a telephone service from Aylesbury, and in Aug 1914 a direct link with Oxford *(285)*.

**1910** GWR opened a "cut-off" line on the London-Birmingham route, from Banbury to Prince's Risborough, with a new station at Bicester North *(238, 476, 503, 621)*.
Village Hall built for Kingham by Charles Baring-Young *(502)*.
Burford Grammar School's scheme was revised to admit a free place element: the very slow approach to girls' admission led in 1921 to the bussing of Burford district girls to Witney Grammar School *(706)*.

**13 APR.** Half-day closure at Brize Norton school for Lew Races *(835)*.

**1911** Caversham parish divided, and part transferred to Berkshire.
Thame High street was first sprayed with tar *(285)*.
St Frideswide and St Edmund's Roman Catholic church opened in Iffley Road, Oxford *(481)*.
Sale broke up the estates, including Albury, of the Earl of Abingdon *(503)*.

**1912** Last summer when Filkins harvesters travelled to the London parks and worked the hayfields back to Wantage *(817)*.
Midland Bank set up a Cornmarket, Oxford branch which soon absorbed the business of the Metropolitan Bank *(295)*.
Gustav Hamel gave exhibition flights at Chipping Norton in a Bleriot monoplane *(502)*.
Walton Street, Oxford buildings for Ruskin College, founded in 1899 by Vrooman completed *(786)*.
Working Men's Club at Nettlebed built to a design "owing much to Arts and Crafts influence" *(786)*.
Oxfordshire County Council's offices at New Road, Oxford, built *(247)*.

**15 MAR.** Oxford meeting of the National League for opposing Woman Suffrage.

**13 JUL.** Pc Gadden apprehended two suspicious ladies in Nuneham Park: Helen Craggs, a militant suffragette, was carrying petrol, meths, and turpentine, and was sentenced to nine months' hard labour *(495)*.

**AUG.** W R M Motors Ltd was registered as a company, and Morris opened a workshop for car production at Cowley *(480)*.

**1913** Jackson built the "Bridge of Sighs" to link the two sites of Hertford

College, Oxford *(786)*.
Workers' Educational Association branch founded at Ascott-under-Wychwood, with membership of 120.
Alexander's Rag-Time Band played at a "loop-the-loop" exhibition in Oxford *(502)*.

**APR.** Disastrous fire at Wrench's plush factory at Shutford.
The first Morris car, a two-seater 8.9 hp at £165, was produced *(480)*.

**NOV.** William Morris operated a "pirate" bus service with coupons between Oxford station and Cowley to draw attention to his application for a licence *(561)*.
A branch of the Workers' Union was formed at Bliss Tweed Mill at Chipping Norton, which brought 250 of the 380 employees on strike when three union leaders were sacked: early in 1914 recriminations increased over the company's terms of reinstatement, as many were not re-employed. The strikers were supported by Ruskin College students and socialist Oxford University teachers, but the only trade unionists in Chipping Norton would have been a few railwaymen *(183)*.

**1914** Picture Palace opened in Chinnor Road, Thame *(285)*: T J H Blinkhorn gave "animated picture shows" in the Corn Exchange, Banbury *(802)*.

**MAR.** Ironstone pits opened at Sydenham Farm, East Adderbury: two locomotives used on the tramway, Gertrude and Margaret, celebrated the manager's daughters. Stewarts and Lloyds dismantled the pit about 1930, and after 1945 Portable Concrete Buildings Ltd., and now Banbury Buildings, took over the loco-shed and site *(707)*.

**9 JUN.** One woman, of six Bliss Tweed Mill strikers charged, chose prison rather than agreeing to keep the peace: on her return to Chipping Norton she was met by a brass band, and received a teapot and speech from C E M Joad *(495)*.

**JUL** Oddfellows' last feast near their barn at Beckley *(541)*.

**AUG.** Culham College was host to a woman's training college, St Gabriel's, while the men students were dispersed: a large number enlisted as second line troops in the 2/4 Battalion of the (then) Oxfordshire & Buckinghamshire Light Infantry *(470, 204)*.

**24 AUG.** The 2nd Battalion of this regiment was involved in 178 mile march in the retreat from Mons until Sep 5 *(204)*.

**8 SEP.** Recruiting began for a Territorial Force of second-line troops: 130 were sworn in at Exeter College, Oxford orderly room on the first day *(204)*.

**20 OCT.** 152 casualties in the 2nd Battalion in an attack on Passchendaele ridge *(704)*.

**1915** Oxford Co-operative Society merged with the Steeple Aston Society (and in 1933 with the Carterton Society) *(411)*.

Headington School, founded as a public school for girls, and entered new buildings in 1930.
Noke and Islip parishes united *(254, 541)*.

**16 MAY** 2nd Battalion lost 395 men at Festubert: almost as many as the 52nd Regiment lost at the siege of Badajoz in 1812 *(704)*.

**17 MAY** Philip Morrell, MP for South Oxfordshire, and Lady Ottoline moved into Garsington Manor House, their home until 1924. War had swept away all London politics and other interest: they sheltered many non-combatants here, including Bertrand Russell and D H Lawrence *(776)*.

**25 SEP.** 2nd Battalion lost 263 men in battle at Loos *(704)*.

**1916** Shell-filling factory opened in the Causeway, Banbury *(654)*.
Morris produced a repair-manual for the Morris Cowley car *(580, 837)*.

**1917** Oxfordshire Ironstone Company founded, in ownership of Brymbo, Baldwin's and Stewarts and Lloyd: tramway built with prisoner-of-war labour led to Wroxton mining by 1919 *(707)*.
Only 315 students in residence at Oxford University, of whom 120 were Officers' Training Corps members waiting to join the army. The Examination Schools were the Third Southern General Hospital *(403)*.

**3 APR.** John Marriott, a university teacher and secretary of the Extension work in Oxford, was elected unopposed as Oxford's MP, having defeated the former Mayor and Bursar of Keble College, Walter Gray, for the Conservative nomination *(403, 664)*.

**11 APR.** 52nd Battalion moved into battle at Arras *(704)*.

**1918** Serious Thames flooding due to aberrant climate *(773)*.
Oxford High School obliged to raise its Free Places to 10% of the girls admitted, in order to claim State support *(558)*.
Work on new Morris buildings began with purchase of new land at Cowley, through Fletcher of Benfield & Loxley *(618)*.
War Office took over Littlemore Hospital and treated 2,807 shell-shock cases, before restoring it in Sep 1922 *(295)*.
Corby's of Headington are reputed to have made the last Oxfordshire wagon *(541)*.

**21 MAR.** 2nd Battalion due for relief from having been in the line since Jan, were prevented by the 5 am bombardment heralding Ludendorff's final German offensive *(704)*.

**MAY** Ironstone pits at Bloxham and Milton opened *(707)*.

**11 NOV.** Armistice Day. During the Great War the Oxfordshire & Buckinghamshire Light Infantry lost 5,878 men killed.

**1919** Neithrop House estate opened as Banbury's "People's Park" using the legacy of a chemist, G V Ball. Banbury's first park and baths near the station were established in 1868 *(510)*.

**17 MAR.** Barclays Bank absorbed Gilletts: the Banbury and Witney notes "with a sheep on" were withdrawn *(565)*.

**6 JUN.** Oxford University voted to apply for a government grant: "So Oxford with the miners, has declared for nationalisation".
Compulsory Greek was also ended *(777)*.

**JUN.** Return of 82 men of the Oxfordshire & Buckinghamshire Light Infantry to Cowley Barracks, after post-war German occupation at Zons near Cologne, and rapid demobilisation *(704)*.

**JUL.** Morris Motors Ltd was formed, taking over the assets of WRM Motors Ltd, chiefly as a device for ending a troublesome agency contract *(480)*.

**1920** Magdalen College School, Oxford became a "Direct Grant" school, independent of local authority plans: in 1976 it chose fully independent status when the Direct Grant List was ended *(511)*.
Wheatley War Memorial was unveiled by a local veteran of the 1848 Punjab War and the Indian Mutiny.
Council housing built at Kingham and Charlbury under the terms of the Addison Act *(408, 502)*.
Otmoor began to be used for practice bombing by the RAF: this lasting until 1958 *(541)*.
Rural industries' survey revealed 8 glove factories, weaving only at Witney, Shutford and Chipping Norton apart from halter headpieces at a few rope-works, and basket-makers at Thame, Eynsham but no longer at Chinnor, where the osier beds were abandoned in favour of keeping ducks *(206)*.

**MAY** Women were allowed to take all Oxford degrees, except Theology: this exception being removed in 1935 *(777)*.

**30 SEP.** Culham College finally re-opened after reversal of a closure decision *(470)*.

**8 OCT.** First Rural Community Council established in Oxfordshire.

**1921** Change at Heythrop: the House was sold by Robert Brassey, and the green plush coats of the hunt servants discontinued *(286)*.
Building began for both Greyfriars and Blackfriars: the Franciscans in Iffley Road, and the Dominicans in St Giles, Oxford *(503, 786)*.
Catholic Workers' College (now Plater College) founded in Oxford.

**15 JUN.** Registration of the Woodstock branch of the Royal British Legion: eight others have survived without a break, at Adderbury, Milton-under-Wychwood, Goring, Clanfield, Stanton Harcourt, Shiplake, Bloxham and Banbury *(538)*.

**1922** Oxfordshire Hussars were converted to Artillery.
Frank Gray won his seat as Oxford's MP from sitting Tory Marriott *(664)*.
Heythrop House became, until 1969, a Jesuit college: it was then taken over by National Westminster Bank *(786)*.
Banbury Rural District Council agreed to build 26 council houses at Hook Norton to replace condemned cottages *(243)*.

**APR.** City of Oxford District Motor Bus services began running to Thame *(285)*.

**NOV.** Morris advertised the reduction in his car prices from £465 to £225 *(480)*. He believed that a motor-car was a standard piece of furniture for the middle and lower classes, not a custom-built job for the upper class fancier *(837)*. He bought engine and component firms, including Hotchkiss, at Coventry *(475)*.
Memorial village hall opened at Hook Norton, encouraging the formation of a Women's Institute *(243)*.

**1923** Morris purchased Osberton Radiators in North Oxford *(480)*.
Burford Grammar School moved towards a girls' department with the help of tea-magnate Horniman, but due to its fees it suffered from competition with other secondary schools such as Northleach *(706)*.

**27 AUG.** Two MPs, Frank Gray and Captain Ainsworth, put their extra-parliamentary athletic talents to the test by competing in a very public road race from Banbury to Oxford, loaded with 70lb packs *(664)*.

**NOV.** Frank Gray's election expenses were overweight: his renewed Liberal success in Oxford was reversed in the courts *(664)*.

**1924** Cowley work-force at Morris car assembly factories was 5,500: by 1934 it was actually lower, but output had doubled *(837)*.
Heyford areodrome built.
Chinnor cement works opened.
Bicester County Secondary School was opened *(621)*.
Cowley sports model withdrew from races after three seasons, in which a maximum speed of 92 mph was achieved *(480)*.
Oxfordshire set up a County Library, having failed to act in 1915 when Carnegie Trust money was available.

**1925** Midland Marts began cattle markets at Banbury *(802)*.
All 16 men of Banbury Police Force were amalgamated with the County Force *(495)*.

**10 FEB.** Former Prime Minister Asquith took the title Earl of Oxford and Asquith: in retirement he lived at Sutton Courtenay.

**16 APR.** British Fascists held a meeting in Oxford Town Hall, with the Town Clerk, Major Hedges, presiding.

**13 JUN.** Woolworth's opened a Cornmarket store in Oxford on the Roebuck site, having recruited 80 women assistants.

**SEP.** Banbury RDC referred back Hook Norton parish's wish to have electric lighting installed in its council houses, as a luxury.

**NOV.** Frank Gray, during a period "on the tramp" in a pre-Shelter campaign, received harsh treatment in Bicester Workhouse, where he later set up the Frank Gray Home for Boys, 1932-4 *(664)*.

**1926** Morris encouraged a car body works at Cowley: Pressed Steel began operations, and diversified into Prestcold domestic refrigerators in 1932

*(295, 480).*
Morris gave way to fashion and the bull-nose radiator disappeared from Morris models: creating a latter-day nostalgia *(480).*
Electric lighting, from Aylesbury, was set up in Thame *(285).*

**2 MAY** Council of Action formed by Oxford Trades Council to direct the TUC strike in support of the miners *(602).* Held 30 meetings in the City, and 60 outside, but the Oxford Council refused the free use of the Town Hall *(843).*

**4 MAY** Printing works (except the Oxford Times), building workers, and railwaymen joined the General Strike in Oxford, but not Morris' workers or the City busmen, with memories of an earlier unsuccessful strike. 3,142 volunteered at the Town Hall for strike-breaking *(602, 843).*

**6 MAY** Council of Action issued a news bulletin to counter the daily editions of the "Oxford Times" *(602).*

**7 MAY** Business much as usual at Early's in Witney, and "life pursuing its normal course" at Chipping Norton *(230).*

**13 MAY** GWR and Clarendon Press backed down after attempting to make returning employees sign a document or accept new conditions *(602).*

**29 JUN.** W R Morris the sole shareholder of Morris Motors (1926) Ltd formed to take on the fresh obligations to Pressed Steel *(480).*

**1927** Sugar beet factory built at Eynsham, which became an RASC depot and NAAFI store 1939-45, then a storage depot for the Colonial Development Corporation, and in 1955 Harding's *(630, 807).*
Sir John Simon joined Fritwell British Legion as an ordinary member *(538).*
Oxford and District Provident Association was set up to aid those outside compulsory health schemes, and thus attracted a benefaction from Morris: BUPA resulted in 1947 from a merger of such bodies *(295, 480).*
Robertson Scott began publishing "The Countryman" from Idbury Manor, and later from Burford *(540).*
Adderbury Village Hall built: 82 villages had such halls.

**1928** "Oxford Mail" began, to give Oxford an evening newspaper *(475).*
Chipping Norton County Secondary School opened *(436).*
St Peter's Hall founded at Oxford, becoming a full college in 1961 *(786),* in premises of the former Wesleyan Day School *(625).*
Portland Cement factory opened at Shipton-on-Cherwell, with a labour force of 280, to exploit the Great Oolite *(476, 627).*
'Cotswold Gateway' Hotel built at Burford to take trade from the GWR Cheltenham-Paddington scenic motor-coaches *(347).*
King's Weir lock made, avoiding 3 hours' lost production at Wolvercote Mill during each weir flash *(497).*
Oxford's city boundaries extended *(475).*

**1929** Bicester received electric lighting *(621).*
Rhodes House, Oxford built by Sir Herbert Baker: by Cecil Rhodes' will

it was a centre for American, British Empire and German scholars *(786).*

**1930** Northern Aluminium Company bought Harewick site at Banbury for a rolling mill which began production in Nov 1931 *(802).*
Filkins council houses were built in Cotswold stone by Witney RDC as Sir Stafford Cripps, owner of Goodfellows, paid the extra expense and had the stone quarried on his own estate *(431).*
Catholic church at Charlbury opened in a former Primitive Methodist chapel *(741).*
Morris bought the Radcliffe Observatory's grounds and buildings at Oxford to house an Institute of Medical Research *(480).*
Oxford Education Committee began experimenting with open-air schooling at Hill End Farm, Wytham *(295).*
New two-seater Minor, the "Morris Eight", costing £100, joined the range of Cowley-produced cars *(480).*

**21 JUL.** MG Car Company registered, its activity centred on Abingdon *(480)* MG Morris Garages originated 1923.

**1931** Population of Oxford city was increasing at the rate of 20% per decade, faster than any town but Bournemouth & Watford *(414).*
GWR built the "hump" marshalling yard at Banbury as a government-assisted measure to relieve unemployment: closed in 1970 *(677).*

**1932** Kingsey became part of Bucks, while Towersey transferred to Oxfordshire *(552).* Shelswell ceased to be a parish separate from Newton Purcell *(573)*, and Hardwick from Tusmore *(520).*
Central schools were established in rural areas at Great Haseley Endowed School and Burford Senior Mixed School, for older pupils *(441. 835).*
Henry Ford visited Cowley works, but Morris avoided a meeting: yet both men had located a motor industry, at Oxford and Detroit, in purely fortuitous locations *(414, 837).*
Frank Gray established Oxford Zoo at Gosford Hill, Kidlington: it closed in 1937 *(709).*

**1933** Morris gave money to rebuild a small convalescent home: this was opened as the "Wingfield-Morris Orthopaedic Hospital" *(295).*
Morris called in Leonard Lord to Cowley, but he left in anger in 1938 for Morris' rival, Herbert Austin *(755).*

**FEB.** Oxford Union debated the circumstances in which they would fight for King and Country: urged by Professor Joad, to the chagrin of Quintin Hogg, they voted "None" by 275 to 153 *(777).*

**MAR.** Samuelson's Britannia Works closed at Banbury *(716).*

**1934** Regal Cinema, Bicester, opened *(621).*
Moving assembly line erected at Cowley, and a New Morris Eight model was produced *(480).*
Transport & General Workers' Union used a press-shop strike as a means of entry to "organise new workers" at Pressed Steel Co at Cowley *(554).*

Christmas Hill brickworks at Thame re-opened as a result of the building boom *(285)*.

**APR.** Automatic traffic lights installed at Carfax, Oxford: the 30 mile per hour speedlimit came in 1933 *(475)*.

**JUN.** Swinford Pumping Station completed *(295, 475)*.

**DEC.** Cutteslowe Wall erected by Clive Saxton of the private developers who found 138 Oxford council houses built in close proximity along Carlton and Wentworth Roads *(554)*.

**1935** Oxford's Northern By-Pass completed, and a new trunk road to Witney opened *(414, 476, 773)*.
Oxford's Bus Company secured a low-slung double-decker bus capable of passing under the railway bridge at Oxford station *(810)*. Perhaps the last straw driving the sole remaining Oxford licensed hackney carriage off the streets *(475)*.
Only 26 of 82 county houses in 1820 *(935)* were owned by the same family, and only 24 of 116 in Gardner's Gazzeteer of 1852 *(285)*.

**MAR.** Closure of Thame Workhouse, following that of Bicester in 1932: the 51 Infirmary and 48 house inmates went to Henley or Woodstock Workhouses *(285)*.

**11 MAY** Direct action demonstration at Cutteslowe Walls, with the Workers' Theatre Group performing to an audience of 2,000: Cutteslowe council tenants formed an organisation to counter the claims of the direct action leaders *(554)*.

**1936** Oxford, together with Luton and Coventry, was the most prosperous part of Britain: 43% of its insured workers were recent immigrants *(414, 476)*.
Youth Hostel opened in Jack Straw's Lane, Headington.
Wessex Electrical Company brought electricity to Ramsden *(535)*.

**11 JUL.** County Record Office opened.

**15 OCT.** Morris, now Lord Nuffield, offered £1¼ million to endow a Medical School Trust at Oxford *(480)*.

**1937** Benfield & Loxley won the contract to build the New Bodleian Library, Oxford to Sir G G Scott's design, in Clipsham and Bladon stone *(618, 786)*. They bought the Bladon quarries from Tolley's *(618)*.
Coronation celebrations at Fifield shared by Neville Chamberlain, who planted a small commemorative oak *(500)*.
Closure of Culham College recommended, but countermanded in 1938 *(470)*.
Nuffield Benefaction for Employees set up at Cowley, earning £2 million for employees by 1954: an unofficial workers' paper, "The Spark" was also begun there *(837)*.

**NOV.** Lord Nuffield gave £1 million to Oxford University for a new college: originally wishing it to be devoted to Engineering, he allowed himself to be persuaded to endow research in social science. Nuffield College was opened in 1949 *(480)*.

**1938** Electricity brought to Wootton *(413)*.

Middleton Park built, probably the last great country house in England, in luxurious neo-Georgian (with bathrooms commensurate with the inter-war 'cult of the tub') by Sir Edward Lutyens for the ninth Earl of Jersey *(786)*.

Another cult, popular among anxious upper classes, and at first known as the Oxford Group, took the title Moral Re-Armament *(489)*.

**7 JUN.** Corporation at Oxford demolished Cutteslowe Walls (as did a private car in 1936 and an "accidental" tank in 1943) but they were re-built *(554)*.

**20 OCT.** Oxford Playhouse, built by Sir Edward Maufe, opened in Beaumont Street *(640)*.

**27 OCT.** Quintin Hogg was elected Tory MP for Oxford in a by-election where student Edward Heath and MP Harold Macmillan supported A D Lindsay, the 'United Front' candidate, supported by Liberal and Labour parties.

**1939** Clough Williams-Ellis "beautified" Cornwell Manor House, its gardens and village *(786)*.

Elementary schools supplied one-quarter of Oxford University's British students, 55% of whom received grants for study *(414)*.

**MAR.** Cowley to be the wartime headquarters of a Civilian Repair Organisation, the only one of six such depots to be run by a private firm. Lord Nuffield's appointment as Director-General of Maintenance, RAF, was ended in 1940 by resignation, in protest at responsibility being moved from the Air Minister to that of Aircraft Production *(480)*.

**22 MAY** Millionth car driven out of Cowley works *(480)*.

**4 SEP.** Basket of incendiary bombs dropped in oats at Steeple Barton *(401)*, where villagers were coping with an influx of evacuees, as were those at Kingham *(502)*, Charlbury, Burford *(347)*, Brize Norton *(835)* and Fifield *(500)*.

**OCT.** School canteen opened at Middle Barton to help those fostering evacuees *(401)*.

**DEC.** City received 2600 and county 4500 evacuees *(410, 788)*.

**1940** George VI visited Burford to inspect troops.

Deer in Holton Park killed, as a Military Hospital was built in the grounds *(503)*.

Gosford Hill Farm (former Zoo) buildings hurriedly adapted for 271 pupils from East Ham Grammar School *(709)*: Girls' Schools from Kent evacuated to Burford and Barton Abbey *(401, 706)*.

Convent and School of St Juliana established at Begbroke *(786)*.

Brakspear's of Henley bought Goring breweries.

New passing loops built at Lechlade and Eynsham on the Witney branch railway, to cope with traffic for Fairford, Broadwell, Brize Norton and Stanton Harcourt aerodromes, Witney and Eynsham army camps, and the Land Army camps at Shilton and Curbridge *(807)*.

**15 MAY** Enrolment began for the "Home Guard" of Local Defence Volunteers *(401)*. Two pill boxes built by county road gangers for the Army at Burford *(412)*.

**25 MAY** Florey demonstrated (on mice) the curative character of penicillin *(777)*.

**26 JUN.** Bombs fell on Weston-on-the-Green aerodrome, damaging two RAF planes *(495)*.

**JUL.** Nuffield Exports, a self-contained unit at Cowley, began to assemble sea mines and sinkers for the Admiralty, giving this up in 1941 for Crusader tanks *(345, 480)*. No 1 CRO at Cowley, with 1200 workers, returned 4000 aeroplanes to battle in six months *(345, 480)*. Tiger Moths at first, then Beanfighter and Lancaster power plants, and finally assembly of tail units for Horsa gliders took place at Cowley *(480)*.

**NOV.** Winston Churchill, as Prime Minister, spent the first of 13 weekend visits to Ditchley, 1940-2, "when the moon was high" and his Kent home at Chartwell less secure: the house belonged to Tory MP Ronald Tree, and was guarded, largely unbeknown, by companies of the Oxfordshire & Bucks. Light Infantry driven there in heavily-curtained buses *(824)*. Bombs were not far away, at Swinbrook on Sep 26, Banbury gasworks on Oct 3, and Witney goods yard on Nov 22 *(654, 786, 807)*.

**1941** Oxford city reached, thanks to evacuation, its peak population of 107,000 *(414)*.

War Office established the Central Ordnance Depot at Ambrosden *(503)*. Burford's Fire Brigade became part of the National Fire Service, and an ATC unit was set up there. Burford lay in the "German corridor" for raids on Coventry and Birmingham *(347)*.

**JUL.** Culham College closed, and used for storing records by the Public Record Office *(470)*.

**1942** The Oratory School moved to Woodcote House *(786)*.

**JUN.** Peak of Barton's War Savings efforts in "Wings for Victory" week: Burford had peaked in "War Weapons" week, Sep 1941 *(412)*.

**OCT.** British Restaurant opened in Charlbury: at its closure in Feb 1945, staff and equipment were used for school dinners.

**1943** Preparations for a Second Front involved heavy traffic through Banbury goods yard, and the building of a yard next to Kingham station *(503, 677)*.

Paul Nash's painting "Totes Meer" records dramatically the acres of scrap from broken aircraft lying beside the Cowley factory *(480)*.

Oxford Co-operative Society disaffiliated from the Co-operative Party

*(411).*
Wolvercote Mill ceased to use water-power: the wheels were removed in 1950 *(497).*

**4 JUN.** Last air raid siren in Charlbury.

**1944** Oxford Co-operative Society only the second in the country to become licensees, buying the Lambert Arms, Aston Rowant *(411).*

**FEB.** United States forces stationed at Ramsden (Anti-Gas unit) and Burford (Sixth Army). The latter left in Jul for Normandy with General Patten.

**JUL.** Parachute production quadrupled at Cowley in preparation for "supply-dropping" for the Arnhem bridgehead *(345).*

**1945** End of Second World War: Oxfordshire and Buckinghamshire Light Infantry lost 1,408 men killed.

**JAN.** Pensioners' Association formed in Oxford.

**9 MAY** Victory in Europe Day: celebrations included tea parties in Oxford side streets.

**JUL.** Narrow Conservative victories in Oxford and the two county divisions in the General Election bringing a Labour Government to power.

**OCT.** Oxford University, as in 1814, honoured allied leaders with honorary degrees: this time it was no Tsar or Kaiser, but Eisenhower and Montgomery, Tedder and Winant, Mark Clark and Alanbrooke.

**1946** Eynsham Hall became one of nine Home Office centres for training police recruits.

**SEP.** Last of the steam traction engines, Wilson's Burrell No. 3273 Queen Mary, at St Giles' Fair, Oxford *(810)* and first lay head of the re-opened Culham College *(470).*

**NOV.** Local impact of Labour, replacing residual Liberal representation on Oxford Council, was recognised when Councillor Smewin became Mayor.

**DEC.** Local option in Oxford went 80% in favour of Sunday opening of its cinemas, four of which lay west of Magdalen Bridge *(414, 567).*

**1947** Amalgamation of 1st and 2nd Battalions of the county regiment *(704).*
Banbury Corporation bought Banbury Water Company: in 1937 it had bought Bloxham Water Company thus drawing on the Sor Brook *(510).*
Thomas Bond died, and his Burford bellfoundry closed *(917).*

**FEB.** Goodfellows at Filkins, Cripps' home after 1919, burned down while used as a Land Army girls' hostel *(620).*

**AUG.** Oxford's new Municipal Restaurant was opened in George Street.

**DEC.** Woodeaton Manor was converted for use as a residential school for backward children.

**1948** Wrench's plush factory at Shutford closed, the business being sold to Walkers of Dewsbury *(802).*

St Antony's College, Oxford founded by a French shipping magnate, Antonin Besse *(786)*.
Unauthorised tenants occupied the hutted ex-RAF camps at Jersey Park and Shilton.

**FEB.** Thomas Sharp produced Oxford planning proposals to remove the Cowley industrial complex from the region, and to build an inner relief road through Christ Church Meadow *(786)*.

**1949** Smith's Motor Accessory Division decided to move to Witney: Windrush Valley Housing for its workers was ready by 1953 *(526)*.
Infant mortality in the county down to 22 per 1000 in the first year of life: the lowest for any county.

**21 APR.** Lord Nuffield finally laid the foundation of Nuffield College, Oxford: "Cotswold Manorial relieved by a book-stack tower" *(475, 786)*.

**MAY** Skies above Oxford saw a new air service to Jersey, and those above Rollright saw the dance of supposed witches round the King's Stone *(742)*.

**SEP.** Unhoused families moved into Slade Camp, Cowley as soon as the Army moved out.
Oxford followed the county in planning the Further Education which the 1944 Act had required: it proposed two "county colleges" in the city, and a Further Education college at Headington, having rejected the Cowley workhouse site.

**1950** Royal Agricultural Show held at Kidlington: again in 1959. Wroxton Abbey was tenanted by Farleigh Dickinson University, New Jersey, about this time *(786)*.
Conservative MPs were elected at the General Election: the occasion nonetheless "providing Banbury a licence to say in public about a political opponent or his policies what it is otherwise taboo to say" *(530)*. Quintin Hogg soon had to resign as Oxford's MP when he succeeded to his father's peerage as Lord Hailsham.
Oxford received South Park as a gift for a playing field and park.

**1 APR.** Blenheim Palace opened to the public at 2*s* 6*d* a time *(451)*.

**SEP.** Shotover School opened at Wheatley, the first post-war purpose-built school in the county. Burford Grammar School shed Saturday morning school, and in 1957 migrated "uphill" *(706)*. Oxford Council rejected the plan to develop the Headington site, but trimmed its sails further in due course *(553)*.

**1951** Pegasus, an Oxford and Cambridge University soccer club, won the FA Amateur Cup, repeating the performance in 1953.

**2 JUN.** Last "Hooky Flier" carried passengers from Kingham to Banbury *(804)*.

**1952** British Motor Corporation formed by the merger of Austin and Morris, with Lord Nuffield briefly as its first chairman *(480)*.
Convent of St Clare, founded at Wantage in 1940, moved to Freeland

*(786).*
New village hall at Islip opened by WI chairman, Lady Brunner.
Execution at Oxford of Banbury murderer, despite jury's strong recommendation for mercy.
Goring Heath and Woodcote were created as separate parishes from Whitchurch and South Stoke.

**MAY** An end to the poor post-war performance of Labour candidates in Oxford, fortified by a party membership of 7,350, a Transport House constituency record.

**1953** Carmel College, founded by Rabbi Rosen at Newbury in 1948, moved to Mongewell: a synagogue was added in 1963, and an Exhibition Hall and Boat House by Sir Basil Spence in 1970 *(786).*
Oxford Masonic Hall Co Ltd bought 333 Banbury Road: the cornerstone of a new Temple was laid in 1960 *(582).*
Fawley Court, Henley became the house of the newly-founded Divine Mercy College of Marian Fathers *(823).*
Debenhams acquired control of Elliston and Cavell's Oxford business.
Lords rejected Oxford's claim of 3200 acres of Bullingdon for its housing expansion.

**MAY** Labour won control of Bicester UDC for the first time.

**2 JUN.** Queen Elizabeth II's Coronation was celebrated by many street parties in Oxford at Wood Farm, Cowmeade, Risinghurst, Sandhills, Rose Hill and many other areas. She formally visited the city in 1976.

**1954** The rabbit in Oxfordshire succumbed to myxomatosis *(502).*
Southern Gas Board at last resolved to build at Cowley to replace the Oxford works at St Ebbe's.
British Association met at Oxford for the first time since 1926 *(475).*

**27 FEB.** The "Woodstock Flier" succumbed to new transport forms *(748).*

**APR.** Lord Nuffield laid the foundation stone of the Headington buildings for Oxford College of Technology. *(553),* designated a Polytechnic in 1970. The new Secondary Technical School on the adjacent site was opened.

**6 MAY** Roger Bannister refused to be blown off course, and assisted by Christopher Chataway and Brasher ran the first four-minute mile on the Iffley-road track at Oxford.

**NOV.** Labour shortage on Oxford buses led to the recruitment of Jamaican conductors: over half of the county population was born outside its boundaries.

**1955** Charlbury stock market moved to a more convenient site next to Kingham station *(741).*
New concrete mill for Wolvercote, by Booth and Ledeboer *(786).*
Oxford's first hostel for non-university foreign students was opened as St

Clare's in Banbury road.
Oxford Council began the "relief road" ball rolling with proposals for a northern "Lamb and Flag" route and a southern "Meadows" route: the Trades Council and University Congregation had other views.
Falling rolls led to closure of St Clements and St Frideswides Infant schools, and of Elsfield school, which was converted to a village hall. 163 parishes had elected councils, the rest annual meetings.

**FEB.** Air Ministry proposal for a USAF radio communications centre at Christmas Common was dropped.

**1956** Prospects of petrol rationing, short-time working at Smith's of Witney, and lay-offs at Cowley, followed the oil crisis in the wake of the Suez campaign.

**APR.** Visit to Oxford of the leaders of the Soviet Union, Nikita Khruschev and Marshal Bulganin.

**SEP.** Duncan Sandys, Transport Minister, announced his support of the "Meadow" inner relief road at Oxford, and the closing of Magdalen Bridge.

**1957** Ring road proposals began to go round in circles with novelties such as a "Barges Boulevard" before Oxford rejected Sandys' proposals. Cowley BMC works recovered rapidly, and the workforce moved decisively towards "union shops" with over 90% appropriate union membership.
St Edmund Hall, Oxford, the last of the mediaeval university halls, became a full college of the university *(777)*.
Regent's Park College, Oxford, which began life as a training college in Stepney for Baptists in 1810, became a permanent private hall in the university *(786)*.

**29 JUN.** Last "Watlington Flier" to run on its branch line *(780)*.

**18 SEP.** Oxford High School's new buildings were erected at Belbroughton Road, Oxford; Epstein's 'Deirdre' was placed in the quadrangle *(558)*.

**18 OCT.** Woolworth's migrated across Cornmarket, Oxford to the Clarendon Hotel site, rebuilt by Lord Holford *(786)*.

**1958** Spendlove County Secondary School built at Charlbury, using the name of a benefactor to the British School whose gift of £100 had disappeared by 1889 *(741)*. In the Banbury and Littlemore areas, the eleven-plus examination was abolished as an experiment.
Banbury gasworks closed, a main line being laid from Kidlington to Banbury *(654)*.
County's "Best-Kept Village" competition was established.
Oxfordshire & Buckinghamshire Light Infantry, whose nucleus celebrated the 200th anniversary of the 52nd at Osnabruck in 1955, now became the First Battalion of the Green Jacket Brigade *(704)*.
Oxford Council "in the interests of maintaining free speech" voted to allow the hiring by a Fascist organisation of the Town Hall. For the first

time, Labour was the major political group, taking the committee chairmanships.
The first families moved into Blackbird Leys estate, Oxford.
Completion of the new £3½m body painting plant at Cowley.

**1959** Oxford College of Technology acquired Cotuit Hall as hostel accommodation despite the prevailing limitation of such provision to the major CATs. It also acquired as neighbour in Gipsy Lane, Headington, Oxford Central Girls' School under its new name as Cheney County Secondary (later Grammar) School *(788)*.

**9 MAR.** Cutteslowe Walls finally demolished *(554)*.

**27 APR.** Oxford's Automatic Telephone Exchange opened.

**OCT.** Oxford Council shared the prevailing admiration for multi-storey flats by deciding to build them at Blackbird Leys.

**1960** Building began on Arne Jacobsen's St Catherine's College, Oxford, on Booth, Ledeboer and Pinckheard's Waynflete Building at St Clements for Magdalen College, Oxford and on Cowley Shopping Centre *(786)*.
Berinsfield (the name a latter-day homage to the Dorchester saint Birinus) was established on the site of a former airfield: its architect was Sir William Holford *(786)*.
Cinema at old Town Hall at Charlbury closed down *(741)*.
Culham Laboratories opened *(786)*.

**9 NOV.** "Free Speech" was not an issue in deciding Oxford Council to allow professional wrestling in the Town Hall.

**DEC.** Sir Frederick Armer held a public inquiry into the Oxford relief road proposals, and supported the "Meadow" route.

**1961** Oxford's Green Belt was established after public inquiry *(820)*.
County re-organisation to provide "secondary education for all" on the 1944 plan was finally achieved. North Oxfordshire Technical College opened at Banbury, to provide further education for some.
Brian Lloyd, senior University proctor (and later Director of Oxford Polytechnic) saying "the proper education of undergraduates at Oxford demands a system of discipline imposed by the government of the University" highlighted issues which were taken up by two committees, on university government (Franks) and relations with junior members (Hart). The juniors were restive, setting up a Students' Representative Council after the proctors suppressed articles in Isis evaluating lecturers' performances *(777)*.
County proposals for a motorway to London with a tunnel at Aston Rowant were rejected by the Transport Ministry as unnecessary.

**2 JAN.** Ending of a passenger service of diesel railcars between Banbury and Buckingham *(804)*.

**MAY** Swerford area saved from large-scale ironstone extraction by the ruling of the Minister of Housing and Local Government.

**1962** Oxford motel built on A40 at Pear Tree roundabout *(786)*.
Oxford United Football Club, under manager Arthur Turner, was elected to the Football League.
New Thames bridge at Donnington in Oxford was opened.
Radar speed check began.
Liberal revival was registered by the return of four councillors to Oxford Council.

**16 JUN.** Last passenger train on the branch from Oxford to Witney and Fairford *(807)*.

**1963** Bird's Foods (since 1947 part of the American-owned General Foods Corporation) decided to move to a site provided by Banbury Council *(802)*.
Merger of Highfield Secondary School and Bicester Grammar School *(621)*.

**1964** Harold Wilson's Industrial Reorganisation Corporation was ready to back mergers with £150 millions, and its conviction that rationalisation of car production must follow that of foreign rivals: thus talks were urged between British Motor Corporation (under chairman Harriman) with Leyland (under Donald Stokes) *(755)*.
Brize Norton was returned to the RAF by USAF: it became the headquarters of Transport Command, with a consequent growth of Carterton *(706)*.
Holy Trinity Church, Blackbird Leys, Oxford begun *(786)*.

**29 FEB.** Oxford United played Preston North End in a cup tie at the Manor Ground, Headington before a record gate of 22,730.

**1965** Local government reorganisation began to be discussed, with local Labour parties supporting the idea of a large "Thameshire" upstream from the new Greater London Council.
"Scampi by candlelight" had become a feature of the saloon bar of some village public houses: a wide survey was a product of the Golden Jubilee celebrations of the Women's Institute movement *(576, 583, 586, 587)*.
Foundation of Linacre College, Oxford for graduate students; Wolfson College, Oxford (founded as Iffley College) for science graduates, and St Cross College, Oxford also for graduate students: all were for both sexes *(786)*.

**24 JAN.** Sir Winston Churchill died and was later buried at Bladon *(808)*.

**1966** Completion of the outer ring of Oxford's by-pass system *(820)*.
Weed Research Council took over Begbroke Hill Farm.
Wheatley buildings erected by F B Pooley to house Lady Spencer-Churchill College of Education (which was founded at Bletchley in 1948 as a post-war emergency training college, and which merged with Oxford Polytechnic in 1976) *(646, 786)*.

**31 MAR.** Evan Luard was elected as the first Labour MP for Oxford.

**MAY** West Oxfordshire Technical College opened in Witney.

**AUG.** County Council proposals emerged for the growth of Banbury to

70,000 by receiving London overspill.

**SEP.**Oxford School was created by the move from its 1880 George Street premises of Oxford High School for Boys to join Southfields School, itself the product of the 1934 flight of schools from Church Street and Gloucester Green.

**1967** Lionel Brett built Tower House, Christmas Common, as his own residence: in Oxford "New Brutalism" was represented by Arup Associates' Nuclear Physics Laboratory in the "Keble triangle".
Brize Norton hangar, the largest in Europe (1045 x 214ft) built *(786)*.

**MAY** Banbury brewing ceased with the closure of Hunt Edmunds brewery *(627)*.

**1968** Thames Valley Police Force established with headquarters at Kidlington *(808)*.
Oxford Canal scheduled as 'a recreational and amenity waterway' *(773)*.
Passenger rail from Oxford to Bicester ended *(820)*.
Oxford area's labour force was the fastest-growing in England, having risen by 34.6% in 16 years *(820)*.
Beginning of three buildings: Maternity Unit (Stage One) of the Radcliffe Infirmary at Headington, the College of Further Education at Oxford's Oxpens by the City Architect, D Murray, and the Florey Building in St Clements, for Queen's College, Oxford by James Stirling *(786)*.

**17 JAN.** Merger announced between BMC Ltd and Leyland Motor Corporation Ltd which united a labour force of 200,000 as British Leyland.

**1969** Westgate Shopping Centre, Oxford begun, planned by D Murray.
New Roman Catholic church for Kidlington, whose congregation had previously used former Methodist and Baptist buildings *(709)*.
Kenton Theatre, Henley produced "The Hanging Wood", Joan Morgan's play based on the Mary Blandy story.

**1970** Checkendon ringers made history with a Checkendon Surprise Major peal of 5056 changes, taking 2 hours 27 minutes.
Oxford Council, overwhelmingly Conservative after voters' local response to Labour's national policies, produced a report on comprehensive reorganisation of secondary education, involving the creation of 9-13 middle schools, and the retention of Milham Ford and Oxford School as single-sex institutions.
Bicester Recreation Centre built *(786)*. Radio Oxford began to broadcast.
Oxford Mail and Times built a new works at Osney Mead *(786)*.
Air transit centre, Gateway House, built at Brize Norton *(786)*. It brought the expelled Asians into Britain from Amin's Uganda.
Open-plan primary school built at Queen's Duke, Witney *(786)*.

**1971** New Commonwealth-born population in Oxford formed 3.7% of the total population *(820)*.
Rejection on traffic grounds of Centramic Properties' plan to build an out-

of-town shopping centre at the A34-A40 interchange north of Oxford *(820)*.
Bloxham School opened Raymond House for Sixth-form boarders: the Education Secretary, Margaret Thatcher, performed the ceremony.

**1972** Proposal made (and dropped) by the Water Resources Board to flood Otmoor *(773)*.
New station at Oxford – "just utilitarian" – opened *(786)*.
Five men's colleges in Oxford University altered their statutes to allow the admission of women in 1974: Brasenose, Hertford, Jesus, St Catherine's and Wadham *(777)*.
New Baptist church in Horsefair, Banbury by G Forsyth Lawson, replacing Underwood's 1850 Unitarian chapel *(786)*.

**5 FEB.** Closure of F Cape and Co Ltd, a department store in St Ebbe's, Oxford, which since 1877 had traded more with Oxford town than gown *(745)*.

**1973** First motorway stretch of M40 opened, from Stokenchurch to Waterstock *(808)*.
Dutch elm disease began to strike in the country.
Oxford Area Arts Council launched: in 1975 Vernon Scannell was given a Fellowship to communicate his poetry in the area.

**MAY** WRVS began a voluntary lift-giving scheme for Taynton, which had lost its bus services *(820)*.

**JUN** Orchard House, Littlemore, an Old People's Home run by the county Social Services Department, (set up in 1971), was closed after the illtreatment of patients and subsequent trial and enquiry.

**1974** Voters were kept busy with two General Elections, in the second of which Oxford again transferred its loyalties to Evan Luard and the Labour party: a third county seat was restored in the mid-Oxfordshire division and this followed the other county seats in electing a Conservative MP.

## 3. The 'New' County of Oxfordshire

**1974 1 APR.** A new authority, including the entire area of the old county council, of Oxford county borough, and much of north Berkshire north of the Downs, was created as a first-tier authority. Robert Weir, representing Stanton St John, became its first chairman. A second tier of district councils was created, of which Cherwell and West Oxfordshire were wholly, and South Oxfordshire based on Wallingford partly, from the area of the historic county. Oxford city became a District Council, as did the Vale of the White Horse. The corporations of Chipping Norton, Woodstock and Banbury were thus brought to an end, though all three retained "town mayors". Banbury had no parish council.

**10 APR.** British Leyland, who had in 1971 introduced measured day-work in place of piecework rates at Cowley, refused to recognise Alan Thornett as a shop steward in the Cowley car assembly plant. A strike followed, in which Cowley wives played a publicised part: Transport Union positions were then elected by members' ballot *(782).*

**1975** Lord Camoys left Stonor Park, which was offered for sale.

**5 JUN.** Oxfordshire voted 73.6% 'Yes' to continued British membership of the European Economic Community, despite the vigorous leadership of the 'No' campaign by Banbury MP, Neil Marten.

**AUG.** A free Pop Festival was held at Watchfield.

**1976** A new county structure plan was published, with imponderables in the Bicester and Banbury areas where final plans on the M40 extension route had not been announced. New perceptions of the future in the wake of a further fuel crisis following the 1973 Yom Kippur war, and of the falling birthrate, affected policies.
Culham College's closure as a centre for the initial training of teachers was announced.

**AUG.** North Sea Gas pipeline between Wisbech and Winchester was planned to cross the county in the Tetsworth area. The Central Electricity's Authority's 1957 plan for a 275kv supergrid pylon from Fleet to Drakelow crossing West Oxfordshire, the Glyme valley and Adderbury, was revived.

**25 AUG.** Dennis Howell, the Minister charged with drought relief, announced that the Thames had stopped flowing, and was a series of ponds.

**OCT.** James Callaghan spoke at Ruskin College, Oxford of the need for an education system to relate to the needs of industry as well as those of society. The media styled this "the Great Debate".

**1977** Peter Shore announced that the Rate Support Grant had stopped its full tide, and that Oxfordshire, as a "shire" county, would receive 7% less than the national average. This contrasted with the third MP given to the "old county" in 1832 as a "champion" county likely to counterbalance the towns politically.

# BIBLIOGRAPHY

## Printed Secondary Sources


| | | | |
|---|---|---|---|
| 1. | The history of the worthies of England | T. Fuller | 1662 |
| 2. | The natural history of Oxfordshire (repr. 1972) . . . . . . . . . . | R. Plot | 1677 |
| 3. | Parochial Antiquities . . . . . . . . . | W. Kennett | 1695 |
| 4. | Itinerarium curiosum . . . . . . . . . | W. Stukely | 1724 |
| 5. | A brief account of . . . the . . . Quakers | J. Besse | 1736 |
| 6. | Ancient and present state of the City of Oxford . . . . . . . . . | A. Wood ed. J. Peshall | 1773 |
| 7. | Specimen of a history of Oxfordshire | T. Warton | 1783 |
| 8. | History and Antiquities of the University of Oxford . . . . . . . . . | A. Wood ed. J. Gutch | 1792-6 |
| 9. | Topographical, historical and descriptive (delineations) of the County | J.N. Brewer | 1813 |
| 10. | An history of the river Thames . . . . | J & J Boydell | 1794 |
| 11. | Magna Britannia . . . . . . . . . | D. Lysons | 1813 |
| 12. | Some account of Great Milton . . . . | T. Ellis | 1819 |
| 13. | The history and antiquities of Bicester and the Hundreds of Bullingdon and Ploughley . . . . . . . . . | J. Dunkin | 1816 1823 |
| 14. | The new British Traveller . . . . | J. Dugdale | 1819 |
| 15. | The genealogical history of the Croke family . . . . . . . . . | Sir A. Croke | 1823 |
| 16. | Memorials of the malignant cholera in Oxford . . . . . . . . . | V. Thomas | 1835 |
| 17. | The history of Banbury . . . . . . . . | A. Beesley | 1841 |
| 18. | A collection of old English customs, and curious bequests and charities | H. Edwards | 1842 |
| 19. | Some account of (Dorchester) Abbey | H. Addington | 1845 |
| 20. | Hunts in the neighbourhood of Oxford | A.M. Venables | 1845 |
| 21. | Antiquities of Steeple Aston . . . . | W. Wing | 1845 |
| 22. | History of Bampton . . . . . . . . . | J.A. Giles | 1848 |
| 23. | Notices of the history of Islip . . . . | J.O. Halliwell | 1849 |
| 24. | History of Witney . . . . . . . . . . | J.A. Giles | 1852 |
| 25. | Additional particulars for the biography of three Oxfordshire writers | Sir T. Phillips | 1854 |
| 27. | Memoir of the cholera at Oxford . . . | H.W. Acland | 1856 |
| 28. | Some account of Yarnton church and parish . . . . . . . . | V. Thomas | 1856-8 |
| 30. | A parochial history of Enstone . . . . | J. Jordan | 1857 |
| 31. | The book of the Thames (Repr. 1975) | S. C. & A.N. Hall | 1859 |

| | | | |
|---|---|---|---|
| 32. | History of Burford . . . . . . . . . | J. Fisher | 1860 |
| 33. | History of Thame and its hamlets | H. Lupton | 1860 |
| 34. | Historical record of the 52nd Regiment (Oxfordshire Light Infantry) from 1775 to 1858 . . . . . . . . . | Ed. W.S. Moorsom | 1860 |
| 35. | The history of Banbury . . . . . . . . | W.P. Johnson | 1860 |
| 36. | A history of Henley-on-Thames . . . . | J.S. Burn | 1861 |
| 37. | Account of Rousham . . . . . . . . . | E. Dormer | 1865 |
| 38. | Annals of Heyford Warren . . . . | W. Wing | 1865 |
| 39. | Historical notices of Swincombe and Ewelme . . . . . . . . . | H.A. Napier | 1858 |
| 40. | An account of the parish of Sandford (St Martin) . . . . . . . . . | E. Marshall | 1866 |
| 41. | Annals of Steeple Barton and Westcot Barton . . . . . . . . . | W. Wing | 1866 |
| 42. | Recollections of Oxford . . . . | G.V. Cox | 1868 |
| 43. | An account of Church Enstone . . . . | E. Marshall | 1868 |
| 44. | Oxfordshire Militia: sketch of the history of the regiment . . . . | Anon. | 1869 |
| 45. | Oxfordshire Annals . . . . . . . . . | J.M. Davenport | 1869 |
| 46. | Memorials of Westcot Barton . . . . | J. Marshall | 1870 |
| 47. | Brief Memorials of the early history of Chipping Norton . . . . . . . . . | C. Kirtland | 1871 |
| 48. | Annals of Bletchingdon . . . . | W. Wing | 1872 |
| 49. | Annals of North Aston . . . . . . . . . | W. Wing | 1867 |
| 50. | The Oxford Methodists . . . . . . . . . | L. Tyerman | 1873 |
| 51. | The early history of Woodstock Manor | E. Marshall | 1873 |
| 52. | Narrative of three prosecutions under the Vaccination Act . . . . | J.E. Malings | 1874 |
| 53. | An account of Iflley . . . . . . . . . | E. Marshall | 1874 |
| 54. | Brief history of the Warneford Lunatic Asylum . . . . . . . . | Anon. | 1875 |
| 55. | Floods in the Thames Valley . . . . | F.I. Palmer | 1877 |
| 56. | Kidlington and its annexes . . . . | W. Wing | 1881 |
| 57. | Memoirs of a Stationmaster, by "Ernest Struggles" (repr. 1974) | H.A. Simmons | 1879 |
| 58. | The story of St Frideswide . . . . | F. Goldie | 1881 |
| 59. | Parliamentary history of the borough of Woodstock . . . . . . . . . | W. Wing | 1873 |
| 60. | History of Oxford Blue Coat Boys' School | H. Hughes | 1881 |
| 61. | History of the Deanery of Bicester | J.C. Blomfield | 1882-93 |
| 62. | A History of Freemasonry in Oxfordshire | E.L. Hawkins | 1882 |
| 63. | Record of the University Boat Race 1829-1880 . . . . . . . . . | G.G.T Treherne & J.H.D. Goldie | 1883 |
| 64. | Health in the Village . . . . . . . . . | Sir H.W. Acland | 1884 |
| 66. | Early History of Oxford . . . . | J. Parker | 1885 |

| | | | |
|---|---|---|---|
| 67. | History of the University of Oxford | M. Lyte | 1886 |
| 68. | Mansfield College: its origins and opening | Anon. | 1890 |
| 69. | Brief Annals of the Bicester Poor Law Union . . . . . . . . . . | W. Wing | 1877-9 |
| 70. | Pyrton Lectures . . . . . . . . . . | H. Coxe | 1890 |
| 77. | Burford . . . . . . . . . . | W.J. Monk | 1891 |
| 78. | History of the Church of St Mary the Virgin, Oxford . . . . . . . . . . | E.S. Ffoulkes | 1892 |
| 79. | The Colleges of Oxford . . . . . . . . . . | Clark | 1891 |
| 80. | The Grey Friars in Oxford. OHS. | A.G. Little | 1892 |
| 81. | Notes on the History of Chipping Norton | A. Ballard | 1893 |
| 82. | Wadham College . . . . . . . . . . | T.G. Jackson | 1893 |
| 83. | Some account of Broughton & North Newington . . . . . . . . . . | G. Metcalfe | 1893 |
| 84. | History of Kidlington, Yarnton, Begbroke, OHS. . . . . . . . . . . | B. Stapledon | 1893 |
| 86. | History of Shiplake . . . . . . . . . . | E.J. Climenson | 1894 |
| 87. | A record of fires in Oxford, 979-1870 | T. Green | 1894 |
| 88. | Temple in the Sun . . . . . . . . . . | P.O. Hill | 1894 |
| 89. | Memories of an Oxfordshire Catholic family . . . . . . . . . . | E.C. Davey | 1898 |
| 90. | History of Witney . . . . . . . . . . | W.J. Monk | 1894 |
| 92. | The Oxfordshire Light Infantry: short history . . . . . . . . . . | Anon. | 1895 |
| 93. | Memorial of Richard Edmunds of Banbury | Ed. T. Champness | 1895 |
| 94. | Early Oxford Press . . . . . . . . . . | F. Madan | 1895 |
| 95. | History of Whitchurch . . . . . . . . . . | J. Slatter | 1895 |
| 97. | Chronicles of the Royal Borough of Woodstock . . . . . . . . . . | A. Ballard | 1896 |
| 98. | History of the church and parish of St Martin, Oxford . . . . . . . . . . | C.J.H. Fletcher | 1896 |
| 100. | A history of the manor of Bensington | M.T. Pearman | 1896 |
| 101. | Brief history of the . . . see of Oxford | P. Dearmer | 1897 |
| 102. | Diocesan histories: Oxford . . . . | E. Marshall | 1897 |
| 103. | Diocesan histories: Lincoln . . . . | E. Venables & G.G. Perry | 1897 |
| 104. | Autobiography . . . . . . . . . . | J. Arch | 1898 |
| 105. | Trinity College . . . . . . . . . . | H.E.D. Blakiston | 1898 |
| 106. | Brasenose College . . . . . . . . . . | J. Buchan | 1898 |
| 107. | Lincoln College . . . . . . . . . . | A. Clark | 1898 |
| 108. | Corpus Christi . . . . . . . . . . | T. Fowler | 1898 |
| 109. | Oxford . . . . . . . . . . | C.W. Boase | 1887 |
| 110. | St. John's College . . . . . . . . . . | W.H. Hutton | 1898 |
| 112. | A History of Oxfordshire . . . . | J.M. Falkner | 1899 |
| 113. | Merton College . . . . . . . . . . | B.W. Henderson | 1899 |
| 114. | All Souls College . . . . . . . . . . | C.G. Robertson | 1899 |
| 115. | Parliamentary history of the county | W.R.J. Williams | 1899 |

| | | | |
|---|---|---|---|
| 116. | Magdalen College . . . . . . . . . | H.A. Wilson | 1899 |
| 117. | Worcester College . . . . . . . . . | C.H. Daniel | 1900 |
| 118. | Oxfordshire Leaders, Social and Political | E. Gaskell | 1900 |
| 119. | Elizabethan Oxford OHS . . . . | Ed. C. Plummer | 1887 |
| 120. | Pembroke College . . . . . . . . . | D. Macleane | 1900 |
| 121. | Oriel College . . . . . . . . . | D.W. Rannie | 1900 |
| 122. | Exeter College . . . . . . . . . | W.K. Stride | 1900 |
| 123. | History of the Oxfordshire regiment of militia, 1778-1900 . . . . | T.S. Willan | 1900 |
| 125. | Studies in Oxford History OHS . . . . | J.R. Green & G. Robinson | 1901 |
| 126. | The Oxfordshire Light Infantry in South Africa . . . . . . . . . | Ed. A.F. Mockler-Ferryman | 1901 |
| 127. | New College . . . . . . . . . | H. Rashdall & R.S. Rait | 1901 |
| 130. | University College . . . . . . . . . | W. Carr | 1902 |
| 131. | Three Centuries in North Oxfordshire . | M.S. Henderson | 1902 |
| 133. | Sir Henry Wentworth Acland: a memoir | J.B. Atlay | 1903 |
| 134. | Reminiscences of Old Banbury . . . . | T.W. Boss | 1903 |
| 135. | Memorials of old Oxfordshire . . . . | P.H. Ditchfield | 1903 |
| 136. | Hertford College . . . . . . . . . | S.G. Hamilton | 1903 |
| 137. | History of Black Bourton . . . . | M.G. Lupton | 1903 |
| 139. | Burford Papers . . . . . . . . . | W.H. Hutton | 1905 |
| 140. | Oxford and its Story . . . . . . . . . | C. Headlam | 1904 |
| 141. | Shelley at Oxford . . . . . . . . . | T.J. Hogg | 1904 |
| 142. | Old Cottages and Farmhouses in the Cotswolds district . . . . | E.G. Dawber | 1905 |
| 143. | Highways & byways in Oxford and the Costwolds . . . . . . . . . | H.A. Evans | 1905 |
| 144. | History of the Congregational churches in the Berks, South Oxon and South Bucks association . . . . | W.H. Summers | 1905 |
| 146. | Memoir of Thomas Hill Green . . . . | R.L. Nettleship | 1906 |
| 147. | A history of the post-reformation Catholic missions in Oxfordshire | B. Stapledon | 1906 |
| 148. | The Lollards of the Chiltern Hills | W.H. Summers | 1906 |
| 149. | Chalgrove . . . and John Hampden | J.H. Swinstead | 1906 |
| 153. | Life & Times of Lucius Cary, Viscount Falkland . . . . . . . . . | J.A.R. Marriott | 1907 |
| 154. | Victoria County History: 2. General | Ed. W. Page | 1907 |
| 157. | The first planting of Quakerism in Oxfordshire . . . . . . . . . | W.C. Braithwaite | 1908 |
| 158. | School History of Oxfordshire . . . . | H.A. Liddell | 1908 |
| 160. | The Reminiscences of Albert Pell | Ed. T. Mackay | 1908 |
| 164. | The Gunpowder Plot and Life of Robert Catesby . . . . . . . . . | M.W. Jones | 1909 |

| | | | |
|---|---|---|---|
| 165. | Chipping Norton in bygone days | M.K. Pearson | 1909 |
| 166. | A history of the Oxford Museum | H.M. & M.D. Vernon | 1909 |
| 168. | History of All Saints' School, Bloxham 1860-1910 | Anon. | 1910 |
| 170. | Cornbury and the Forest of Wychwood | V.J. Watney | 1910 |
| 172. | The Village Labourer | J.L. & B. Hammond | 1911 |
| 175. | The Place-names of Oxfordshire | H. Alexander | 1912 |
| 176. | Social Conditions in Oxford | C.V. Butler | 1912 |
| 177. | Berkshire & Oxfordshire: historical biographical and pictorial | Ed. J. Grant | 1912 |
| 178. | The old Colleges of Oxford | A. Vallance | 1912 |
| 179. | Early History of the Abbey of Abingdon | F.M. Stenton | 1913 |
| 180. | Kingham Old and New | W. Fowler | 1913 |
| 181. | New Road Chapel Sunday School Society 1813-1913 | H. Paintin | 1913 |
| 183. | The strike at Chipping Norton | G.N. Clark & G.D.H. Cole | 1914 |
| 184. | A corner of the Cotswolds, through the nineteenth century | M.S. Gretton | 1914 |
| 185. | The Thames Highway | F.S. Thacker | 1914-20 |
| 186. | The story of the Oxfordshire & Buckinghamshire Light Infantry | Sir H.J. Newbolt | 1915 |
| 187. | Agriculture in Oxfordshire | C.S. Orr | 1916 |
| 191. | Allotments & small holdings in Oxfordshire | A.W. Ashby | 1917 |
| 192. | Memoirs of Sir William Markby | L. Markby | 1917 |
| 194. | St Barnabas, Oxford: record of fifty years | A.T. Bassett | 1919 |
| 198. | Dr John Radcliffe | J.B. Nias | 1918 |
| 201. | War Record of the 1/4th Battalion, Oxfordshire and Buckinghamshire Light Infantry | P. Pickford | 1919 |
| 202. | Record of Oxford YMCA's war work 1914-19 | Anon. | 1920 |
| 203. | The Burford Records | R.H. Gretton | 1920 |
| 204. | The story of the 2/4th Oxfordshire & Buckinghamshire Light Infantry | G.K. Rose | 1920 |
| 205. | Memorial records of the 7th (Service) Battalion, Oxfordshire & Buckinghamshire Light Infantry | Ed. C. Wheeler | 1921 |
| 206. | Rural Industries round Oxford | K.S. Woods | 1921 |
| 208. | History of Crowmarsh Gifford | T.S. Clack | 1922 |
| 210. | The Oxfordshire Dashwoods | J. Townsend | 1922 |
| 211. | Lady Margaret Hall: a short history | Anon. | 1923 |
| 212. | Glympton | H. Barnett | 1923 |
| 213. | Tom Tower, Christ Church | W.D. Caröe | 1923 |
| 214. | Oxford outside the Guide Books | F. Madan | 1923 |
| 217. | Adderbury | H.J. Gepp | 1924 |

| | | | |
|---|---|---|---|
| 218. | History of the University of Oxford | C.E. Mallett | 1924-7 |
| 219. | Early Science in Oxford . . . . | R.T. Gunther | 1922 |
| 220. | Round about the Mitre . . . . . . . . . . | R.A.H. Spiers | 1924 |
| 221. | The early history of Mapledurham | A.H. Cooke | 1925 |
| 222. | Long Barrows of the Cotswolds . . . . | O.G.S. Crawford | 1925 |
| 223. | Short history of the Oxfordshire & Buckinghamshire Light Infantry 1741-1922 . . . . . . . . . | R.B. Crosse | 1925 |
| 224. | Oxford and Neighbouring Churches | C. Headlam | 1925 |
| 225. | Catholics in Oxford. 1581 to the present day . . . . . . . . . | C.C. Martindale | 1925 |
| 227. | The Radcliffe Infirmary . . . . | A.G. Gibson | 1926 |
| 228. | A village on the Thames . . . . | R.J. Godlee | 1926 |
| 230. | Action taken in the General Strike | National Citizens' Union | 1926 |
| 232. | A Short History of Thame School | J.H. Brown | 1927 |
| 233. | The manor of Elsfield . . . . . . . . . | G.N. Clark | 1927 |
| 234. | An Oxford hall in medieval times | A.B. Emden | 1927 |
| 235. | Twixt Cherwell and Glyme . . . . | M.E. Freeborn | 1927 |
| 236. | The Oxfordshire Hussars in the Great War . . . . . . . . . | A. Keith-Falconer | 1927 |
| 237. | Historical and other notes . . . . | J. Kibble | 1927 |
| 238. | History of the Great Western Railway | E.T. Macdermot | 1927 |
| 242. | The Bicester and Warden Hill . . . . | A.S. Barrow | 1928 |
| 243. | The history of Hook Norton . . . . | M. Dickins | 1928 |
| 244. | Historical and other notices on Wychwood Forest . . . . . . . . . | J. Kibble | 1928 |
| 245. | Short notice of the charities of Henry Allnutt . . . . . . . . . | G.E.B. Rogers | 1928 |
| 246. | Coaching Days in Oxford and at the Mitre . . . . . . . . . | R.A.H. Spiers | 1928 |
| 247. | In West Oxford . . . . . . . . . | T.W. Squires | 1928 |
| 251. | History of Steeple Aston & Middle Aston | C.C. Brookes | 1929 |
| 253. | Cuddesdon College 1854-1929 . . . . | Anon. | 1930 |
| 254. | The history of the village of Islip . . . | E. Miller | 1930 |
| 255. | Banbury Cross and the Rhyme . . . . | W. Potts | 1930 |
| 257. | The story of the Chiltern Heathlands | J.H. Baker | 1931 |
| 258. | Oxfordshire: regional planning report | Earl of Mayo, et al | 1931 |
| 263. | Manchester College . . . . . . . . . | V.D. Davis | 1932 |
| 264. | Famous Women of Oxfordshire . . . . | E. Mansfield | 1932 |
| 265. | The Siege of Oxford . . . . . . . . . | F.J. Varley | 1932 |
| 268. | A history of Headington Quarry and Shotover . . . . . . . . . | G.A. Coppock & B.M. Hill | 1933 |
| 270. | Saxon Oxfordshire . . . . . . . . . | Ed. G.B. Grundy | 1933 |
| 271. | Oxford: its place in national history | J.A.R. Marriott | 1933 |
| 272. | History of Kidmore End . . . . | J.E. Smith-Masters | 1933 |

| | | | |
|---|---|---|---|
| 273. | Martyrs of Oxfordshire .... | Students of Heythrop College | 1933 |
| 274. | Story of Deddington ......... | M.V. Turner | 1933 |
| 276. | Oxfordshire Justices of the Peace in the seventeenth century .... | M.S. Gretton | 1934 |
| 277. | History of Shipton-under-Wychwood | M. Groves | 1934 |
| 278. | Oxford Theology and Theologians | A.G. Little & F. Pelster | 1934 |
| 280. | Brief history of the parish of Kiddington | P. Norwood | 1934 |
| 281. | Godes Peace and the Queenes .... | H.J. O'Conor | 1934 |
| 282. | The Witney Blanket Industry .... | Ed. A Plummer | 1934 |
| 283. | History of Churchill ......... | L. Rose | 1934 |
| 284. | The map of medieval Oxford .... | H.E. Salter | 1934 |
| 285 | History of Thame ......... | J.H. Brown & W. Guest | 1935 |
| 286. | The Heythrop Hunt ......... | G.T. Hutchinson | 1935 |
| 287 | History of Dean and Chalford .... | M.D. Lobel | 1935 |
| 288 | Oxfordshire by-ways ......... | R.M. Marshall | 1935 |
| 290 | Oxford (for World Education Conference: previous publications by National Union of Teachers for 1907 and 1925 meetings) ......... | Anon. | 1935 |
| 291. | Notes on the history of Charlbury | J.D. Payne | 1935 |
| 292. | Church and parish of St Nicholas, Abingdon ......... | A.E. Preston | 1935 |
| 293. | Lawrence: the story of his life .... | E. Robinson | 1935 |
| 294. | Companion into Oxfordshire .... | E.C. Williams | 1935 |
| 295. | The Book of Oxford (for BMA Conference) ......... | Anon. | 1936 |
| 296. | The Quatremains of Oxfordshire ... | W.F. Carter | 1936 |
| 297. | Eynsham under the Monks .... | E.K. Chambers | 1936 |
| 298. | Sir Henry Lee: an Elizabethan Portrait | E.K. Chambers | 1936 |
| 300. | Fifty Years of Kingham Hill, 1886-1936 | A.P. Jarvis | 1936 |
| 301. | The Universities of Europe in the Middle Ages: 3 ......... | H. Rashdall | 1936 |
| 302. | Medieval Oxford ......... | H.E. Salter | 1936 |
| 310. | Garsington ......... | Garsington Women's Institute | 1937 |
| 314. | Weston-on-the-Green Methodist Church Centenary ......... | Anon. | 1938 |
| 315. | An Oxford University Chest .... | J. Betjeman | 1938 |
| 316. | A history of Chastleton .... | M. Dickins | 1938 |
| 321. | The history of Nuffield ......... | P.M. Briers | 1939 |
| 322. | Oxford as it was and as it is today | C. Hobhouse | 1939 |
| 323. | Victoria County History: 1 General | Ed. L.F. Salzman | 1939 |
| 329. | Village Life ......... | Oxfordshire Rural Community Council | 1937 |

| | | | |
|---|---|---|---|
| 330. | Memories of Victorian Oxford .... | Sir C. Oman | 1941 |
| 336. | Oxford and Industrial Education.... | J. Johnson | 1943 |
| 340. | Technical and Art Education in Oxford | C. Batey | 1944 |
| 341. | Towards a plan for Oxford City .... | L. Dale | 1944 |
| 342. | The Place-Names of Oxfordshire .... | M. Gelling | 1944 |
| 344. | Newman and Littlemore .... | Cowley Salesian Fathers | 1945 |
| 345. | Calling All Arms .......... | E. Fairfax | 1945 |
| 346. | Record of the 4th Oxfordshire (Bullingdon) Battalion Home Guard, 1940-4 .......... | C. Graham | 1945 |
| 347. | Burford Past and Present .... | M.S. Gretton | 1945 |
| 348. | Lark Rise to Candelford .... | F. Thompson | 1945 |
| 349. | Guide to the Eagle Brewery 1839-1939 | Clinch & Co Ltd. | 1939 |
| 401. | It happened in the Dorn valley .... | Barton Women's Institute | 1946 |
| 402. | A Christ Church Miscellany .... | W.G. Hiscock | 1946 |
| 403. | Memories of Four-Score Years .... | Sir J.A.R. Marriott | 1946 |
| 408. | Oxford Stone .......... | W.J. Arkell | 1947 |
| 410. | London Children in Wartime Oxford | Barnett House | 1947 |
| 411. | 75 Years' Cooperation in Oxford & District .......... | D. Barnie | 1947 |
| 412. | Burford in the war .......... | Burford & Fulbrook Women's Institute | 1947 |
| 413. | Wootton: the history of an Oxfordshire parish .......... | C. Ponsonby | 1947 |
| 417. | Oxford & District Gas Company 1818-1948 .......... | Anon. | 1948 |
| 418. | The Pre-Raphaelites and Oxford .... | J.E. Alden | 1948 |
| 420. | Records of Milton & Shipton-under-Wychwood during the war 1939-45 .......... | M. Groves | 1948 |
| 421. | Shoemaker's Window. .......... | G. Herbert Ed. C.R. Cheney | 1948 |
| 422. | The Golden Cross and its Guests ... | E.A.G. Lamborn | 1948 |
| 423. | War Record .......... | Leafield Women's Institute | 1948 |
| 424. | Life & work of Humphrey Gainsborough | G.H. Peters | 1948 |
| 425. | Oxford Replanned .......... | T. Sharp | 1948 |
| 426. | The Baptists of New Road, Oxford | W. Stevens & W.W. Bottoms | 1948 |
| 431. | Sir Stafford Cripps .......... | E. Estorick | 1949 |
| 432. | The story of Lewis Carroll .... | R.L. Green | 1949 |
| 433. | Six centuries of an Oxford college | R.H. Hodgkin | 1949 |
| 434. | The Amorial Glass of the Oxford Diocese | E.A.G. Lamborn | 1949 |
| 435. | Cooperation in the Thames Valley | A. Lockwood | 1949 |
| 436. | History of Chipping Norton .... | E. Meades | 1949 |

| | | | |
|---|---|---|---|
| 437. | The Oxfordshire Election of 1754 | R.J. Robson | 1949 |
| 441. | Rural Education | A.B. Allen | 1950 |
| 442. | The Origins of the Austin Canons | J.C. Dickinson | 1950 |
| 443. | Life of Dr John Radcliffe 1652-1714 | C.R. Hone | 1950 |
| 444. | Charles Baring Young of Daylesford | A.P. Jarvis | 1950 |
| 445. | Recollections of T.G. Jackson 1835-1924 | B.H. Jackson | 1950 |
| 446. | A Backward Glance | H. Wyndham | 1950 |
| 449. | Excavations at Dorchester | R.J.C. Atkinson et al | 1951 |
| 450. | Combe . . . church and village | C.S. Emden | 1951 |
| 451. | Blenheim Palace | D. Green | 1951 |
| 452. | Re-cognitions | M.S. Gretton | 1951 |
| 453. | Historic Oxfordshire | Oxfordshire Rural Community Council | 1951 |
| 454. | Jews of Medieval Oxford | C. Roth | 1951 |
| 455. | Introduction to Woodstock | J.M. Shelmerdine | 1951 |
| 456. | Stonor, a Catholic sanctuary in the Chilterns | R.J. Stonor | 1951 |
| 458. | History of the Bodleian Library 1845-1945 | Sir E. Craster | 1952 |
| 460. | New College and its Buildings | A.H. Smith | 1952 |
| 464. | Some Early Bishops of Oxford | C.M. Ady | 1953 |
| 465. | Hanborough | R.C.S. Bailey | 1953 |
| 466. | Medicine in Oxford | M. Davidson | 1953 |
| 467. | Kings and Queens at Oxford | M.E. Freeborn | 1953 |
| 468. | St Frideswide the Patron Saint of Oxford | E.F. Jacob | 1953 |
| 470. | Culham 1853-1953 | L. Naylor | 1953 |
| 471. | Father Benson, founder of the Cowley Fathers | M.V. Woodgate | 1953 |
| 473. | Oxford City Libraries 1854-1954 | Anon. | 1954 |
| 474. | The Founding of Cuddesdon | O. Chadwick | 1954 |
| 475. | A History of the City of Oxford | R. Fasnacht | 1954 |
| 476. | The Oxford Region | Eds. A.F. Martin & R.W. Steel | 1954 |
| 477. | Victoria County History: 3 The University of Oxford | Eds. H.E. Salter & M.D. Lobel | 1954 |
| 479. | Guide to St Mary's Church, Ewelme | A. Bolton | 1954 |
| 480. | Life of Lord Nuffield | P.W.S. Andrews & E. Brunner | 1955 |
| 481. | St Aloysius, Oxford: the first eighty years | D.A. Bischoff | 1955 |
| 482. | Canals of Southern England | C. Hadfield | 1955 |
| 483. | Wheatley Stone | W.O. Hassall | 1955 |
| 487. | Whitchurch-on-Thames | J.H. Baker | 1956 |
| 488. | Jubilee Record | Milham Ford School | 1956 |
| 489. | The Oxford Group | W.H. Clark | 1951 |
| 490. | Family and Neighbourhood | J.M. Mogey | 1956 |

| | | | |
|---|---|---|---|
| 491. | Labour and Learning | H.P. Smith | 1956 |
| 495. | Oxfordshire Constabulary Centenary 1857-1957 | Anon. | 1957 |
| 496. | Henley Regatta: a history | R.D. Burnell | 1957 |
| 497. | Wolvercote Mill | H. Carter | 1957 |
| 498. | The School in our Village | J.M. Goldman | 1957 |
| 500. | Fifield Merrymouth | E. Goshawk | 1957 |
| 501. | St Denys' School, Oxford | G. Hargrave | 1957 |
| 502. | Kingham, the beloved place | E. Lainchbury | 1957 |
| 503. | Victoria County History: 5 Bullingdon Hundred | Ed. M.D. Lobel | 1957 |
| 504. | Story of a Music Shop 1857-1957 | C. Taphouse & Son Ltd | 1957 |
| 507. | St John's College 1598-1860 | W.C. Costin | 1958 |
| 508. | Jowett: portrait with a background | G.C. Faber | 1958 |
| 509. | Minster Lovell Hall | A.J. Taylor | 1958 |
| 510. | A History of Banbury | W. Potts | 1958 |
| 511. | A History of Magdalen College School, Oxford | R.S. Stanier | 1958 |
| 512. | Georgian Oxford | W.R. Ward | 1958 |
| 513. | The King's War 1641-7 | C.V. Wedgwood | 1958 |
| 517. | The Ipsden Country | J.H. Baker | 1959 |
| 518. | Rural England 1086-1135 | R. Lennard | 1959 |
| 520. | Victoria County History: 6 Ploughley Hundred | Ed. M.D. Lobel | 1959 |
| 523. | All Saints' School, Bloxham | Anon. | 1960 |
| 525. | Occupation, education and housing in an English city | P. Collison | 1960 |
| 526. | Witney Grammar School 1660-1960 | M.A. Fleming | 1960 |
| 527. | Oxfordshire Clergy 1777-1869 | D. McClatchey | 1960 |
| 528. | Brief description and history | Pressed Steel Co Ltd | 1960 |
| 529. | Oxford and Cambridge in Transition 1558-1642 | M.H. Curtis | 1959 |
| 530. | Tradition and Change | M. Stacey | 1960 |
| 531. | Some reminiscences of an Oxford builder | W.C. Walker | 1960 |
| 535. | Ramsden | D.H. Allpot | 1961 |
| 536. | Joseph Ashby of Tysoe | M.K. Ashby | 1961 |
| 537. | Watlington . . . branch-line handbook | J.E.S. Gadsden | 1961 |
| 538. | British Legion, Oxfordshire: the first 50 years | F.R.L. Goadby | 1961 |
| 540. | Idbury History | E. Goshawk | 1961 |
| 541. | Otmoor and its Seven Towns | M.G. Hobson & K.H.L. Price | 1961 |
| 546. | A History of Deddington | H.M. Colvin | 1962 |
| 547. | History of Spelsbury | E. Corbett | 1962 |
| 548. | The Story of Woodstock Gloves | F. Grierson | 1962 |
| 550. | Victoria County History: 7 Dorchester and Thame Hundreds | Ed. M.D. Lobel | 1962 |

| | | | |
|---|---|---|---|
| 553. | City of Oxford College of Technology | Anon. | 1963 |
| 554. | The Cutteslowe Walls | P. Collison | 1963 |
| 555. | A History of the King's Works | H.M. Colvin | 1963 |
| 556. | A History of Balliol College. | H.W.C. Davis<br>R.H.C. Davis rev. | 1963 |
| 557. | A History of St Edward's School | R.D. Hill | 1963 |
| 558. | Oxford High School 1875-1960 | Ed. V.E. Stack | 1963 |
| 560. | Traditional domestic architecture in the Banbury region | R.B. Wood-Jones | 1963 |
| 561. | The Nuffield Story | R. Jackson | 1964 |
| 562. | Victoria County History: 8 Lewknor and Pyrton Hundreds | Ed. M.D. Lobel | 1964 |
| 563. | The Oxfam Story | T.R. Mitford | 1964 |
| 565. | Gillett's, bankers at Banbury and Oxford | A.M. Taylor | 1964 |
| 566. | A Century of Summer Fields | Ed. R. Usborne | 1964 |
| 573. | The deserted villages of Oxfordshire | K.J. Allison et al | 1965 |
| 574. | The Eagle Ironworks, Oxford | P.W.S. Andrews &<br>E. Brunner | 1965 |
| 575. | Landscape in Distress | L. Brett | 1965 |
| 576. | Golden Jubilee Scrapbook | Haseley Women's Institute | 1965 |
| 577. | A medieval . . . village: Cuxham | P.D.A. Harvey | 1965 |
| 578. | The Oxford Union | C. Hollis | 1965 |
| 580. | The Bullnose Morris | L.P. Jarman &<br>R.I. Barraclough | 1965 |
| 581. | Big men, little men and men in between | R.C. Keen | 1965 |
| 582. | History of freemasonry in Oxfordshire | A.J. Kerry | 1965 |
| 583. | Golden Jubilee Year Scrapbook | Marston Women's Institute | 1965 |
| 584. | Alvescot and its Past | O.R. Mason | 1965 |
| 585. | The sociology of housing: studies at Berinsfield | R.N. Morris &<br>J. Mogey | 1965 |
| 586. | Golden Jubilee Year scrapbook | Over Norton Women's Institute | 1965 |
| 587. | Golden Jubilee Year scrapbook | Sandhills Women's Institute | 1965 |
| 588. | A history of Methodism in Banbury | B.S. Trinder | 1965 |
| 590. | Victorian Oxford | W.R. Ward | 1965 |
| 599. | Canals of the East Midlands | C. Hadfield | 1966 |
| 601. | City of Oxford Redevelopment | D. Benson & J. Cook | 1966 |
| 602. | Oxford Workers in the Great Strike | R. Hyman | 1966 |
| 603. | Radcot and its Bridge | E.A. Pocock | 1966 |
| 608. | Clockmaking in Oxfordshire 1400-1800 | C.F.G. Beeson | 1967 |
| 611. | Oxford | F. Markham | 1967 |
| 612. | Church and parish of St Michael at the Northgate, Oxford | R.R. Martin | 1967 |

| | | | |
|---|---|---|---|
| 618. | Benfield and Loxley Ltd | Anon. | 1968 |
| 620. | History of Broadwell . . . with Filkins, Kelmscott and Holywell | A.S.T. Fisher | 1968 |
| 621. | Bicester wuz a little town | S. Hedges | 1968 |
| 622. | The Living Village | P. Jennings | 1968 |
| 623. | Paris and Oxford Universities in the Thirteenth and Fourteenth Centuries | G. Leff | 1968 |
| 624. | The departed village: Berrick Salome at the turn of the century | R.E. Moreau | 1968 |
| 625. | A History of Wesley Memorial Church, Oxford | J.E. Oxley | 1968 |
| 626. | Wootton: anatomy of a village 1945-68 | C. Ponsonby | 1968 |
| 627. | Bells, blankets, baskets and boats | C. Sibbitt | 1968 |
| 642. | Swynford Toll Bridge 1769-1969 | Eynsham History Group (de Villiers E.) | 1969 |
| 643. | How Summertown Started | R. Fasnacht | 1969 |
| 644. | Drink and Sobriety in an Early Victorian County Town: Banbury 1830-60 | B Harrison & B.S. Trinder | 1969 |
| 645. | Captain Swing | E.J Hobsbawm & G. Rude | 1969 |
| 646. | The Lady Spencer-Churchill College of Education 1948-69 | M. Hodges | 1969 |
| 647. | Oxford Past and Present | C.W. Judge | 1969 |
| 648. | Victoria County History: 9 Bloxham Hundred | Eds. M.D. Lobel & A. Crossley | 1969 |
| 649. | The Ironstone Railways and Tramways of the Midlands | E.S. Tonks | 1959 |
| 650. | The Two Britwells | B. O'Sullivan | 1969 |
| 651. | The Blanket Makers 1669-1969 | A. Plummer & R.E. Early | 1969 |
| 652. | Through the Lych Gate | R. Rainsberry | 1969 |
| 661. | St Giles' Fair 1830-1914 | S. Alexander | 1970 |
| 662. | Holton through the Centuries | M. Durran | 1970 |
| 663. | Short history of the War Memorial Hospital at Chipping Norton 1920-70 | D.T.G. Eddershaw | 1970 |
| 664. | The Other Oxford | C. Fenby | 1970 |
| 665. | History of Kencot | A.S.T. Fisher | 1970 |
| 666. | The Chartist Land Company | A.M. Hadfield | 1970 |
| 667. | The Oxford Martyrs | D.M. Loades | 1970 |
| 668. | The Class Struggle in Nineteenth Century Oxfordshire: the social | | |

| | | | |
|---|---|---|---|
| | and communal background to the Otmoor disturbances of 1830 to 1835 | B. Reaney | 1970 |
| 670. | Short History of the Radcliffe Infirmary | A.H.T. Robb-Smith | 1970 |
| 671. | Cropredy Bridge 1644 | M.R. Toynbee & P. Young | 1970 |
| 701. | Arthur's Britain | L. Alcock | 1971 |
| 702. | Jesus College | J.N.L. Baker | 1971 |
| 703. | Victorian and Edwardian Oxford | J. Betjeman & D.G. Vaisey | 1971 |
| 704. | The Oxfordshire & Buckinghamshire Light Infantry | P. Booth | 1971 |
| 705. | Street Lighting in Oxford | T. Braun | 1971 |
| 706. | Burford Grammar School | E.M. Rylands & A.M. Simpson | 1971 |
| 707. | Oxford Now and Then | D. Balsdon | 1970 |
| 708. | Gathorne Robert Girdlestone | J. Trueta | 1971 |
| 709. | A History of Kidlington | V. Offord | 1971 |
| 718. | The Oxford Industry | Ed. S. Bowden & E. Morgan | 1972 |
| 720. | History of Westwell | A.S.T. Fisher | 1972 |
| 721. | Oxford: the city beneath your feet | T.G. Hassall | 1972 |
| 722. | Oxford Buildings | D.A. Hinton | 1972 |
| 723. | 100 Years of Cooperation in Oxford | A. Ledger | 1972 |
| 724. | Story of Bloxham Parish Church | C.O. Moreton | 1972 |
| 725. | Oxford Life in Oxford Archives | W.A. Pantin | 1972 |
| 726. | The Trade in Lunacy | W.L. Parry-Jones | 1972 |
| 739. | The Iron Age in the Upper Thames Region | D.W. Harding | 1972 |
| 740. | Oxford Shops and Shopping | M.L. Turner & D.G. Vaisey | 1972 |
| 741. | Victoria County History: 10 Banbury Hundred | Ed. A. Crossley | 1972 |
| 742. | Witchcraft in the Thames Valley | T. Barham | 1973 |
| 743. | Oxfordshire: a handbook for students of local history | D.M. Barratt & D.G. Vaisey | 1973 |
| 744. | Southern England: an archaeological guide | J. Dyer | 1973 |
| 745. | F. Cape & Co of St Ebbe's Street | R. Foster | 1973 |
| 746. | Henry Taunt of Oxford | M. Graham | 1973 |
| 747. | Whitsun in Nineteenth Century Oxfordshire | A. Howkins | 1973 |
| 748. | The Woodstock Branch | R. Lingard | 1973 |
| 749. | Life in the Cotswolds | E. Brill | 1973 |
| 750. | Workers on the Move | M. Mann | 1973 |
| 751. | Oxford in the Age of John Locke | W.N. Hargreaves-Mawdsley | 1973 |

| | | | |
|---|---|---|---|
| 752. | The Age of Arthur | J. Morris | 1973 |
| 753. | St Antony's College | A Saint & M. Kaser | 1973 |
| 754. | Strangers in Oxford | M. Toynbee & P. Young | 1973 |
| 755. | The Leyland Papers | G. Turner | 1971 |
| 759. | Stonesfield Slate | M. Aston | 1974 |
| 766. | Chaucer at Oxford and Cambridge | J.A.W. Bennett | 1974 |
| 767. | The Upper Thames Valley: an archaeological survey of the river gravels | D. Benson & D. Miles | 1974 |
| 768. | Useful Toil | Ed. J. Burnett | 1974 |
| 770. | The Oxfordshire area in the Civil War | A. Carter & J. Stevenson | 1974 |
| 771. | Iron Age Communities of Britain | B. Cunliffe | 1974 |
| 772. | History of Oxford Telecommunications | R.A.J. Earl | 1974 |
| 773. | The Oxfordshire Landscape | F.V. Emery | 1974 |
| 774. | Britannia | S.S. Frere | 1974 |
| 775. | Youth and History | J.R. Gillis | 1974 |
| 776. | Ottoline at Garsington | Ed. R. Gathorne-Hardy | 1974 |
| 777. | A History of Oxford University | V.H.H. Green | 1974 |
| 778. | The Iron Age in Lowland Britain | D. Harding | 1974 |
| 780. | The Watlington Branch | J.S. Holden | 1974 |
| 781. | The Victorian Country Child | P.R.L. Horn | 1974 |
| 782. | Victimization at Cowley | S. Johns | 1974 |
| 783. | Glovemaking in West Oxfordshire | N.L. Leyland & J.E. Troughton | 1974 |
| 784. | A Family of Rectors | R.N. Mann | 1974 |
| 785. | British Prehistory | C. Renfrew | 1974 |
| 786. | The buildings of England: Oxfordshire | J. Sherwood & N. Pevsner | 1974 |
| 787. | Civil strife in the Midlands 1642-51 | R. E. Sherwood | 1974 |
| 788. | History of the Oxford Central Girls' School and Cheney Girls' Grammar School | M. Spackman | 1974 |
| 790. | Finance of Canal Building in the eighteenth century | J.R. Ward | 1974 |
| 802. | The Book of Banbury | C. Bloxham | 1975 |
| 803. | The Tolsey at Burford | K. Briggs | 1975 |
| 804. | Forgotten Railways: Chilterns and Cotswolds | R Davies & M.D. Grant | 1975 |
| 805. | Between the White Gates | H.M. Harris | 1975 |
| 806. | A short history of Charlbury | R. Hill | 1975 |
| 807. | The Witney and East Gloucestershire Railway | S.C. Jenkins | 1975 |
| 808. | Oxfordshire | M. Jessup | 1975 |

| | | | |
|---|---|---|---|
| 810. | Memories of St Giles' Fair .... | V. Kirk | 1975 |
| 811. | Oxford: the City and County as it used to be ......... | C. Long | 1975 |
| 812. | A century of Rosegrowing .... | J. Mattock Ltd | 1975 |
| 813. | The archaeology and economic history of English clay tobacco pipes | A. Oswald | 1975 |
| 814. | The Church of St Aloysius, 1875-1975 | H.M. Palmer | 1975 |
| 815. | Historic Towns in Oxfordshire .... | Ed. K. Rodwell | 1975 |
| 816. | Oxford in the History of the Nation | A.L. Rowse | 1975 |
| 817. | Village Life and Labour .... | Ed. R. Samuel | 1975 |
| 818. | The story of Hethe ......... | J.M. Sergeant | 1975 |
| 820. | Oxford and its Region ......... | C.G. Smith & D. I. Scargill | 1975 |
| 821. | Power, persistence and change: a second study of Banbury .... | M. Stacey et al | 1975 |
| 822. | The University in Society .... | Ed. L. Stone | 1975 |
| 823. | The Book of Henley-on-Thames .... | G.H.J. Tomalin | 1975 |
| 824. | When the Moon was High .... | R. Tree | 1975 |
| 833. | Warneford Hospital 1826-1976 .... | Anon. | 1976 |
| 834. | The Barton Project ......... | P. Evens | 1976 |
| 835. | Brize Norton County Primary School 1876-1976 ......... | G. Lohmann | 1976 |
| 836. | An Oxford Childhood ......... | C. Oman | 1976 |
| 837. | William Morris, Viscount Nuffield | R.J. Overy | 1976 |
| 838. | Eliza of Otmoor ......... | P. Surman | 1976 |
| 846. | The Oxford Canal ......... | H.J. Compton | 1976 |

## Journal and other articles

| **Abbreviation** | **Full journal title** |
|---|---|
| Ag HR | Agricultural History Review |
| Antiq | The Antiquary |
| Antiq J | Antiquaries Journal |
| Archaeol J | Archaeological Journal |
| CC | Cake & Cockhorse (Banbury Historical Society) |
| EcHR | Economic History Review |
| EHR | English Historical Review |
| Gen | Genealogist |
| Geog J | Geographical Journal |
| JmodH | Journal of Modern History |

| | |
|---|---|
| JRagS | Journal of the Royal Agricultural Society |
| JRCHS | Journal of the Railway & Canal History Society |
| NDFCT | Newbury District Field Club Transactions |
| OHS | Oxford Historical Society |
| ORS | Oxfordshire Record Society |
| Ox | Oxoniensia |
| POxAHS | Proceedings of the Oxford Archaeological and Historical Society |
| RlyM | Railway Magazine |
| ROxArchS | Reports of the Oxfordshire Archaeological Society |
| TOxArchS | Transactions do. |
| TO | Top Oxon |
| TRHS | Transactions of the Royal Historical Society |

| | | | |
|---|---|---|---|
| 26. | 'Farming of Oxfordshire' JRagS . . . . | C.S. Read | 1855 |
| 29. | 'Account of certain (supposed) British & Saxon remains. . .' Proceedings of the Society of Antiquaries of London . . . . . . . . . | S. Stone | 1856-9 |
| 65. | 'The Banbury Peerage' Gen. . . . . | M.T. Pearman | 1884-5 |
| 71. | 'University of Oxford in the twelfth century' OHS . . . . . . . . . | T.E. Holland | 1890 |
| 72. | 'Note on Jews in Oxford' OHS . . . . | A. Neubauer | 1890 |
| 73. | 'Oxford Market' OHS . . . . . . . . . | O. Ogle | 1890 |
| 74. | 'Friars Preachers of the University' OHS | H. Rashdall | 1890 |
| 75. | 'Historical account of the hundred of Chiltern in Oxfordshire' TOxArchS | M.T. Pearman | 1890 |
| 76. | 'Chronological summary of the Civil War in Oxfordshire, Buckinghamshire and Berkshire' POxArchS . . . . | C.H. Firth | 1890 |
| 85. | 'Notices . . . of the parish of Checkendon' ORS . . . . . . . . . | M.T. Pearman | 1893 |
| 91. | 'Historical notes of Caversham' ORS | M.T. Pearman | 1894 |
| 96. | 'The Fettiplace Family' NDFCT . . . . | J. Renton-Dunlop | 1895-1901 |
| 99. | 'Traces of the early Britons in the neighbourhood of Oxford' POxArchS . . . . . . . . . | W. Boyd-Dawkins | 1860-4 |
| 111. | 'Oxfordshire traces of the northern insurgents of 1065' EHR . . . . | F. Baring | 1898 |
| 124. | 'Murderous affray near Stonor 1535' ROxArchs . . . . . . . . . | M.T. Pearman | 1900 |

| | | | |
|---|---|---|---|
| 128. | 'Notices . . of the parish of Nuffield' ORS . . . . . . . . . | M.T. Pearman | 1901 |
| 132. | 'Stray Notes on Oxfordshire Folklore' Folklore . . . . . . . . . | P. Manning | 1902 |
| 138. | 'Dedications of churches, feasts . . ' ROxArchS . . . . . . . . . | C.E. Prior | 1903-6 |
| 145. | 'Description of Oxford from the Hundred Rolls of Oxfordshire 1279' OHS | Ed. R. Graham | 1905 |
| 150. | 'Notes on Swyncomb' ORS . . . . | M.T. Pearman | 1906 |
| 151. | 'John Milton and Foresthill' ROxArchS | E. Greaves | 1906 |
| 152. | 'Seven Somerton Court Rolls' ORS | A. Ballard | 1906 |
| 155. | 'An Oxfordshire village in the thirteenth century' Antiq . . . . . . . . . | A. Ballard | 1907 |
| 156. | 'Charlton . . . open fields' ORS . . . . | C.E. Prior | 1907 |
| 161. | 'Oxford Downs, history of the breed' JRagS . . . . . . . . . | J.T. Hobbs | 1908 |
| 162. | 'Notes on open fields of Oxfordshire' ROxArchs . . . . . . . . . | A. Ballard | 1908 |
| 167. | 'The Black Death at Witney' ROxArchS | A. Ballard | 1909 |
| 171. | 'Yeoman farming in Oxfordshire from the sixteenth to the nineteenth century' Quarterly Journal of Economics . . . . . . . . . | H.L. Gray | 1910 |
| 173. | 'Tackley in the sixteenth and seventeenth centuries' ROxArchS . . . . | A. Ballard | 1911 |
| 174. | 'Chancellors & their relationships to the Bishops of Lincoln' EHR . . . . | S. Gibson | 1911 |
| 182. | 'Oxfordshire village folklore, 1840-1900' Folklore . . . . . . . . . | A. Parker | 1913-23 |
| 188. | 'Black Death in manors of Witney, Brightwell and Downton': Levett A.E: Black Death on the estates of the see of Winchester . . . . | A. Ballard | 1916 |
| 190. | 'Old Meeting House, Banbury' Transactions of the Unitarian Historical Society . . . . | A.D. Tyssen | 1916-8 |
| 193. | 'Woodeaton' ROxArchS . . . . . . . . | M.V. Taylor | 1917 |
| 207. | '. . . History of Watlington' ROxArchS | H.E. Salter | 1921-2 |
| 209. | 'Presbyterians of Bloxham and Milton' Transactions of the Unitarian Historical Society . . . . | A.D. Tyssen | 1920 |
| 215. | 'Sport and pastimes in Stuart Oxford' OHS . . . . . . . . . | P. Manning | 1923 |
| 216. | 'Oxford Tradesmen's Tokens': H.E. Salter: Surveys and Tokens . . . . | E.T. Leeds | 1923 |
| 226. | 'Open Fields and Inclosure at Marston' ORS . . . . . . . . . | G.N. Clark | 1925 |

| | | | |
|---|---|---|---|
| 229. | 'The Poure family of Oxfordshire' Miscellanea Genealogica et Heraldica . . . . . . . . . | G.A. Moriarty | 1926-8 |
| 231. | 'The Rollright Stones . . .' ROxArchS | T.H. Ravenhill | 1926 |
| 239. | 'Campaign of Radcot Bridge in December 1387' EHR . . . . | J.N.L. Myres | 1926 |
| 240. | 'Alcester' Antiq J . . . . . . . . . | C.F.C. Hawkes | 1927-9 |
| 241. | 'An Oxford Hall in 1424': H.W.C. Davis Essays in History Presented to R.L. Poole . . . . . . . . . | H.E. Salter | 1927 |
| 248. | 'Halifax Builders in Oxford' Transactions of the Halifax Antiquarian Society | T.W. Hanson | 1928 |
| 249. | 'A prehistoric settlement on Hinksey Hill . . .' Journal of the British Archaeological Association | J.N.L. Myres | 1930 |
| 250. | 'The manor of Headington' ROxArchS | E. Evans | 1928-32 |
| 252. | 'Beckley Park' Country Life . . . . | C. Hussey | 1929 |
| 256. | 'Dispossessed religious in Oxfordshire ROxArchS . . . . . . . . . | G. Baskerville | 1930 |
| 259. | 'Grim's Ditch in Wychwood. . .' Antiq | O.G.S. Crawford | 1930 |
| 260. | 'Chastleton Camp, a hillfort of the Early Iron Age' Antiq. J . . . . | E.T. Leeds | 1931 |
| 261. | 'Printers & Printing in Oxford & district' Our Bulletin . . . . . . . . . | J. Cheney | 1931 |
| 262. | 'Oxford, Witney & Fairford Railway' RlyM . . . . . . . . . | C.L. Mowat | 1931 |
| 266. | 'Adventures among . . . villagers' Contemporary Review . . . . | H.J. Massingham | 1932 |
| 267. | 'Oxfordshire Poor Laws' EcHR . . . . | C.R. Oldham | 1932-4 |
| 275. | 'Building of All Souls': J.G. Edwards: Essays in honour of James Tait | E.F. Jacob | 1933 |
| 303. | 'Navigation of Thames & Kennet, 1600-1750' Berkshire Archaeological Journal . . . . . . . . . | T.S. Willan | 1936 |
| 304. | 'The Hundred outside the North Gate of Oxford' Ox . . . . . . . . . | H.M. Cam | 1936 |
| 305. | 'St Frideswide and Her Times' Ox | F.M. Stenton | 1936 |
| 306. | 'The Royal Visit to Oxford in 1636' Ox | A.J. Taylor | 1936 |
| 307. | 'Oxford Jewry in the Thirteenth Century' Transactions of the Jewish Historical Society of England | S. Cohen | 1936 |
| 308. | 'Rev John Thorley of Chipping Norton' ROxArchs . . . . . . . . . | H.E. Salter | 1936 |
| 309. | 'Excavations on Grim's Dyke, North Oxfordshire' Ox . . . . . . . . . | D.B. Harden | 1937 |
| 311. | 'Factors in the development of the Cotswold woollen industry' Geog J . . . . | R.P. Beckinsale | 1937 |

| | | | |
|---|---|---|---|
| 312. | 'River Navigation at Oxford during the Civil War and Commonwealth' Ox | I.G. Philip | 1937 |
| 313. | 'Alien Priory of Minster Lovell' Ox | A.J. Taylor | 1937 |
| 317. | 'Mason's marks in Oxfordshire' ROxArchS | R.H.C. Davis | 1938 |
| 318. | 'Medieval domestic architecture in Oxfordshire' ROxArchS | E.T. Long | 1938 |
| 319. | 'Prehistoric & Roman Site on Mount Farm, Dorchester' Ox | J.N.L. Myres | 1937 |
| 320. | 'Castle Hill, Swerford' ROxArchS | E.M. Jope | 1938 |
| 324. | 'Peel & the Oxford University election of 1829' Ox | N. Gash | 1939 |
| 325. | 'Domesday Water Mills' Antiq | M.T. Hodgen | 1939 |
| 326. | 'Gothic Revival in Oxford . . .' Oxford | J. Betjeman | 1940 |
| 327. | 'Oxford Architectural and Historical Society and the Oxford Movement' Ox | S.T. Ollard | 1940 |
| 328. | 'Brian Twyne' Ox | S. Gibson | 1940 |
| 331. | 'Alchester: Archaeological notes' Ox | Anon. | 1941 |
| 332. | 'An Oxford Convict in Maryland' Maryland Historical Magazine | P.B. Gove | 1942 |
| 333. | 'Place-names and topography in the upper Thames country' Ox | W.J. Arkell | 1942 |
| 334. | 'Reminiscences of a Quaker community' Friends' Quarterly Examiner | C.M. Albright | 1942 |
| 335. | 'Tackley's Inn, Oxford' Ox | W.A. Pantin | 1942 |
| 337. | 'Study of Archdeacons' Court records illustrated from Oxford court records 1556-1759' TRHS. | E.R.C. Brinkworth | 1942 |
| 338. | 'The Alleged Migration of the University of Oxford to Northampton in 1264' Ox | F.M. Powicke | 1943-4 |
| 339. | 'The Woodstock Glove Industry' Ox | T.E. Schultz | 1938 |
| 343. | 'Sineta Lambourne & Sineta Smith' Journal of Gipsy Lore Society | E.O. Winstedt | 1944 |
| 350. | 'Geology and prehistory from the train' Ox | W.J. Arkell | 1945 |
| 351. | 'Oxford career of Robert Grosseteste' Ox | D.A. Callus | 1945 |
| 352. | 'Civil war battery at Cornbury' Ox | B.H. St J. O'Neil | 1945 |
| 353. | 'Archaeological sites in Port Meadow. . ' Ox | R.J.C. Atkinson | 1942 |
| 354. | 'Early Iron Age Site at Allen's Pit . .' Ox | J.S.P. Bradford | 1942 |
| 355. | 'Early Iron Age settlement at Standlake' Antiq J | J.S.P. Bradford | 1942 |
| 356. | 'Archaeology from the air in the upper Thames valley' Ox | D.N. Riley | 1943-4 |
| 357. | 'Excavations at Stanton Harcourt, 1940' Ox | W.F. Grimes | 1943-4 |

| | | | |
|---|---|---|---|
| 404. | 'Chronology of Perpendicular Architecture in Oxford' Ox | R.H.C. Davis | 1946-7 |
| 405. | 'The family of Dormer in Oxfordshire and Buckinghamshire' Ox . . . . | M. Maclagan | 1946-7 |
| 406. | 'Saxon Oxford' Ox and 'Dark Age Britain' Ed. D.B. Harden (1956) | E.M. Jope | 1947-7 |
| 407. | 'Gloucester College' Ox . . . . | W.A. Pantin | 1946-7 |
| 409. | 'Excavations at Langford Downs . . .' Ox | A. Williams | 1946-7 |
| 414. | 'The industrialisation of Oxford' Geog J | E.W. Gilbert | 1947 |
| 415. | 'Development of domestic architecture in Oxford' Antiq J . . . . | W.A. Pantin | 1947 |
| 416. | 'Charles I and the Perrots of Northleigh' Ox . . . . . . . . | M.R. Toynbee | 1947 |
| 427. | 'Building Stones of Blenheim Palace, Cornbury Park, Glympton Park and Heythrop House' Ox . . . . | W.J. Arkell | 1948 |
| 428. | 'Port Meadow Races' Ox . . . . | E.H. Cordeaux & D.H. Merry | 1948 |
| 430. | 'Papists in early eighteenth century Oxfordshire' Ox . . . . . . . . | W.O. Hassall | 1948 |
| 438. | 'MPs and their personal relations to Enclosure . . . with special reference to Oxfordshire enclosures' AgHR . . . . | W.E. Tate | 1949 |
| 439. | 'Bronzes from Woodeaton' Ox . . . . | J.R. Kirk | 1949 |
| 440. | 'Radcot Bridge and Newbridge' Ox | M.R. Toynbee | 1949 |
| 447. | 'Jews in Oxford after 1290' Ox . . . . | C. Roth | 1950 |
| 448. | 'Oxford Down Breed . . .' Agriculture | H.C. Stilgoe | 1950 |
| 457. | 'Oxfordshire Enclosure Commissioners 1737-1856' JmodH . . . . | W.E. Tate | 1951 |
| 459. | 'Late Saxon pits under Oxford Castle mound' Ox . . . . . . . . | E.M. Jope | 1952-3 |
| 461. | 'Oxford Carpenters' 1370-1530' Ox | E.A. Gee | 1952 |
| 462. | 'John Allen & Sons (Oxford) Ltd 1868-1952' Allen's Activities | G.T. Launchbury | 1952-4 |
| 463. | 'Cost of parliamentary enclosures in England' EcHR . . . . . . . . | W.E. Tate | 1952-3 |
| 469. | 'Romano-Celtic temple at Woodeaton' Ox | R.G. Goodchild & J.R. Kirk | 1954 |
| 472. | 'Oxford Masons 1370-1530' Archaeol J | E.A. Gee | 1953 |
| 478. | 'Early Iron Age camp on Bozedown, Whitchurch . . .' Ox . . . . | P. Wood | 1954 |
| 484. | 'Banbury & Cheltenham Direct Railway' RlyM . . . . . . . . | J.S. Gilkes | 1955 |
| 485. | 'Typhus in Oxfordshire billets 1643-4' Royal Army Medical Corps Bulletin . . . . . . . . | W.O. Hassall | 1955 |

| | | | |
|---|---|---|---|
| 486. | 'The Golden Cross, Oxford' Ox . . . . | W.A. Pantin | 1955 |
| 492. | 'Account for building of the Divinity School' Ox . . . . . . . . . | A.D.M. Cox | 1956 |
| 493. | 'Watlington & Princes Risborough Railway' RlyM . . . . . . . . . | R.K. Kirkland | 1956 |
| 494. | 'Rectorial Barn at Church Enstone' Ox | R.B. Wood-Jones | 1956 |
| 499. | 'Account-book of an Oxford undergraduate 1619-22' Ox . . . . | H.V.F. Somerset | 1957 |
| 505. | 'Excavation at Callow Hill, Glympton & Stonesfield . . .' Ox . . . . | N. Thomas | 1957 |
| 506. | 'Buckinghamshire & Oxfordshire rising of 1549' Ox . . . . . . . . . | A.V. Woodman | 1957 |
| 514. | 'Pioneer maps of health and disease in England' Geog J . . . . . . . . . | E.W. Gilbert | 1958 |
| 515. | 'Farming in the Oxford region from the Napoleonic to the First World War. JRagS . . . . . . . . . | J. Higgs | 1958 |
| 516. | 'Clarendon Hotel, Oxford' Ox . . . . | E.M. Jope & W.A. Pantin | 1958 |
| 519. | 'The six new towns of the Bishops of Winchester 1200-1255' Medieval Archaeology . . . . . . . . . | M. Beresford | 1959 |
| 521. | 'Excavation at Lyneham Camp . . .' Ox | N. Bayne | 1957 |
| 522. | 'Twelfth century castle at Ascott d'Oilly . . .' Antiq J . . . . | E.M. Jope & R.I. Threlfall | 1959 |
| 532. | 'Parliamentary representation of the City of Oxford 1754-1790' Ox . . . . | J. Cannon | 1960 |
| 533. | 'Excavations at Madmarston Camp, Swalcliffe, 1957-8' . . . . | P. Fowler | 1960 |
| 534. | 'City of Oxford and Restoration of 1660' Ox . . . . . . . . . | M.R. Toynbee | 1960 |
| 539. | 'William Kimber, a Portrait' Journal of English Folk Dance and Song Society . . . . . . . . . | T.W. Chaundy | 1959 |
| 542. | 'Bicester in the seventeenth and eighteenth centuries' Ox . . . . | G.H. Dannatt | 1961-2 |
| 543. | 'Agricultural progress in open-field Oxfordshire' Ag HR and 'Agricultural and Economic Growth in England 1650-1815' Ed: E.L. Jones (1967) . . . . | M.A. Havinden | 1961 |
| 544. | 'Sir Bernhard Samuelson, pioneer of technical education' CC . . . . | A Potts | 1961 |
| 545. | 'Economic & Social Change in Banbury 1830-70' CC . . . . . . . . . | B.S. Trinder | 1961 |
| 549. | 'Excavations at Purwell Farm, Cassington' Ox . . . . . . . . . | G.J. Dawson | 1961-2 |

| | | | |
|---|---|---|---|
| 551. | 'Excavations at Dorchester. .' Archaeol J | S.S. Frere | 1962 |
| 552. | 'Oxfordshire': Domesday Geography of South-Eastern England . . . . | E.M. Jope & I.B. Terrett Ed. H.C. Darby | 1962 |
| 559. | 'Agricultural change in the Chilterns 1875-1900' AgHR . . . . | J.T. Coppock | 1961 |
| 564. | 'Halls & Schools of Medieval Oxford': Oxford Studies presented to Daniel Callus . . . . . . . . . | W.A. Pantin | 1964 |
| 567. | 'Super Cinema Organ, Oxford' Journal of Cinema Organ Society . . . . | C.S. Manning | 1964 |
| 568. | 'Excavations at City Farm, Hanborough' Ox . . . . . . . . . | H. Case et al | 1964-5 |
| 569. | 'Excavations of Ring-Ditches and other sites at Stanton Harcourt' Ox | A. Hamlin | 1963 |
| 570. | 'Carfax Conduit' Ox . . . . . . . . . | C. Cole | 1964-5 |
| 571. | 'Some Documentary Sidelights on the Deserted Medieval Village of Brookend' Ox . . . . . . . . . | T.H. Lloyd | 1964-5 |
| 572. | 'Parish Government of Tadmarton in the eighteenth and nineteenth century' CC . . . . . . . . . | J. Mason | 1964 |
| 589. | 'Plush Industry of Oxfordshire' Ox | R.P. Beckinsale | 1963 |
| 591. | 'Halle Place in West Adderbury and its Occupants' CC . . . . . . . . . | C.F.G. Beeson | 1965 |
| 592. | 'Alexander Samuelson: a Victorian engineer' CC . . . . . . . . . | A. Potts | 1965 |
| 604. | 'Historical Geography of Woodstock' Northern Universities Geographical Journal . . . . . . . . . | C.J. Bond | 1966 |
| 605. | 'Cassington Canal' JRCHS . . . . | H. Compton & K. Belsten | 1966 |
| 606. | 'Where was Banbury Cross?' Ox . . . . | P.D.A. Harvey | 1966 |
| 607. | 'Banbury's Poor in 1850' CC . . . . | B.S. Trinder | 1966 |
| 609. | 'Pottery from Kirtlington . . .' Ox | D.W. Harding | 1966 |
| 613. | 'Last phase of the enclosure of Otmoor' Ox . . . . . . . . . | A.V. Brown | 1967 |
| 614. | 'Cheney & Sons: two centuries of printing in Banbury' CC . . . . | C.R. Cheney | 1967 |
| 615. | 'The Farm Workers, the Dockers and Oxford University' Ox . . . . | P.R.L. Horn | 1967 |
| 616. | 'Banbury and the riots of 1830' CC | P.R.L. Horn | 1967 |
| 617. | 'Demographic & genetic study of group in Oxfordshire' Human Biology and Applied Historical Studies Ed: M. Drake (1973) . . . . | C.F. Kuchemann et al | 1967 |
| 619. | 'Early Iron Age sites at Stanton Harcourt' Ox . . . . . . . . . | A Hamlin | 1966 |

| | | | |
|---|---|---|---|
| 628. | 'Nuneham Courtenay . . . an Oxfordshire eighteenth century deserted village' Ox . . . . | M. Batey | 1968 |
| 629. | 'Iron Age Hillforts . . . in Oxfordshire' Ox | J.E.G. Sutton | 1966 |
| 630. | 'Eynsham Wharf' JRCHS . . . . | K Belsten & H. Compton | 1968 |
| 631. | 'The south Oxfordshire Grim's Ditch. . ' Ox . . . . . . . . . | R. Bradley | 1968 |
| 632. | 'An Oxford charter of 1191 and the beginnings of municipal freedom' Ox . . . . . . . . . | R.H.C. Davis | 1968 |
| 633. | 'Bicester Priory' Ox . . . . . . . . . | D.A. Hinton | 1968 |
| 634. | 'Christopher Holloway: an Oxfordshire trade union leader' Ox . . . . | P.R.L. Horn | 1968 |
| 635. | 'Farmers' defence associations in Oxfordshire 1872-4' History Studies . . . . . . . . . | P.R.L. Horn | 1968 |
| 636. | 'The Chartist Land Company' CC | P.R.L. Horn | 1968 |
| 637. | 'The Banbury Weavers' Union of 1834' CC | P.R.L. Horn | 1968 |
| 638. | 'First fields in an Oxfordshire parish' AgHR . . . . . . . . . | E.A. Pocock | 1968 |
| 639. | 'Education in an Oxfordshire village' Catholic Education Today. . . . | P.R.L. Horn | 1968 |
| 640. | 'Oxford Playhouse 1923-68' Oxford | E. Sweeting | 1968 |
| 641. | 'Banbury Fair in the nineteenth century' CC . . . . . . . . . | B.S. Trinder | 1968 |
| 653. | 'Boat-building yard at Banbury' CC | G.C.J. Hartland | 1969 |
| 654. | 'Gas-making in Banbury' CC . . . . | G.C.J. Hartland | 1969 |
| 655. | 'Banbury': Historic Towns 1 (Ed: M.D. Lobel) . . . . | P.D.A. Harvey | 1969 |
| 656. | 'The Burghal Hidage' Medieval Archaeology . . . . . . . . . | D. Hill | 1969 |
| 657. | 'Methodism & Agricultural Trade Unionism in Oxfordshire in the 1870's' Proceedings of the Wesley Historical Society . . . . | P.R.L. Horn | 1969 |
| 658. | 'Daniel Pidgeon and the Britannia Works' CC . . . . . . . . . | A. Potts | 1969 |
| 660. | 'Sanderson Miller of Radway' CC | A.C. Wood | 1969 |
| 672. | 'Advent of the telephone in Oxford' TO | G. Barber | 1970 |
| 673. | 'Banbury Power Station 1901-35' CC | C.C.J. Hartland | 1970 |
| 674. | 'The Country Child' CC . . . . | P.R.L. Horn | 1970 |
| 675. | 'Minchery Farm, Littlemore' Ox . . . . | W.A. Pantin | 1970 |
| 676. | 'Three Oxford Architects' Ox . . . . | A. Saint | 1970 |
| 677. | 'Railway Marshalling Yard at Banbury' CC . . . . . . . . . | B.S. Trinder | 1970 |
| 710. | 'Fawler Industrial Site' Bulletin of Industrial Archaeology Group 9 (CBA) | M. Aston | 1971 |

| | | | |
|---|---|---|---|
| 711. | 'Banbury – pattern of local government, 1554-1835' CC | R.N. Gilkes | 1971 |
| 712. | 'A Fulling Mill at Standlake' TO | F.R.L. Goadby | 1971 |
| 713. | 'The Building of Magdalen Bridge' Ox | T.W.M. Jaine | 1971 |
| 714. | 'Littlemore Hospital 1846-1970' TO | H. Leopoldt | 1971 |
| 715. | 'The Friars and Paradise: essay in the building history of Oxford, 1801-61' Ox | R.J. Morris | 1971 |
| 716. | 'Ernest Samuelson & Britannia Works' CC | A Potts | 1971 |
| 717. | 'Agricultural experiment at Great Tew' TO | J.R. Walton | 1971 |
| 727. | 'An Oxfordshire enclosure 1791-4' TO | M.R. Bruce | 1972 |
| 728. | 'Raid on Chinnor & Fight at Chalgrove' Ox | A Carter & J Stevenson | 1972 |
| 730. | 'Excavations at Dorchester Abbey' Ox | C.J.K. Cunningham & J.W. Banks | 1972 |
| 731. | 'Roman finds at Glyme Farm, Chipping Norton' Ox | D.T.G. Eddershaw | 1972 |
| 732. | 'The Buildings of Godstow Nunnery' Ox | D. Ganz | 1972 |
| 733. | 'Oxford in the 1850s: reminiscences of Henry Taunt' TO | Ed: M. Graham | 1972 |
| 734. | 'Horse-trams of Oxford, 1881-1914' Ox | H.W. Hart | 1972 |
| 735. | 'Pillow Lacemaking in Victorian England: the experience of Oxfordshire' Textile History | P.R.L. Horn | 1972 |
| 736. | 'Agricultural Trade Unionism & Emigration 1872-1881' Historical Journal | P.R.L. Horn | 1972 |
| 737. | 'Pauper Fortunes in Oxfordshire 1660-1760' Ox | J.A. Redwood | 1972 |
| 738. | 'The Oxford Potteries' Current Archaeology | C. Young | 1972 |
| 756. | 'Mock Mayor-Making Ceremony in Old Woodstock' TO | F.A. Bevan | 1973-4 |
| 757. | 'The Ford, the River and the City' Ox | R.H.C. Davis | 1973 |
| 758. | 'Chipping Norton – the riot of 1845, and the policing of the town 1836-56' TO | D.T.G. Eddershaw | 1973-4 |
| 760. | 'Oxford and the Licensing Act 1872' TO | M. Graham | 1973-4 |
| 761 | 'Excavations on the route of M40' Ox | D.A. Hinton & R.T. Rowley | 1973 |
| 762 | 'Old Age & Oxfordshire Agricultural Labourer – 1870-1914 Ox | P.R.L. Horn | 1973 |
| 763. | 'Banbury Workhouse Children during the 1890s' CC | P.R.L. Horn | 1973 |
| 764. | 'The Buildings of Burford: a Cotswold Town in the fourteenth to nine- | | |

teenth centuries': Perspectives in
English Urban History
(Ed: A.N. Everitt) . . . . M. Laithwaite 1973
765. 'First reports on the excavations at
Middleton Stoney' Ox . . . . R.T. Rowley 1973
769. 'Road-digging and aestheticism: Oxford
in 1874' Studio International T. Hilton 1974
779. 'Oxfordshire recusants 1580-1640' CC A. Davidson 1974
791. 'Cuddesdon & Dorchester-on-Thames:
two Saxon princely sites in
Wessex' British Archaeological
Reports 1 . . . . . . . . . T.M. Dickinson 1974
792. 'The Banburys of England' Urban
History Yearbook . . . . A.N. Everitt 1974
793. 'Tooley's Boatyard' Oxfordshire Rural
and Environmental Studies
Association Journal . . . . M. Gelling 1974
794. 'Urban Surveys: Medieval Oxford':
Landscapes and Documents
(Eds: A. Rogers & R.T. Rowley) T.G. Hassall 1974
795. 'Agricultural Trade Unionism in
Oxfordshire': Rural Discontent
in Nineteenth Century Britain
(Ed: J.P.D. Dunbabin) . . . . P.R.L. Horn 1974
796. 'Aspects of Labouring Life: the Model
Farm at Ditchley 1856-73' CC P.R.L. Horn 1974
797. 'Landowners & Agricultural Trade
Unionism in the 1870s' Local
Historian . . . . . . . . . P.R.L. Horn 1974
798. 'Legatine Award to Oxford in 1214 and
Robert Grosseteste' Ox . . . . G. Pollard 1974
800. 'Vernacular building in the Oxford
region in the sixteenth and
seventeenth centuries':
Rural Change and Urban Growth
1500-18-- (Eds: C.W. Chalklin &
M.A. Havinden) . . . . . . . . . D. Portman 1974
801. 'Early Saxon Settlements in Dorchester'
Anglo-Saxon Settlement and
Landscape (Ed: R.T. Rowley) R.T. Rowley 1974
825. 'Hogarth's Fable and the Oxfordshire
Election of 1754' TO . . . . G.A. Dannatt 1975
826. 'Bliss Mills & the Bliss Family in
Chipping Norton 1758-1920' TO R.L. Evans 1975
827. 'The Medieval Hall at Lewknor' Ox J. Fletcher 1975
828. 'Evolution of Juvenile Delinquency in England
1890-1914' Past and Present J.R. Gillis 1975

| | | | |
|---|---|---|---|
| 829. | 'The Plush Industry in Shutford' CC | V. Hodgkins | 1975 |
| 830 | 'Building of St Clements church, Oxford' TO . . . . . . . . . | M. Graham | 1975 |
| 831. | 'Roman Towns of Oxfordshire: Alchester & Dorchester: The 'Small Towns' of Roman Britain (Eds: W.J. Rodwell & R.T. Rowley) . . . . . . . . . | R.T. Rowley | 1975 |
| 832. | 'Victorian Middle Barton: Open Village' CC . . . . . . . . . | G.R. Stevenson | 1975 |
| 839 | 'Development of nineteenth century private preparatory schools' History of Education . . . . . | D.P. Leinster-Mackay | 1976 |
| 840 | 'Oxfordshire Village School Teachers 1800-80' CC . . . . . . . . . | P.R.L. Horn | 1976 |
| 841. | 'Banbury Bluecoat Foundation' CC | J. Portergill | 1976 |
| 842. | 'A Victorian parson and his people. .' CC | F.D. Price | 1976 |
| 843. | 'Revolution gone awry – or just a Wage Dispute?' Orbit (Oxford College of Further Education) . . . . | R. Sephton | 1976 |
| 844. | 'Court records and the social history of seventeenth century England' History Workshop Journal . . . | D.G. Vaisey | 1976 |
| 845. | 'The small shopkeeper in industrial and market towns: . . . . . . . . . The Lower Middle Class in Britain (Ed: G. Crossick) . . . . . . . . . | T. Vigne & A. Howkins | 1977 |


## Printed Primary Sources


| | | | |
|---|---|---|---|
| 900. | Dictionary of National Bibliography | | |
| 901. | Abingdon Chronicle . . . . . . . . . | Ed: J.S. Stevenson | 1858 |
| 902. | Adderbury Rectoria ORS . . . . | Ed: T.F. Hobson | 1926 |
| 903. | Agricultural Trade Unionism in Oxfordshire 1872-81 ORS . . . | Ed: P.R.L. Horn | 1974 |
| 904. | Anglo-Saxon Chronicle . . . . . . . . . | intro: G.N. Garmonsway | 1953 |
| 905. | Archdeacon's Court: Liber Actorum 1584 ORS . . . . . . . . . | Ed: E.R.C. Brinkworth | 1942-6 |
| 906. | Bampton Hundred Rolls 1279 ORS | Ed: E. Stone | 1968 |
| 907. | Banbury: Baptism and Burial Register 1558-1653 . . . . . . . . . | | 1965-6 |
| | 1653-1723 BHS; (1968) Marriage | | |

| | | | |
|---|---|---|---|
| | Register 1558-1724 (1960), 1724-1790 (1961), 1790-1837 (1963) BHS; Wills and Inventories 1621-50 (1976) BHS. | | |
| 908. | Baker, Galfridi le, Chronicon | Ed: E.M. Thompson | 1889 |
| 909. | Belcher, Richard Boswell of Banbury and Blockley, autobiography Blockley Antiquarian Society | Ed: Anon | 1976 |
| 910. | Coaching in and out of Oxford, 1820-40 OHS | W. Bayzand | 1905 |
| 911. | Crosfield, Diary of Thomas | Ed: F.S. Boas | 1905 |
| 912. | Boartstall Cartulary OHS | Ed: H.E. Salter | 1930 |
| 913. | Bodicote Parish Accounts 1700-1822 BHS | Ed: J.H. Fearon | 1975 |
| 914. | BMC and Pressed Steel Ltd: report on merger (HMSO) | | 1966 |
| 915. | Islip, Custumal (1391) and bye-laws of the Manor (1386-1540) ORS | Ed: B.F. Harvey | 1959 |
| 916. | Burford district of Witney Union, report on sanitary condition | T.H. Cheatle | 1872 |
| 917. | Church Bells of Oxfordshire ORS | comp. F. Sharpe | 1949-53 |
| 918. | English Agriculture in 1850-1 | J. Caird | 1852 |
| 919. | Calamy Revised | Ed: A.G. Matthews | 1934 |
| 920. | Britannia (trans: R. Gough 1789) | W. Camden | 1586 |
| 921. | A plan for the employment of labourers as adopted in Cropredy | W.H. Chamberlin | 1820 |
| 922. | Chantry Certificates & Edwardian Inventories of Church Goods ORS | Ed: R. Graham | 1919 |
| 923. | Godstow Cartulary (Early English Text Society) | | 1905 |
| 924. | Church Plate of Oxfordshire | Ed: J.T. Evans | 1928 |
| 925. | Rural Rides | W. Cobbett | 1830 |
| 926. | Portion of Magna Britannia relating to Oxfordshire | T. Cox | 1720 |
| 927. | A Tour through the whole Island of Great Britain (repr. 1924-7) | D. Defoe | c1720 |
| 928. | General View of the Agriculture of the County of Oxford | R. Davis | 1794 |
| 929. | A Freshman's Diary | W. Elmhirst | 1911-2 |
| 930. | Eynsham Cartulary OHS | Ed: H.E. Salter | 1907-8 |
| 931. | Journeys (Morris C ed 1949) | C. Fiennes | c1690 |
| 932. | Flemings at Oxford OHS | Ed: J.R. Magrath | 1904-24 |
| 933. | Frideswide, Cartulary of St. OHS | Ed: S.R. Wigram | 1895-6 |
| 934. | Godstow Nunnery: English Register | Ed: A. Clark | 1905-11 |
| 935. | Gentlemen's Magazine: extracts relating to Oxford 1731-1800 OHS | Ed: F.J. Haverfield | 1890 |

| | | | |
|---|---|---|---|
| 936. | Goring Charters ORS . . . . . . . . . | Ed: T.R. Gambier Perry | 1931-2 |
| 937. | Great Rollright, manors & advowsons | Ed: R.W. Jeffrey | 1927 |
| 938. | Henley Borough Records ORS . . . . | Ed: P.M. Briers | 1960 |
| 939. | Inclosures, Handlist of Oxfordshire | rev. County Record Office | 1976 |
| 940. | Inclosures, Domesday of (1517) . . . . | Ed: I.S. Leadam | 1897 |
| 941. | Inventories, Oxfordshire: 1550-1590 ORS | Ed: M.A. Havinden | 1965 |
| 942. | Pages in the life of an Oxford lady 1843-62 . . . . . . . . . | M.D. Jeune | 1932 |
| 943. | Johnson W.P: Early description of Britannia Works CC . . . . | Ed: B.S. Trinder | 1969 |
| 944. | Leland J (c1535-1543) Itinerary . . . . | Ed: L Toulmin-Smith | 1907-10 |
| 945. | Lincoln Diocesan Visitations 1517-31 | Lincoln Record Office | 1940-7 |
| 946. | Hearne's Collections OHS . . . . | (various eds.) | 1884-1906 |
| 947. | Lords Lieutenant, High Sheriffs . . . | Ed: J.M. Davenport | 1888 |
| 948. | Luke Sir S: Journal ORS . . . . | Ed: I.G. Philip | 1950-3 |
| 949. | Lybbe Powys P: Passages from diaries, 1756-1808 . . . . . . . . . | Ed: E.J. Cleminson | 1899 |
| 950. | Oxfordshire Tokens . . . . . . . . . | J.G. Milne | 1935 |
| 951. | Travels in England, 1782 . . . . | C.P. Moritz | 1886 |
| 952. | Newington, South: Churchwarden's Accounts 1553-1684 BHS | | 1964 |
| 953. | Oseney Cartulary OHS . . . . . . . . . | Ed: H.E. Salter | 1929-34 |
| 954. | Over Norton: report on coal prospects | J. Lucas | 1891 |
| 955. | Oxford Council Acts 1583-1626 OHS | Ed: J. Carter | 1928 |
| | 1626-65 OHS . . . . . . . . . | Ed: M.G. Hobson | 1933 |
| | 1666-1701 OHS . . . . . . . . . | Ed: M.G. Hobson | 1939 |
| | 1701-52 OHS . . . . . . . . . | Ed: M.G. Hobson | 1954 |
| | 1752-1801 OHS . . . . . . . . . | Ed: M.G. Hobson | 1962 |
| 956. | Oxford Topography OHS . . . . | H. Hurst | 1899 |
| 957. | Oxford by Oxford Men, Reminiscences 1559-1850 . . . . . . . . . | Ed: L.M. Quiller-Couch | 1892 |
| 958. | Oxford St Michaels: Churchwarden's Accounts OHS . . . . | Ed: H.E. Salter | 1933 |
| 959. | Oxford, Biographical Register to 1500 | A.B. Emden | 1957-9 |
| 960. | Oxford: St John the Baptist Hospital Cartulary OHS . . . . . . . . | Ed: H.E. Salter | 1914-6 |
| 961. | Oxford City Documents, Financial & Judicial 1268-1665 OHS . . . . | Ed: J.E. Thorold-Rogers | 1891 |
| 962. | Oxford City Properties . . . . . . . . . | Ed: H.E. Salter | 1926 |
| 963. | Oxford City (Royal Commission on Historical Monuments) . . . . | | 1939 |

| | | | |
|---|---|---|---|
| 964. | Oxford, Sanatory Condition of . . . . | W.P. Ormerod | 1848 |
| 965. | Oxford City Records, 1509-83, selections . . . . . . . . . | Ed: W.H. Turner | 1880 |
| 966. | Oxford, Public Health Report 1849-50 | Greenhill & Allen | 1850 |
| 967. | Oxfordshire, Feet of Fines 1195-1291 OHS . . . . . . . . . | Ed: H.E. Salter | 1930 |
| 968. | Oxfordshire: History, Eminent Natives. (Gentleman's Magazine) . . . . | | 1820 |
| 969. | Parish Registers, Oxfordshire: Marriages . . . . . . . . . | Ed: W. Phillimore | 1909-10 |
| 970. | Parochial collections of A. Wood & R. Rawlinson ORS | Ed: F.N. Davis | 1920-2 |
| 971. | Railways, Handlist of plans etc. for Oxon proposals 1825-1936 (County Record Office) . . . . | | 1964 |
| 972. | Royalist Ordnance Papers 1642-6 ORS | Ed: I. Roy | 1964, 1975 |
| 973. | Sandford Cartulary ORS . . . . | Ed: A.M. Leys | 1938-41 |
| 974. | Secker Visitation 1738 ORS . . . . | Ed: H.A.L. Jukes | 1957 |
| 975. | Sidney S (1851) Rides on Railways | Ed: B.S. Trinder | 1973 |
| 976. | Tancred H.W: A Victorian MP & his constituents . . . . . . . . . | Ed: B.S. Trinder | 1969 |
| 977. | Thame Cartulary ORS . . . . . . . . . | Ed: H.E. Salter | 1947-8 |
| 978. | Tusmore Papers ORS . . . . . . . . . | Ed: L.G. Wickham Legg | 1939 |
| 979. | Uffenbach Z.C. von (1710) Travels | | 1928 |
| 980. | Hearth Tax Returns, 1665 ORS | Ed: M. Weinstock | 1939 |
| 981. | Wheatley Records ORS . . . . . . . . . | Ed: W.O. Hassall | 1956 |
| 982. | Wilberforce's Visitation 1854 ORS | Ed: E.P. Baker | 1954 |
| 983. | Who's Who in Oxfordshire | | 1936 |
| 984. | Wigginton Constable's Book 1691-1836 BHS . . . . . . . . . | Ed: F.D. Price | 1973 |
| 985. | Wilberforce, Samuel: Letter-books 1843-68 ORS . . . . . . . . . | Ed: R.K. Pugh | 1970 |
| 986. | Wood A: Life and Times OHS . . . . | Ed: A. Clark | 1891-1900 |
| 987. | Wood A: Athenae Oxoniensis 1500-1695 . . . . . . . . . | Ed: P. Bliss 1721 | 1848 |
| 988. | Woodforde at Oxford 1759-76 . . . . | Ed: W.N. Hargreaves-Mawdsley | 1969 |
| 989. | Woodward: Progress notes round New College estates 1659-75 ORS | Ed: R.L. Rickard | 1945 |
| 990. | Young A Six weeks' tour through the Southern Counties . . . . | | 1772 |
| | View of the Agriculture of Oxfordshire . . . . . . . . . | | 1809 |
| | General View of the Agriculture of Oxfordshire . . . . . . . . . | | 1813 |
| 991. | Wood A: Survey of Antiquities of City of Oxford OHS . . . . . . . . . | Ed: A. Clark | 1889-99 |

| | | | |
|---|---|---|---|
| 992. | Merton College, Early Rolls of. OHS | Ed: J.R.L. Highfield | 1964 |
| 993. | Marshall W. Rural Economy of the Southern Counties; . . . . | | 1789 |
| | do. of the Midland Counties: | | 1790 |
| | General remarks on agriculture in the Southern Counties; . . . . | | 1799 |
| | Review and abstract of the county reports to the Board of Agriculture: 4 Midlands . . . . . . . . . | | 1815 |
| 994. | Oxford District Social Services, a Survey of . . . . . . . . . | A.F.C. Bourdillon | 1938 |
| 995. | Sutton, Rolls & Register of Bishop, 1280-99 . . . . . . . . . | Ed: R.M.T. Hill | 1958 |
| 996. | Protestation Returns for Oxfordshire 1641-2 ORS . . . . . . . . . | Ed: Dodson | 1955 |
| 997. | Enactments in Parliament: OHS . . . . | Ed: L.L. Shadwell | 1911 |
| 999. | British Parliamentary Papers: House of Commons. | | |

a. 1819 iv: Select Committee on the Education of the Lower Orders.
b. 1834 ix: Select Committee on education.
c. 1835 xxiii-xxvi: Royal Commission on Municipal Corporations
d. 1847 xi: Select Committee on Settlement and Poor Law Removal
e. 1852-3 lxxxix: Religious census of 1851.
f. 1868-9 xiii: Royal Commission on Children & Women in Agriculture
g. 1874 lxxii: Return of owners of land in each county
h. 1892 xxiv: Royal Commission on Labour

# ILLUSTRATIONS

Space and the desire to retain an essential simplicity of reference have dictated the omission of index-linked entries for manuscript primary sources, printed directories, local newspapers and maps. The illustrations which follow give an indication of the potential of such sources.

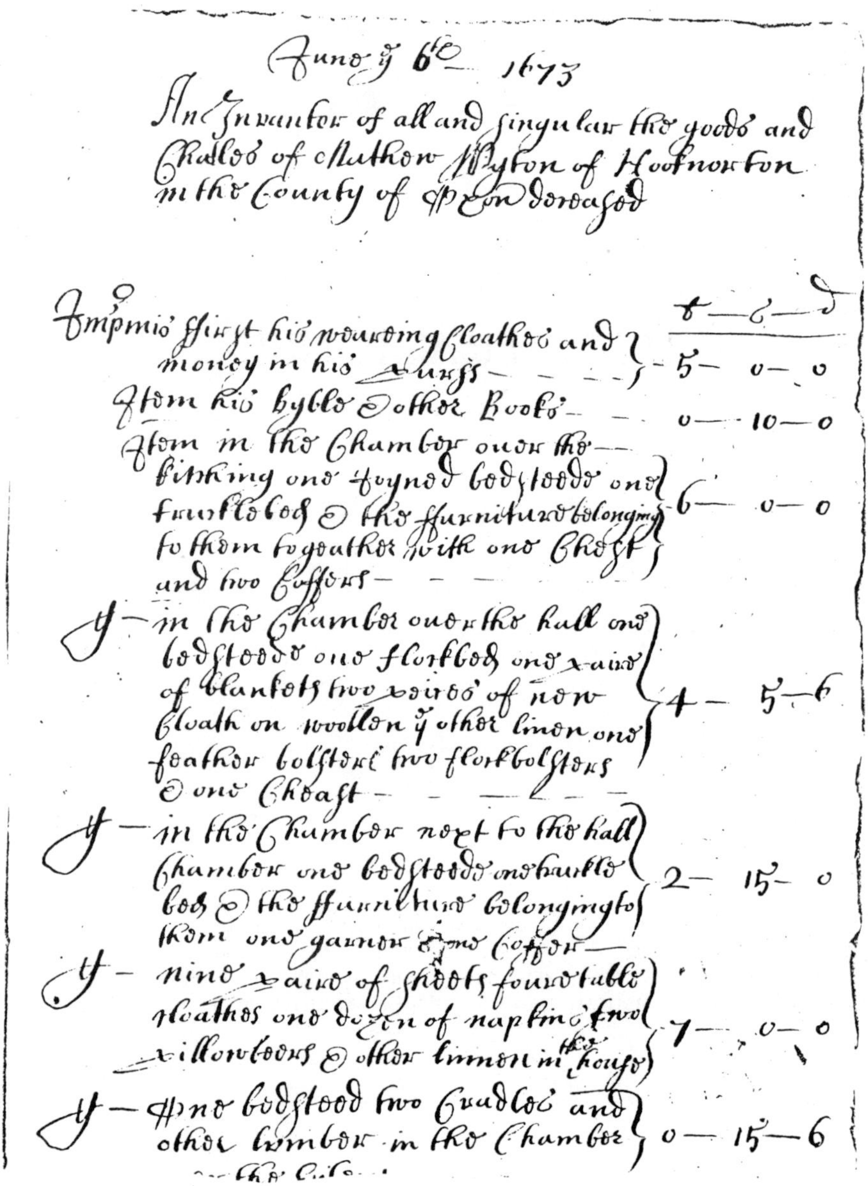

June ye 6th 1673

An Inventory of all and singular the goods and Chattles of Mathew Wyton of Hooknorton in the County of Oxon deceased

| | £ | s | d |
|---|---|---|---|
| Imprimis ffirst his wearing cloathes and money in his purse | 5 | 0 | 0 |
| Item his byble & other Books | 0 | 10 | 0 |
| Item in the Chamber over the kitching one joyned bedsteede one truckle bed & the ffurniture belonging to them togeather with one Chest and two coffers | 6 | 0 | 0 |
| It in the Chamber over the hall one bedsteede one flockbed one paire of blankets two paires of new cloath on woollen ye other linen one feather bolster two flockbolsters & one Cheast | 4 | 5 | 6 |
| It in the Chamber next to the hall chamber one bedsteede one truckle bed & the ffurniture belonging to them one garner & one coffer | 2 | 15 | 0 |
| It nine paire of sheets foure table cloathes one dozen of napkins two pillowbeers & other linnen in the house | 7 | 0 | 0 |
| It one bedstead two cradles and other lumber in the Chamber [illegible] | 0 | 15 | 6 |

1673 Inventory of Mathew Wyton of Hook Norton, *(Bodleian Library)*.

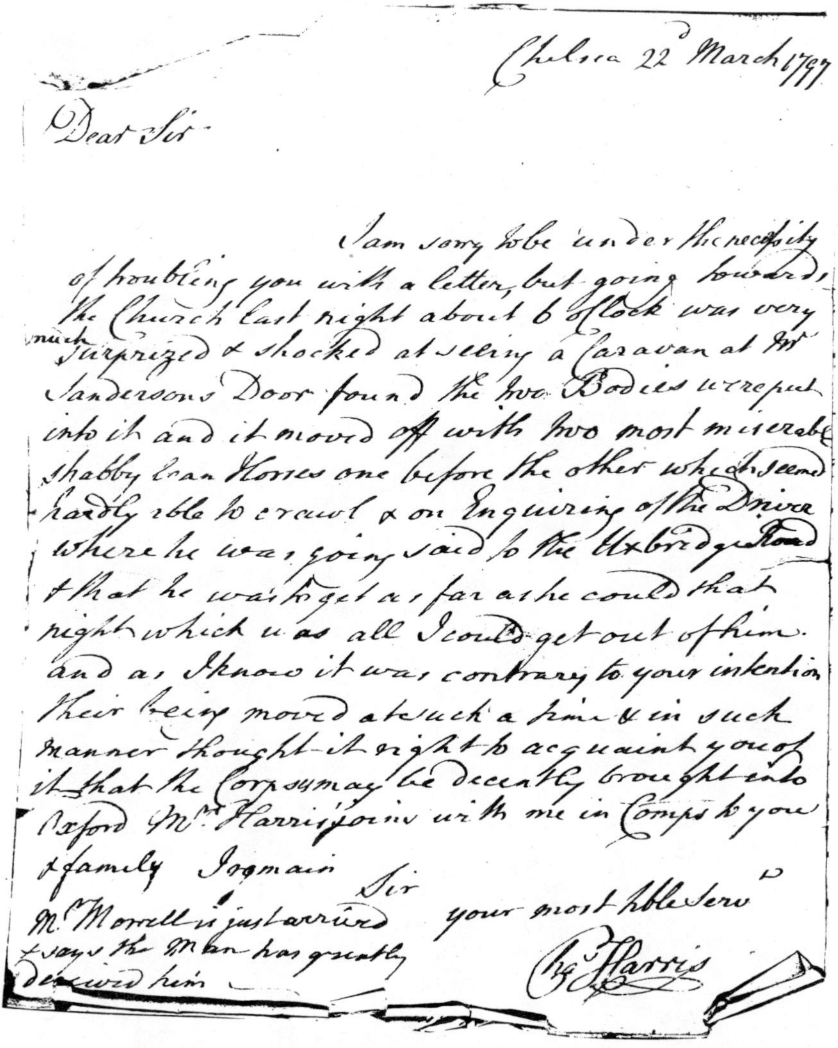
Chelsea 22d March 1797

Dear Sir

I am sorry to be under the necessity
of troubling you with a letter, but going towards
the Church last night about 6 oClock was very
much surprized & shocked at seeing a Caravan at Mr
Sandersons Door found the two Bodies were put
into it and it moved off with two most miserable
shabby lean Horses one before the other which seemed
hardly able to crawl & on Enquiring of the Driver
where he was going said to the Uxbridge Road
& that he was to get as far as he could that
night which was all I could get out of him.
and as I know it was contrary to your intention
their being moved at such a time & in such
manner thought it right to acquaint you of
it that the Corps may be decently brought into
Oxford Mrs Harris joins with me in Comps to you
& family I remain

Sir

your most hble Servt

Chas Harris

Mr Morrell is just arrived
& says the Man has greatly
deceived him

1797 private correspondence between Chelsea and Oxford on a mortal matter, *(Clive Birch)*.

Indenture of 1835 binding George Johnson of Henley-on-Thames apprentice to Joseph Higgins of Rotherfield Greys, *(Mrs. C. Tomalin)*.

## CHIPPING-NORTON, OXFORDSHIRE.

Market Day, Wednefday.

BANBURY, Wm. *Manufacturer of Harrateens, Chinas, &c.*
Biggerftaffe, Stephen, *ditto*
Builey, Edward, *Surgeon*
Eades, Thomas, *Ironmonger and Tin-plate-worker*
Fardou, Mrs. *Linen-draper*
Field, Jofeph, *Sadler*
Fowler, Wm. *Manufacturer of Tilts for Waggons, & Malfter*
Freeman, Jofeph, *Manufacturer of Harrateens and Duffils*
Haynes, Charles, *Surgeon*
Haynes, Nathaniel, *Ironmonger*
King, John, *Linen and Woollen-draper*
King, William, *Grocer*
Mackinefs, Mr. *Surgeon*
Matthews, William, *Grocer and Ironmonger*
Smith, ———, *M. D.*
Wagftaff, Richard, *Draper and Auctioneer*
Walford, Theophillus, *Attorney at Law*
Witts, Edward, Efq; *Woolftapler*

Bailey's Western and Midland Directory, 1784.

## JACKSON'S OXFORD JOURNAL,

**ESTABLISHED IN MAY, 1753.**

*PUBLISHED ON FRIDAY EVENING IN TIME FOR THE MAILS TO ALL PARTS, BY* HUGH HALL, *AT THE OFFICE, 65, CORN MARKET STREET, OXFORD.* **PRICE 2D.**

THE OXFORD JOURNAL is one of the very few Papers in the United Kingdom that can boast of an existence of *more than* 130 *Years.* It is an Agricultural, Commercial, and Family Newspaper, which enjoys a very influential and extensive circulation in the University, City, and County of Oxford, as well as in the adjoining Counties of Berks, Bucks, Northampton, Gloucester, Warwick, Worcester, and Wilts.

It has a very large Business Connection, being the

**CHIEF ADVERTISING MEDIUM OF THE DISTRICT,**

as its Columns sufficiently testify, and it has long been the leading and most widely circulated Paper in the County. As it devotes a large portion of its space to Agricultural Matters, and contains the Advertisements of every Auctioneer and Land Agent in the District, it is much read by Land Owners and Farmers.

It is sent to many of the Clubs, Literary Institutes, and News Rooms in London and the large Towns in the Kingdom, and is regularly filed by the following London Agents:—Messrs. Barker and Sons; Mr. R. F. White; Mr. Deacon; Messrs. Reynell and Co.; Messrs. Knight and Company; Messrs. G. Street and Co.; Messrs. Street Brothers; Messrs. Mitchell and Co.; Messrs. Clarke, Son, and Platt; Mr. T. B. Browne; Mr. H. Green; Mr. F. Algar; Messrs. F. L. May and Co.; Laughton and Co.; and Messrs. Crossley and Co. &c., by whom Advertisements are received.

(15)

Jackson's Oxford Journal as advertised in 1887.

Part of the 1773 Map of

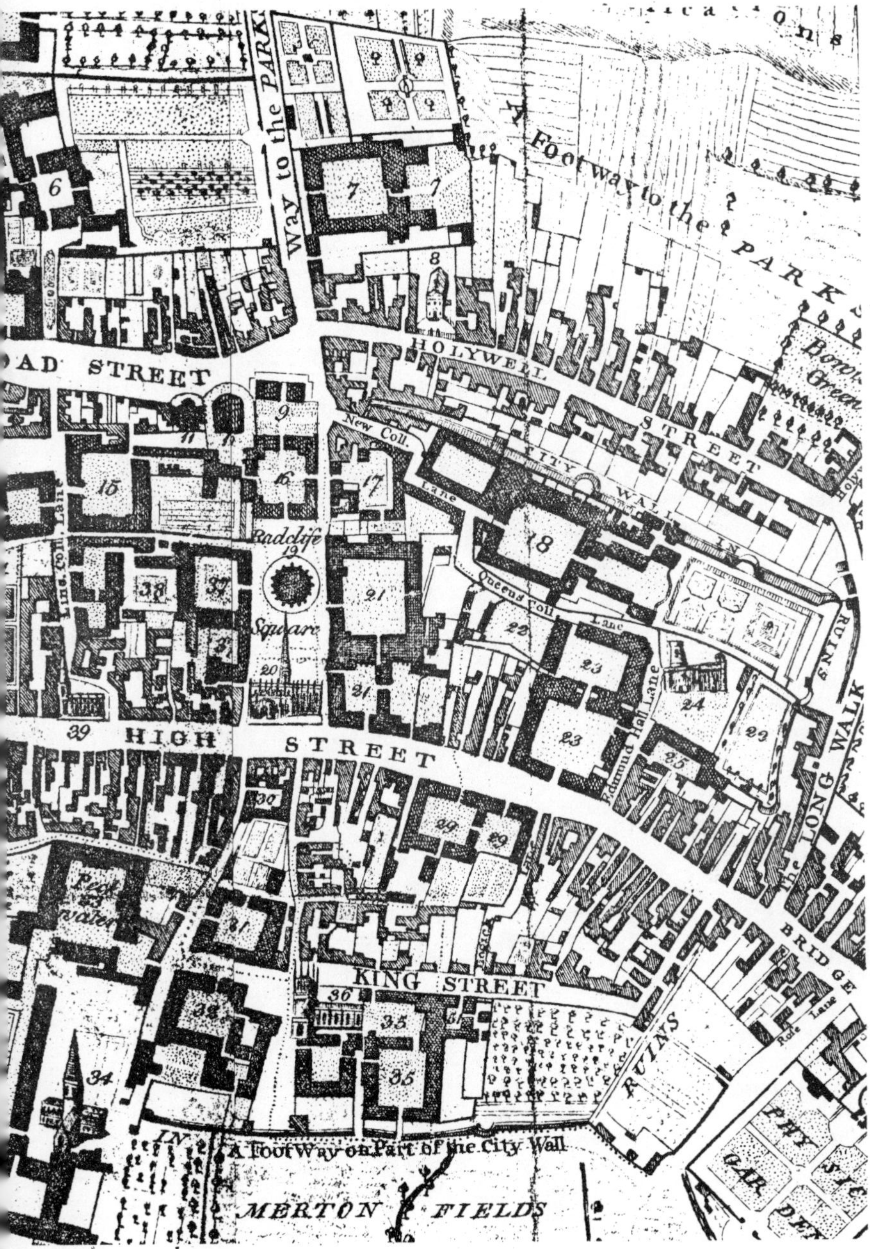


xfordshire County Library).

# 1841.

BOROUGH OF BANBURY, IN THE COUNTY OF OXFORD. } LIST OF PERSONS upon the REGISTER OF ELECTORS for the BOROUGH OF BANBURY, on the 30th Day of June.

H. Holbech. T. Tancred. | V. Vincent. *N.* Neutral. | *R.* Removed. *D.* Deceased. | *A.* Absent.

| NAMES. | RESIDENCE. | TRADE, PROFESSION, &c. | VOTED FOR H | T | V | |
|---|---|---|---|---|---|---|
| Abbott, Thomas ... | North-bar-street ... | Grocer ... ... | | — | | |
| Abraham, James ... | Fish-street ... | Tailor ... | | | — | |
| *Adkins, William* ... | *Market-place* ... | *Publican* ... | | | | *R* |
| *Adkins, John* ... | *South-bar-street* ... | *Surveyor* ... | | | | *R* |
| Allgood, James ... | Bridge-street ... | Ironmonger ... | | — | | |
| Amos, Thomas ... | Bridge-street-south | Butcher ... | — | | | |
| *Anderson, James* ... | *Parson's-street* ... | *Tailor* ... ... | | | | *N* |
| Aplin, Benjamin ... | Chalcombe ... | Solicitor ... | — | | | |
| Aplin, Benjamin William | Bridge-street-south ... | Solicitor ... | — | | | |
| *Aplin, John* ... | *South-bar-street* ... | *Gentleman* ... | | | | *A* |
| *Appletree, Frederick* | *South-bar-street* ... | *Butcher* ... | | | | *R* |
| *Armitt, John, senior* | *Back-lane* ... | *Carpenter* ... | | | | *R* |
| *Armitt, John, junior* ... | *High-street* ... | *Butcher* ... | | | | *N* |
| Armitt, Samuel, senior | Water-lane ... | Gardener ... | | — | | |
| Astell, George ... ... | Parson's-street ... | Victualler ... | — | | | |
| Austin, Barnes ... | South-bar-street ... | Common Brewer | | | — | |
| Austin, John, senior ... | Bodicote ... | Mealman ... | | — | | |
| *Austin, John, junior* | *Bodicote* ... | *Mealman* ... | | | | *N* |
| Bailey, Richard ... | Market-place ... | Tailor ... ... | — | | | |
| Baker, William ... | Parson's-street ... | Tailor ... | | — | | |
| Ball, Joseph ... | Parson's-street ... | Boot-maker ... | | — | | |
| Ball, Vincent ... | Parson's-street ... | Saddler ... | | — | | |
| Barford, John ... | Market-place ... | Ironmonger ... | — | | | |
| Barrett, William ... | Market-place ... | Maltster ... | — | | | |
| Barton, John ... | Parson's-street ... | Jeweller ... | — | | | |
| Baughen, Richard | North-bar-street ... | Plush-manufacturer | | — | | |
| Baughen, Thomas ... | North-bar-street ... | Plush-manufacturer | | — | | |
| Baxter, Robert ... | Parson's-street ... | Shoemaker ... | | | — | |
| Bayliss, Edward ... | Crouch ... ... | Farmer ... | — | | | |
| *Bazeley, John* ... | *Market-place* ... | *Innkeeper* ... | | | | *R* |
| Beale, James ... | South-bar-street ... | Baker ... | | — | | |
| *Bearsley, John* ... | *North-bar-street...* | *Plush-manufacturer* | | | | *D* |
| *Beck, William* ... | *London-yard* ... | *Watchmaker* ... | | | | *D* |
| Beere, Thomas ... | North-bar-street ... | Grazier ... | | — | | |
| *Beere, George* ... | *Parson's-street* ... | *Tailor* ... | | | | *N* |

Banbury Poll-Book of the 1841 Election.

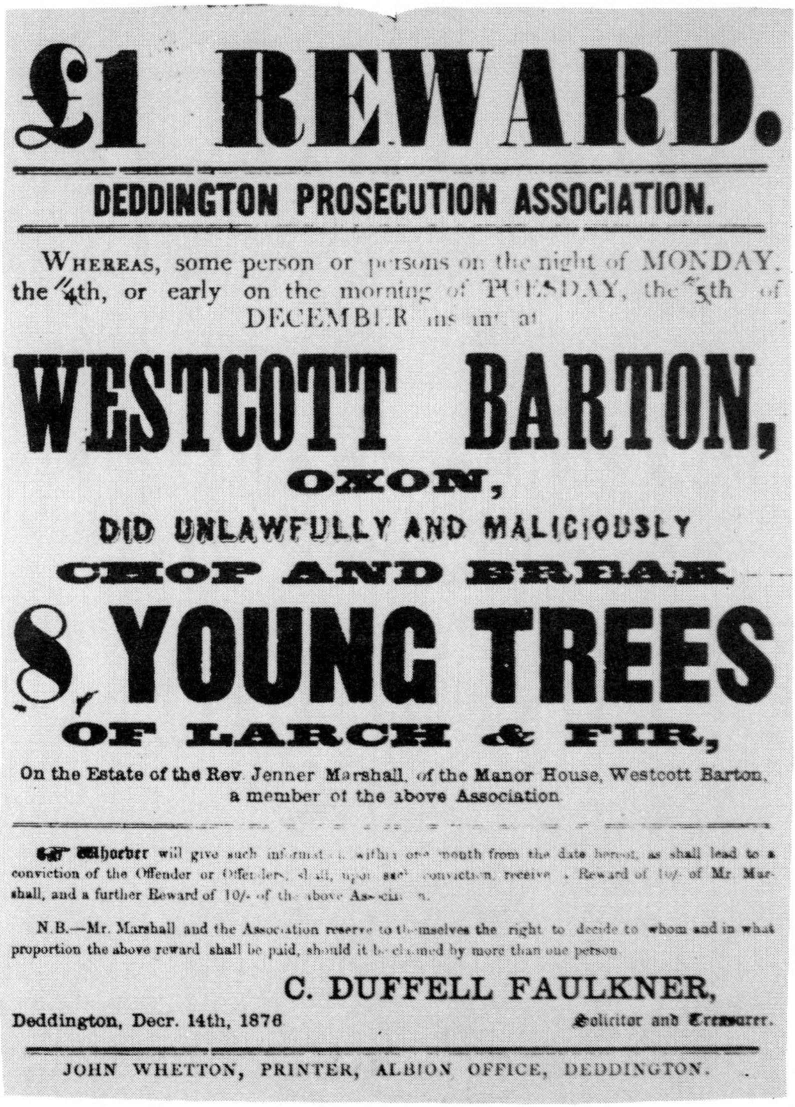

# £1 REWARD.

## DEDDINGTON PROSECUTION ASSOCIATION.

WHEREAS, some person or persons on the night of MONDAY, the 4th, or early on the morning of TUESDAY, the 5th of DECEMBER instant, at

# WESTCOTT BARTON,

## OXON,

DID UNLAWFULLY AND MALICIOUSLY

CHOP AND BREAK

# 8 YOUNG TREES

OF LARCH & FIR,

On the Estate of the Rev. Jenner Marshall, of the Manor House, Westcott Barton, a member of the above Association.

☞ Whoever will give such information within one month from the date hereof, as shall lead to a conviction of the Offender or Offenders, shall, upon such conviction, receive a Reward of 10/- of Mr. Marshall, and a further Reward of 10/- of the above Association.

N.B.—Mr. Marshall and the Association reserve to themselves the right to decide to whom and in what proportion the above reward shall be paid, should it be claimed by more than one person.

C. DUFFELL FAULKNER,

Deddington, Decr. 14th, 1876 — Solicitor and Treasurer.

JOHN WHETTON, PRINTER, ALBION OFFICE, DEDDINGTON.

Poster issued by Deddington Prosecution Association, 1876.

| | | | | |
|---|---|---|---|---|
| | School subs | | 10 | |
| | Padbury bill for thrashing | 10 | 10 | 0 |
| 4 | Edmunds seed bill | | | |
| " | Kibbles rent | 12 | 0 | 0 |
| 7 | Wages men & boys | 2 | 2 | 2 |
| 13 | bill artificial manure | 14 | 10 | |
| 14 | wages men & boys | 2 | 4 | 0 |
| | x sold Mr Walford qr peas | 14 | 12 | 6 |
| 21 | wages men & boys | 2 | 4 | 0 |
| 28 | do do do | 2 | 4 | 0 |
| | wages for cleaning ditch | 1 | 5 | 0 |
| | | | 6 | |
| | March | | | |
| 7 | wages men & boys | 2 | 4 | 0 |
| 14 | do do do | 2 | 4 | 0 |
| " | bill Butchers | 3 | 1 | 0 |
| | sold Mr Harris horse beans | 12 | 18 | 9 |
| | sold Mr Jas Harris | 3 | 6 | |
| | sold 3 qr oats V. T. Wyton [?] | | 8 | 3 |
| 21 | wages men & boys | 2 | 1 | 4 |
| | steaming 3 days 4 men | 1 | 10 | 0 |
| | Dd [?] | | | |
| 28 | wages | 2 | 9 | 8 |

Page from an Almanack used at Six Ash Farm, Hook Norton, 1883-5, *(Mrs. J.M. Hiatt and Reading University Library).*

# OXFORD CHRONICLE AND BERKS AND BUCKS GAZETTE.

ESTABLISHED 1837.

*Price 1d.; Half yearly by Post, Prepaid, 3s. 4d.*

**Is published every Friday Afternoon, and circulated the same evening in all the Towns and Villages in the District.**

An Agricultural, Commercial, and Family Newspaper. The local and district reports are more full and complete than in any other Newspaper in the locality. Being the only Liberal Newspaper in the County, it has a special circulation not possessed by any other journal. It has a larger circulation among the trading, professional, and commercial classes than any other Newspaper in the County, and is, therefore, the best medium for Auction, Business, Official, and other Advertisements.

**The "OXFORD RAILWAY GUIDE" is published on the 1st of every month, price One Penny.**

*ADVERTISEMENT CONTRACTORS FOR THE OXFORD TRAM CARS.*

Printed and published every Friday Afternoon for the OXFORD CHRONICLE COMPANY (Limited), by DAVID AUGUSTUS PEACHEY, at 119, High Street, Oxford. [12]

# WM. F. MATTHEWS,

## Carting Agent for the G. W. R.,

Furniture, &c., Removed

by Road or Rail.

**PRIORY ST., BURFORD, OXON.**

PICTURES, GLASS & CHINA CAREFULLY PACKED.

**Estimates Free, and Testimonials upon Application.**

# THE BEAR HOTEL, WOODSTOCK.

(CLOSE TO BLENHEIM PARK.)

*First-class Family and Hunting Establishment.*

*Good Fishing and every Accommodation.*

POSTING and LIVERY STABLES. + BILLIARDS.

**H. PRATT, Proprietor.**

The Oxford Chronicle advertised in 1887, together with other communications at Burford and Woodstock.

# INDEX: PLACES

# INDEX: PEOPLE

ABBREVIATIONS - a = Architect; Abp of C = Archbishop of Canterbury, or as Bishops, (below); b = Builder; bp of D = Bishop of Dorchester; bp of L = Bishop of Lincoln; bp of O = Bishop of Oxford; bp of Y = Bishop of York; c = Charitable Bequest; Capt. = Captain, Army and Navy; Cllr. = Councillor; Col. = Colonel; e = Employer; f = Family; j = Judge; Kg = King; JP = Justice of the Peace; m = Mayor; Maj. Genl. = Major General; MP = Member of Parliament; Pc = Police Constable; pr = Printer; Q = Queen; SJ = Society of Jesus; St = Saint.

OXFORDSHIRE 1977
District Council Boundaries
Former Boroughs
Other places mentioned
Pre-1974 County Boundary
WEST
OXON
CHERWELL
BANBURY
CHIPPING NORTON
WOODSTOCK
Bicester
Claydon
Clattercote
Mollington
Prescote
Cropredy
Wardington
Bourton
Hornton
Horley
Hanwell
Alkerton
Shenington
Drayton
Epwell
Wroxton
North Newington
Shutford
Bodicote
Swalcliffe
Broughton
Sibford
Milton
Bloxham
Tadmarton
Adderbury
Wigginton
Hook Norton
Barford
South Newington
Deddington
Mixbury
Finmere
Cottisford
Newton Purcell
Souldern
Tusmore
Hethe
Great Rollright
Swerford
North Aston
Chastleton
Duns Tew
Somerton
Fritwell
Great Tew
Little Tew
Over Norton
Salford
Fringford
Cornwell
Heythrop
Sandford St. Martin
Westcote Barton
Steeple Aston
Upper Heyford
Ardley
Stoke Lyne
Godington
Churchill
Enstone
Steeple Barton
Bucknell
Stratton Audley
Lower Heyford
Kingham
Rousham
Caversfield
Sarsden
Middleton Stoney
Kiddington
Chadlington
Spelsbury
Glympton
Lyneham
Chesterton
Launton
Charlbury
Wootton
Tackley
Idbury
Wendlebury
Blackthorn
Ascott-under-Wychwood
Fifield
Kirtlington
Ambrosden
Weston-on-the-Green
Shipton-on-Cherwell
Milton-under-Wychwood
Stonesfield
Arncott
Bletchingdon
Merton
Piddington
Shipton-under-Wychwood
Fawler
Hampton Gay
Charlton-on-Otmoor
Hampton Poyle
Finstock
Combe
Taynton
Ramsden
Bladon
Islip
Oddington
Murcott